THE TAO OF TAI-CHI CHUAN

(or Tai ji quan in Pinyin)

Way to Rejuvenation

Jou, Tsung Hwa

Edited by:
Shoshana Shapiro, Ph.D.

太極拳之道

TAI CHI FOUNDATION
Warwick, New York

First Printing in Taiwan, April, 1981.
Second Printing, December, 1982.
Third Revised Edition, March, 1983.
Forth Printing November, 1985.
Fifth Printing in Taiwan May 1988

ISBN 0-8048-1357-4
Published by: Tai Chi Foundation
            Jou, Tsung Hwa
            POB. 828
            Warwick, NY. 10995

THE TAO OF
TAI-CHI CHUAN
Way to Rejuvenation

Dedicated to :

the friendship of Chinese and American peoples.

$17.00(U.S.)
Author's Dream

It has long been my dream that one day Americans of all ages, creeds and colors will be practicing Tai-Chi Chuan in the beautiful parks of this country, as they do in China. Few places in the world have lovely open spaces which can and should be used productively, and at no expense. The result would be tremendous improvement in mental and physical well-being.

To realize this dream. I have for the past ten years been teaching Tai-Chi Chuan on a voluntary basis using the open facilities of Rutgers University in New Brunswick, New Jersey. For the past five years I have also been working on this volume which has a dual purpose: first, to guide people in the understanding of Tai-Chi and its philosophy; and second, to raise funds for a Tai-Chi college which will train Tai-Chi teachers and introduce Chinese culture to Americans.

CHANG, SAN-FENG
The founder of Tai-Chi Chuan.

Chen, Yen-Lin (陳炎林 1906–) published an excellent book about Yang's Tai-Chi Chuan during the 1930's. In his book he wrote about the Tai-Chi Chi-Kung, sword form, knife form, staff form and Tai-Chi sparring. He also stressed a different kind of Chin which no one had explained previously. He remained an enigma to his readers because he provided no background information about himself.

While practicing Tai-Chi Chuan in a Shanghai park in the spring of 1980, I met one of Chen Yen-Lin's students who brought me to visit his teacher. Master Chen gave me a new insights into Push-hands techniques.

Master Chen, who is a doctor of Chinese medicine, began the practice of Tai-Chi at four years of age and has practiced every day since then. This picture was taken at his home in Shanghai, China.

When I visited Taiwan in the summer of 1972, I appeared on
television show with Master Cheng Man-Ching. This picture
was taken at the Grand or Yuan-San Hotel in Taipei, Taiwan.

Chu, Ju-Hsun (朱汝訓)

In the spring of 1980, when I returned to my native town Chu Chi (諸暨), Chekiang (浙江) in China, I met Mr. Chu, Ju-Hsun a Chinese doctor, acupuncturist and acrobat who is 53 years old . He showed tremendous internal strength such as I had never seen before. He broke off a piece of a ceramic bowl and with his thumb and forefinger crushed it to a fine powder. He assured me if I remained with him for six months he could transmit the body of his knowledge to me. It is my intention to take advantage of Mr. Chu's offer at the earliest opportunity.

The birthplace of Tai Chi Chuan is the Chen Village, Ho Nan Province, China. The author has visited here twice to exchange greetings and share in perpetuating Tai Chi.

Chen Chang-Wen (陳振文) and Chen Tzeh-Tzy (陳者才) two olders of the Chen family, enjoy health and happy lives. Both are in their eighties and continue to practice the traditional Chen Form with spirit and enthusiasm. They are a living document from which all Tai Chi players can learn.

Though Wu Do-Nan (吳圖南 1883 –) is 102 years old, his sight is normal, his hearing is keen and his memory is sharp. He can easily speak out his old friend's name without thinking. His spine remains erect when sitting and standing.

He lived in an apartment on the nineth floor, but goes to park to practice Tai Chi Chuan twice a day. We ask him what is the secret of his longevity. His answer is simple:

Tai Chi, Tai Chi and Tai Chi!

In American senior citizens are discovering Tai Chi as the way to rejuvention, In all parts of the United States my students are showing old Americans how to develop the spiritual energy or Chin, so a state of relaxed alertness can be maintained at all times, once again "like a young kitten."

The kittenlike seniors pictured here do breathing Exercise or Chi-Kung in the Piscataway senior citizen Center, N.J. with their instructor, my student, Paul Albe.

The Tai Chi Foundation sponsors a Tai Chi Tour to China, Hong Kong and Taiwan each year. Our group spends two weeks in China, where we exprience an academic opportunity through our stay in the dormitory of the Beijing Institute of Physical Education. we visit the Great Wall, Shaolin Temple, Chen Village etc. We visit many world known Tai Chi masters. We also spend one week visiting Hong Kong and Taiwan, joining Tai Chi players in the local parks. The Chinese Tai Chi Institute (above) were our host in Taipei, Taiwan, 1985.

CONTENTS

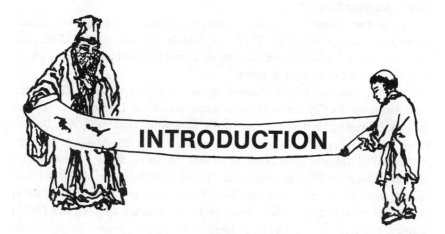

INTRODUCTION

I was a math teacher who had published about thirty books on mathematics in Chinese. In 1964 at the age of forty-seven, I became very ill with an enlarged heart and a gastroptosis, because of years of hard work and vigorous schedules. My doctor told me that my condition was incurable using available medication. At the same time, one of my friends, Lou Tzu-Feng (婁子豐), told me about Tai-Chi Chuan (太極拳) and introduced me to his Tai-Chi teacher, Yuan Tao (袁道). Mr. Yuan is a Hsiung-I specialist; his picture had been used in Robert Smith's book, *Hsiung-I Chuan* (形意拳). Although Mr. Yuan at that time was in his sixties with white hair and beard, his movements were youthful and agile. When I compared Mr. Yuan's alert and good health in his sixties to my ill health at age forty-seven, I became aware of how people take care of themselves can enjoy a healthy and happy life. I stopped smoking and started to practice Tai-Chi Chuan.

I first learned Yang's Tai-Chi Chuan (楊式太極拳). Two years later, I learned the Wu style (武式). For three years, I practiced the Wu style constantly day and night. Then I learned the first routine of Chen's Tai-Chi Chuan (陳家太極第一路). I did not, however, practice this routine to the degree I practiced the Yang and Wu styles. I now practice at least three hours a day and have been doing so for the past fifteen years. At first, I had only enough strength to practice a half hour at a time. In only two weeks, my appetite improved and the frequency and severity of my stomach pain lessened. In three years time, my stomach was completely healed. In five years my heart returned to normal, and I regained total good health without the use of drugs. Because of my personal experience, I decided to devote much of my time to teaching Tai-Chi Chuan.

There are thousands of people today who desire good health but do not know how it can be acquired. They seek doctors, take pills and try all kinds of methods. Since Tai-Chi Chuan can provide a way to regain good health, I want to share Tai-Chi Chuan with all people.

In 1972, one year after my arrival in the United States, Daniel Goode, my first American Tai-Chi student and a music teacher at Livingston College of Rutgers University, introduced me to the Livingston Music and Arts Department, where I began teaching a credit course in Tai Chi Chuan. In 1973, Professor Phil Shinick, in an effort to enlarge the Sports Study Program into a Physical Education Program, took the Tai-Chi class from the Music and Arts Department and included it in the Sports Study Program. The original Tai-Chi course was expanded to include classes in Tai-Chi sword (太極劍) and Tai-Chi sparring (太極散手). About three hundred students registered for the Tai-Chi classes during each semester. However, since each class was limited to thirty students, most students were unable to enroll. Unfortunately, in 1975, because of financial and other reasons, the Sports Study Program was not developed into a Physical Education Program, and consequently, the Tai-Chi classes had to be cancelled.

The Livingston College Curriculum Committee, based on their reading of existing Tai-Chi texts, felt that Tai-Chi Chuan was a form of exercise, rather than an area of study worth academic credit. The committee relied on various books available on Tai-Chi Chuan at that time which through pictures and illustrations emphasized only Tai-Chi's postures and physical aspects.

Having read all of the Tai-Chi books, both in English and Chinese, I would tend to agree with the Curriculum Committee. The books currently available do not explain the philosophy of Tai-Chi Chuan or how the Tai-Chi philosophy relates to one's daily life. Thus I decided to work on a book which could serve as a college textbook for courses in Tai-Chi Chuan. However, I initially had a lot of difficulty because I tried to write in English. Dr. Shoshana Shapiro Adler, one of my students, suggested that I begin writing the text in Chinese and then translate it into English. It was this suggestion that encouraged me to write this book, Wu-Chi to Tai-Chi (無極而太極).

Tai-Chi Chuan is a Chinese art with a history dating back thousands of years. The movements are graceful, the tempo is slow, and the benefits are great. It is the only form of exercise in which a person should not use outward strength (拙力) or force in their movements. Improvement depends not on outer strength, but inner awareness. Behind every Tai-Chi movement is the philosophy of Yin and Yang (陰 陽). In the Western world, exercise concentrates on outer movements and the development of the physical body. On the other hand, Tai-Chi Chuan develops both the mind and body. It embodies a philosophy that not only promotes health but also can be applied to every aspect of daily life. For example, the posture of Lu (握), or roll-back, teaches the student not to resist or try to escape. Simply, the student, with total awareness of the opponent, relaxes. This movement could be compared to the graceful and precise reactions of the bullfighter. When the bull attacks, he does not meet the bull head-on, because it would mean certain death. Nor does the bullfighter run from the bull and try to escape, because the bull would follow and kill him. The bullfighter simply steps aside or "rolls-back", allowing the bull to pass him, and thus the bullfighter maintains control and awareness of the bull. It is important to note that the bullfighter's position allows him to withdraw yet stay in a position to attack the bull as it passes by. This ability to attack as one withdraws is known in Taoism as the Yang among the Yin (陰 中有陽).

The teachings of Tai-Chi Chuan can also be incorporated into one's daily life. To carry the above example further, consider the verbal attacks encountered from day to day. If a person criticizes you or makes an unfair or disparaging remark, you can react in several ways. If you meet resistance with resistance and attack by returning the criticism, conflict naturally develops; you become upset, and nothing is settled. Alternatively, if you retreat from the person's statement, you become fearful and assume the statement must be accepted; you again become upset, frustrated and hurt. However, Taoist philosophy provides an alternative to either total attack or total retreat. The philosophy of "the Yang among the Yin" teaches you how to become acutely aware of what is said, consider its meaning, and act accordingly. You will dismiss the statement if it is false, and learn from it if it is true. Having this understanding, you realize that you are in control of yourself and your own reactions.

Clearly, there are many aspects involved in the practice of Tai-Chi Chuan. To concentrate merely on the physical aspect places limits on what one can gain from its practice. College students will particularly benefit from a holistic study of Tai-Chi philosophy. Since they are at a period in life when they are developing a greater awareness of themselves, their world and their future, Tai-Chi practice will help college students open their minds to a new way of thinking and viewing life. In addition, since every aspect of Tai-Chi Chuan can be applied to daily life, they will be better able to cope with the challenges presented by their academic studies and their extracurricular activities. Tai-Chi emphasizes the development of the whole person, promoting personal growth in all areas of life. Consequently, the study of Tai-Chi Chuan not only enhances students' academic careers, but provides a philosophy that will benefit students for the rest of their lives, whatever career they may pursue. Since the objectives of our colleges are to prepare our young people for a happy and successful life and to open up new ways of thinking and growing as individuals, the opportunity to learn Tai-Chi Chuan could be an important part of the college curriculum.

Thousands of people have been practicing Tai-Chi Chuan throughout South-east Asia, in places such as China, Taiwan, Hong Kong, Japan, and Korea. In recent years, the practice of this art has become increasingly popular in the United States and throughout the Western world. Tai-Chi Chuan's long tradition and widespread popularity have led to the development of various Tai-Chi schools, each with different types, or styles, of Tai-Chi Chuan. However, each school still follows the same basic Tai-Chi principle; the *I-Ching* (易經) philosophy with its emphasis on "change". Within the framework of constant change, moreover, there exists the idea that some things, such as basic principles, do not change. This is especially applicable to the Tai-Chi Chuan postures. In the interest of the widespread development of Tai-Chi Chuan, standard sets of postures need to be practiced, and the student should seek out a teacher who teaches one of these forms. These standard forms will provide a basis for communication among Tai-Chi practitioners everywhere.

In this book three main schools of Tai-Chi Chuan are discussed and illustrated: Chen, Yang and Wu. The *Chen* family's Tai-Chi Chuan is described using illustrations from Shen Chia Cheng's (沈家楨) book *Chen's Tai-Chi Chuan* published in the 1960's. Depicted in the illustrations are the famous Master Chen Fu-Ku (陳發科 1887-1957) and his son Chen Chia-Kuei (陳照奎). The first routine of Tai-Chi Chuan and the second routine Pao-Twi (砲捶) are shown. The *Yang* family's Tai-Chi Chuan is illustrated using the postures of the great Master Yang Chen-Fu (楊澄甫 1883-1936), Wu Chian-Chyan (吳鑑泉 1870-1940) and Chen Man-Ching (鄭曼青 1901-1975). The *Wu* family's Tai-Chi Chuan is illustrated with the postures of Master Hay Way Jen's (郝爲眞 1849-1920) grandson, Hay Shao-Ju (郝少如) who is still teaching Tai-Chi Chuan in Shanghai. I did not use my postures in the book because I feel students should see and learn from the original masters, and since these postures illustrate the optimal standards, students will avoid pursuing variations.

When I began my study of Tai-Chi in Taiwan, Master Cheng Man-Ching had just arrived in New York to teach Tai-Chi Chuan. When I came to America in 1971 for my graduate degree in mathematics education at Rutgers University in New Jersey, Master Cheng Man-Ching had returned to Taiwan to teach the *I-Ching* at the Chinese Cultural College (中國文化學院). I made three visits to

Taiwan. During these visits, I spent much time visiting Master Cheng's home in Taipei, especially on Saturdays and Sundays, when he taught his students how to practice Push-hands. Master Cheng's appearance was small and very gentle, but one had the sense that he was very strong internally. In the practice of Push-hands, he could easily throw a student far away. Although I was not a formal student of Master Cheng, I called him my Master and had great respect for him. With each individual, the question is not who one's teacher is, or how many years one has studied, but how well one understands the philosophy and persists throughout life in the practice of Tai-Chi Chuan.

There is only one warning I would like to give; although the practice of Tai-Chi Chuan can promote good health, it cannot help people who do not take care of themselves. For example, the great master, Yang Chen-Fu, achieved a very high level in Tai-Chi Chuan. In a book on Tai-Chi Chuan, which was published in 1939, Tseng Chao-Jen (曾昭然), Yang Chen-Fu's last student, described his master's posture of Golden Pheasant Stands on One Leg (金雞獨立) as follows: "My master, when he was young, met his elbow to his knee in the posture. However, as he grew older, his stomach became as big as a drum. Thus, he was unable to touch elbow and knee. In fact, they were several inches apart." In the preface of Tseng's Tai-Chi book he states: "I asked my master about the meaning of every posture, and he explained each posture and its meaning very clearly to me. What he could not explain in words, he would show me by demonstrating the postures. After a few movements, he would become short of breath. I recall those times as if they were happening now, and thinking of my master, I am brought to tears." When he was young, Yang Chen-Fu lived in Beijing and had an orderly daily life. Hsu Yu-Sen (許禹生) points out in his Tai-Chi Chuan book published in the 1930's that Yang and Hsu practiced the Tai-Chi Chuam solo exercise at least twelve times daily in the Pao-Fu Temple (保福寺)in Beijing. Later, Yang went to Nanking, Shanghai, etc. to teach Tai-Chi. The move to the south part of China from the pleasant countryside of Beijing meant a change of environment and lifestyle. Because of increased travel and social activities, Yang Chen-Fu did not have as much time for his daily practice of Tai-Chi Chuan. He gradually became very fat and died in his fifties.

Another example of the importance of taking care of oneself is provided by Cheng Man-Ching, who was not only a renowned master of Tai-Chi Chuan but also a poet, artist, Chinese doctor and famous chess player. Master Cheng in the preface of his Chinese Tai-Chi Chuan book, published in 1946, talks about himself: "When I was young, I suffered from rickets and rheumatism. However, by the practicing Yin-Gin Ching(易筋經) or "the change of tendons," I developed my strength and regained my health. When I neared twenty, I contracted tuberculosis and suffered from a serious cough and vomited blood. I learned

Tai-Chi Chuan and consequently regained my health and strength once again." Later in his book, Master Cheng talks about drinking: "At about age seven or eight, I could drink one or two bottles of wine; at age eighteen, I nearly died from a twenty-four hour drinking binge. My mother then forced me to stop drinking. I stopped for six years, but at age twenty-four, I began drinking again. My frequency and capacity for drink increased greatly. Until about age forty, I could drink large amounts and not become drunk. In 1946, at age forty-five, my tolerance for drink began to decrease, and I easily and frequently became drunk."

Master Cheng taught Tai-Chi Chuan in Taiwan for free. His students, knowing he liked to drink, often gave him gifts of fine wines. He soon developed an outstanding wine collection in his home. Finally, his doctor told him that his blood pressure had become too high and advised him to stop drinking. Master Cheng continued to practice Tai-Chi, but he also continued to drink. In 1975, at age seventy-four, he was struck with a heart attack and died.

I have used these two examples not to criticize these great masters, but to point out that, along with the practice of Tai-Chi Chuan, one must always take care of oneself and avoid harmful habits. My dream is for all Americans to practice Tai-Chi Chuan each day in order to promote health and well-being throughout their country. For this reason, I have taught Tai-Chi free to students for eight years. Likewise, this dream is the inspiration for my writing this book. The backyards of this nation are ideal places for the practice of Tai-Chi Chuan, and as people experience the many benefits of Tai-Chi Chuan, its practice will continue to spread. I envision a day when Tai-Chi teachers will be trained in a Tai-Chi college to instruct them in the practice of Tai-Chi Chuan. Everywhere people will have the opportunity to learn how the practice of Tai-Chi Chuan improves the health of the body, mind and spirit.

Because English is a second language for me, the writing of this book has been a great challenge. After my Chinese text was translated into English, some of my students helped me to improve the English. It was difficult to find students who were proficient in both Tai-Chi philosophy and the skills required to write and publish a book.

Five years of work on the book resulted in a basic text which reflected my research and experience as well as accurately described the Tai-Chi philosophy. First I standardize Chen's, Yang's, and Wu's forms to promote the common practice of Tai-Chi Chuan throughout the world. Second, I go beyond the physical forms and talk about the philosophy. Although Tai-Chi philosophy is not easily explained, I feel it is important to give readers an understanding of how Tai-Chi Chuan effects one's view of space and time. My book is the first to deal with this subject in any detail. Eventually,. after years of practice of Tai-Chi Chuan, one will gradually feel that every movement of Tai-Chi Chuan is a movement of the universe. The separation between mind, body and spirit begins to disappear, and the Tai-Chi student attains "oneness". Likewise, the Tai-Chi student ceases to feel apart from other people and the rest of creation. Finally, the Tai-Chi student will be on the threshold of the four-dimensional world by learning that our present understanding of time is limited to our perception of this moment and gradually becoming aware of the continuum of past, present, and future. Tai-Chi will show us a new awareness of space and time and our place in that continuum.

There are a number of people who have been helpful in the writing of this book. Without their advice, assistance and encouragement, writing this book would have been much more difficult.

I especially would like to thank the following:

Daren Driscoll, Elisabeth Boeke, Estelle Lader, James Birney, Jay Dunbar, Hess, Laurie Heddy, Leonard Hollander, Marsha Rosa, Mindy Sheps, Paul Albe Richard Green, Shana, Stephen Berman, Sidney Austin, Susanna Thompson, Vector Franco, Suzanne, Wagner, Zollo; C.C. Chan (詹), 陳嘉素 , 邰小姐 . And, I extend a special gratitude to Wang, Chien-Chang (王建章) for his work on the drawings.

Jou, Tsung-Hwa

PREFACE
TO THE
THIRD EDITION

Since the publication of the first edition of this book, I have received letters from around the world, and many teachers and students of Tai-Chi Chuan have visited me. I am grateful for their favorable response, but now I feel as if a thousand pound burden has been set upon my shoulders. I am sixty-five years old: a "senior citizen." In other forms of physical activity I might be expected to retire, having been surpassed by younger people. Tai-Chi Chuan, however, is unique. If people visited me and found I had nothing further to show them, they might justifiably feel that though my book is good, its author is unable to demonstrate that Tai-Chi can be used by people of any age to fight, develop energy, and rejuvenate the body. They would say that Tai-Chi Chuan is only talk. Consequently, over the past three years I have redoubled my efforts to make progress, and as a result, have achieved a breakthrough from my previous ability to a new level of understanding and practice.

There is no secret, no key piece of information which if revealed would instantly confer enlightenment and expertise. If you do not make progress, you cannot blame your teacher, because no teacher can transfer awareness to you. If you have no teacher, do not place your highest priority on finding the "right" one. None of my teachers were famous Tai-Chi masters, and for over ten years I have not had a personal teacher. In that time, I have discovered the only real secret: you must develop on your own. If you continue to depend on a teacher, or merely try to reproduce and preserve a particular teacher's

approach, you will not reach your highest potential. Anyone wishin. ₒ◡
further must be willing to re-examine the classical principles of Tai-Chi,
explained in chapter four, and intensify his or her efforts to embody them.

In order to improve my own ability, I knew I needed to devote more time
to Tai-Chi; yet I thought I could not possibly fit more practice into my schedule.
When I reviewed my daily habits, though, I realized that I was spending two or
more hours a day reading a variety of Chinese newspapers. I cancelled all my
subscriptions, and ordered only the Sunday Times. In this way I could improve
my English, keep up with the news, and have more time for Tai-Chi Chuan.
Now I do not subscribe to the Times, either. It is always possible for people
to make time for activities they really value.

Also, I thought about the stories of early Yang style masters: how one
could throw the strongest boxer to the ground using only the force in his
abdomen, and how another would lie on his back, place grains of rice on his
abdomen, and launch them to the ceiling. Clearly this kind of prowess is not
the result of performing the Tai-Chi forms softly and gracefully a few times a
day. Another Yang master used to practice his inner strength at night, making
the bed shake suddenly. I realized then that to attain the highest levels in
Tai-Chi Chuan, it would be necessary for me to strengthen myself even at
night. Now, I sleep only two or three hours every night, catnapping between
sessions of meditation and Ch'i-Kung.

The breakthrough I have attained is most obvious to others in the practice
of push-hands. I now realize that true ability is not a trick, or simply better
technique. It results from the cultivation of a real, non-muscular energy, Tai-Chi
"Chin," and from learning how to mobilize this energy with a minimum of
effort. From my own experience over the past three years, I would like to
place a renewed emphasis on three aspects of Tai-Chi Chuan, which I feel will
lift any good Tai-Chi player to new levels if practiced diligently.

First, practice Ch'i-Kung breathing, described in Chapter 3, as often as
possible. Hold the abdominal positions for longer intervals, concentrating
with your mind on the Tan-Tien. Ch'i will begin to gather in the belly, like
money deposited in a savings bank. As you are gradually able to give up the
use of muscular force, you will be able to draw upon this reserve of inner
strength. Unless you cultivate this energy, your Tai-Chi will be like writing
checks on an empty account. You may be able to push people around, but
you are only fooling yourself.

Second, practice repeatedly the Chan Ssu Chin in the Silk Cocoon exercises,
described in Chapter 3. You can practice these movements with each of the
joints in the body, striving to emulate the soft, powerful sensitivity of a cat.

Third, merge your practice of Ch'i-Kung and the Chan Ssu Chin with your performance of any Tai-Chi Chuan solo form. Let the body's outer movements and inner energy become responsive to the kind of spiral pathways you develop for the Chan Ssu Chin. For awhile, this may impel you to change the appearance of the form so that, for example, the hands in "Single Whip" twist outward simultaneously, or the feet rotate dynamically. Eventually, as you internalize the energy patterns, the form will look much as it did at first. This is reminiscent of the story of a Zen master for whom a mountain was a mountain before his enlightenment; upon his enlightenment a mountain was not a mountain; after his enlightenment, a mountain became a mountain again.

Gradually you will be able to sink the movements of Silk Cocoon into your body, until they become natural and automatic. Then, when you practice push-hands, your arm can be still while your whole body expresses the Chan Ssu Chin. You will not have to disengage the attack with a forceful block, or withdraw by stepping back. Instead, differentiating emptiness and solidity, your inner response to his first touch will already have defeated your opponent.

I would like to assure my readers that the Tao, the way, of Tai-Chi Chuan leads to mastery today as surely as it did in former times. The old stories and principles are authentic guides to the kind of faithful, persevering study and practice required. I trust that this book will also continue to serve as a dependable guide. Another source of encouragement is the growing sense of community among Tai-Chi players. In the southeast, for instance, one of my students, Jay Dunbar, established a newly-formed society to help players from all schools and backgrounds communicate and share with each other. Tai-Chi is not something we should attempt to guard jealously. Generosity does not deplete us, and may help others to make progress. Let us open old doors wide, and work together for a true Tai-Chi society.

Jou, Tsung-Hwa

PREFACE
TO THE
FOURTH EDITION

There is a Master Key to Tai-Chi Chuan. Possessing it, if we are willing to devote time and energy to practice, we can continue to make progress throughout life to the limits of our natural ability. Without this key, we can only hope to improve our technique to a certain level, and then will "sigh away our time," (枉費功夫貽嘆息) as the Song of Thirteen Postures says. The Master Key defines the art of Tai-Chi Chuan. We can do the forms, the "ch'uan," and even practice a variety of principles such as slowness, relaxation, straight spine, and certain hand positions. We can even reach high technical achievement; but without the Master Key, we should not call our art "Tai-Chi Chuan."

The Master Key is not related to any particular style. Instead, it makes one family of all diverse forms of Tai-Chi. The forms and styles are analogous to rooms in the same hotel. Each room has a key whose superficial appearance differentiates it from all others, and provides the guest with access to that room, and to no other Problems arise when guests begin thinking their room is best, and the particular bumps and valleys, notches and grooves, straight or contoured edges in their key are essential, and should appear in everyone's key. As the external differences are given greater significance, "Tai-Chi Hotel" turns into "Chuan Condominiums." All the guests try their keys in one another's doors and say, "Your room is no good because my key doesn't open your door, and I know my key works" This is happening among some Tai-Chi players today. Adherents of various styles become involved in describing individual differences as if they were fundamental. One might say, "The key to Tai-Chi Chuan has five notches of increasing depth in its upper edge"; another might counter. "The upper edge of the key must be smooth to permit it to turn either way." When instructors, who may have been misled by their teachers, focus on the unique configuration of their own "keys," students are easily fooled, and mimic the person at the front of the class instead of seeking to apply the Master Key for themselves. However, just as the manager of a hotel has one master key which unlocks all doors, there is one Master Key to Tai-Chi Chuan that reveals which bumps and valleys in individual keys are merely superficial differences, and which are common to all other styles, and therefore define the essence of the art.

The Master Key to Tai-Chi Chuan, is so complete that it contains all other principles within it, yet so simple that some people will hear and laugh, some will acknowledge it yet forget to practice it, and only a few will achieve mastery with it. Yet anyone can hear and immediately have some understanding of it. What is the Master Key? You do not have to take my word for it: I did not originate it. It has existed since ancient times, distinguishing Tai-Chi from other "ch'uan." I only wish to emphasize it so Tai-Chi players of all styles can see the common ground defining their practice, and can work together toward mastery.

In the Tang Dynasty (618-905 A.D.), a hermit named Hsu Suan-Ping (許宣平) is said to have practiced a martial art similar to Tai-Chi Chuan "with the eight trigrams in the arms and five elements under the feet,"(手抱八卦, 脚踏五行) which means all movement according to the principles of the I Ching. In the tenth century, Chen Lin Hsi (程靈洗) stated that no one can master Tai-Chi Chuan without studying the I Ching. These are early statements of the Master Key to Tai-Chi Chuan.

In the fourteenth century, Chang San Feng (張三豐), who synthesized earlier forms of Tai-Chi boxing, Taoist breathing techniques or ch'i kung, and the principles of the I Ching to define the art now known as Tai-Chi Chuan, wrote a treatise called "The Theory of Tia-Chi Chuan." (太極拳經). At the end of that work he emphasizes the importance of thirteen postures, which correspond to the eight trigrams of the I Ching and the five elements. (五步，八門十三勢) These concepts can be considered the Master Key to Tai-Chi Chuan. All subsequent variations are based on this foundation.

Around 1970, Chi Chang Tao (綦江濤), an advanced student of the great modern master Cheng Man-Ch'ing, told me that his teacher had said there were "eight trigrams in the hand," Chi did not understand this saying, and asked me about it because he thought my background in mathematics would enable me to explain the dynamics of hand movements in terms of the eight trigrams. I didn't understand then, but now, fifteen years later, I do.

From before Chang San Feng to the present, experts have recognized the Master Key which can transform any "ch'uan" into Tai-Chi Chuan. If karate practitioners applied the Master Key, their karate would become Tai-Chi. This sounds mysterious, but actually it is quite simple. There is a Chinese expression,

"The highest thing is the simplest." As soon as I show you, you can see it immediately, for it seems natural. I might say initially "the eight trigrams in the arms" means that your hands move in unison, and your movements match perfectly those of your opponent; the "five elements under the feet" means to be able to step forward or back, to turn left or right, while remaining poised at the center. This may seem too simple; but the Master Key is not an academic or intellectual comprehension. The only way to understand it is to do it. Do not expect to get this by following a teacher. Practice again and again by yourself to gain tong chin (懂勁). "understanding energy" or self-knowledge; one day you will know, and will no longer feel the need to ask anyone about this or that.

The Master Key is not a short cut. "The highest is the simplest, but the simplest is also the most difficult." Practice in applying the Master Key is the work of a lifetime. Whether you have been studying thirty years or three months, ask yourself if your practice incorporates an effective method for embodying "the eight trigrams in the arms, the five elements under the feet."

If you want to understnad the eight trigrams in the arms, for instance, you must practice the Chan Ssu Chin, which I have described in chapter three of The Tao of Tai-Chi Chuan. If you want to understand the Chan Ssu Chin, you must understand the Tai-Chi Diagram, discussed in chapter two. Your practice might develop through three stages. First, you must learn not to move your arms independently of your body. Cheng Man-Ch'ing used to say that if the arms moved independently, one was just "doing exercise, not Tai-Chi." The arms must move around a center as the earth orbits around the sun. Study this by tracing the Tai-Chi Diagram with each hand singly, paying attention to the relationship between the palm (Yin) and the back of the hand (Yang). When the palm is facing straight up, the hand shows the trigram "Kun" (≡ ≡). When the palm is facing down, the hand shows the trigram "Chien" (≡). Each hand manifests all eight trigrams as it passes around the circle, like the monthly cycle of the moon from new to full and back again.

Second, all parts of the body must exhibit revolution, similar to the rotation of the earth on its axis, which, when added to the circularity of its orbit, results in a spiralling motion through space. Study the Chan Ssu Chin exercise with both hands matching one another, like the sun and the moon. Matching may be complementary, where for instance the left hand shows the trigram "Tui" (≡≡) and the right hand shows "Ken" (≡≡); each hand showing Yin in an equal proportion to the Yang in the other hand. Matching may also be corresponding, where the hands move as identical or mirror images of one another. Third, your two hands must match one another in the solo form in preparation for being able to match the energy of a partner.

All arts have a "master key." For example, most people can learn to dance by taking lessors, following a teacher, or imitating others around them on the dance floor, and some dance professionally for years; but only a few become great dancers. The others learn the outer movements, but the great dancer possesses a "master key." Many people take piano, and of these, some are disciplined enough to become professional players, piano teachers, or even concert pianists; but only a few become great. The others may learn to put their fingers in the "right" places; the great pianist possesses a "master key." It is the same in the martial arts.

Long ago, someone got the idea for the art of monkey fist by watching a monkey. Now, a person may study "monkey fist" (猴拳) for twenty years and reach a high level of proficiency; but if he has never watched a monkey, his art cannot truly be called monkey fist. The master key to the art of Pa Kua (八卦) is the circular arrangement of the eight trigrams. Practitioners may imitate circular walking, but they must understand the eight trigrams for their art to truly be "Pa Kua." The master key to Hsing-I (形意) is the relation of the five elements in each movement. In Tai-Chi, we have the same problem as other arts. Most students learn only to follow, and do not acquire knowledge of the Master Key. The Tai-Chi player must learn both the eight trigrams and the five elements. Lacking the Master Key, even after twenty years of study with the best teacher, you may have "ch'uan" but it will not be Tai-chi Chuan.

Some practitioners of monkey fist, Pa Kua, Hsing-I, and Tai-Chi would exclaim loudly against this, saying it is too theoretical, and useless for fighting. They would be right if the goal were form, but it is formlessness. They would be right if the Master Key were complicated: too abstract to be applied effectively. It is not. In Tai-Chi Chuan, the Master Key is the conscious embodiment of the fundamental way in which change occurs naturally in this world. This mechanism is exercised in Ch'i kung, expressed in the five elements, and pictured in the Tai-Chi Diagram, which is the basis of the I Ching. The Tai-Chi Diagram is our "monkey".

Beware of being satisfied with your own level of understanding of these things. If you are willing to accept a platitude about the "natural harmoney of opposites" as a summary of the Tai-Chi Diagram, you will never make progress. Take the Tai-Chi Diagram as your teacher, practice "Tai-Chi" as revealed in it, and you will begin to be able to read the trigrams and hexagrams as patterns of energy in yourself and others. If you haven't yet made the effort to understand these things, then no matter how many years you have studied, until you have made the effort to understand the master key, you cannot say you have begun to be a student of Tai-Chi Chuan.

JOU, TSUNG HWA

CHAPTER ONE
ROOTS

After careful and intensive study of the world around them, the ancient Chinese philosophers developed the concept of "Tai-Chi" (太極) or "The Grand Terminus." Understanding this Tai-Chi philosophy that influenced traditional Chinese culture provides a necessary foundation for the study of Tai-Chi Chuan (太極拳). Unlike fragmented and apparently unrelated branches of knowledge, Tai-Chi can offer a comprehensive explanation for all the phenomena in the universe. Thus, Tai-Chi may be seen as the root of the tree of wisdom, in its ability to enrich every branch of knowledge.

Tai-Chi principles describe practical approaches to solving problems in natural as well as human realms. During the Ein Dynasty (殷朝 1200 B.C.), these concepts were used to create the Chinese calendar and to predict lunar and solar eclipses. Acupuncture, invented in the Chow Dynasty (周朝 696 B.C.), applied Tai-Chi philosophy to curing illness and maintaining health. Tai-Chi Chuan was another practical application of Tai-Chi philosophy.

Tai-Chi Chuan can be translated as the ultimate or highest of the martial arts. It is based on three major principles of Tai-Chi philosophy: the changing trigrams of the *I Ching* (易經), the Tai-Chi diagram (太極圖), and the five elements (五行). The objectives of Tai-Chi Chuan include harmony of the mind, promotion of health, and the attainment of rejuvenation and longevity. Through the constant practice of Tai-Chi Chuan one begins to comprehend more fully some of the profound concepts in Chinese philosophy which are impossible to explain clearly in words.

1-1. CHANG SAN-FENG AND TAI-CHI CHUAN

*A*lthough there are various stories about the founding of Tai-Chi Chuan, Chang San-Feng (張三丰), who certainly was the greatest teacher of the system, is generally given the major credit. Chang San-Feng was also known as Chang Tung (張通) and Chang Chun-pao(張君寶).His ancestors lived on Dragon-Tiger Mountain (龍虎山), a Taoist historical site in Kiang-Hsi (江西) Province in the southeast of China. His grandfather moved to Yi Hsien (懿州), in Liao-Lin (遼寧), a northeast province. His father, Chang Chun-Jen (張居仁), a very intelligent man, passed the examination given by the government of the Emperor Tai-Chung (太宗) of the Yuan Dynasty (元朝 1279-1368) and was thereby eligible for a high government position. However, he was devoid of worldy ambition and preferred to live in the mountains. This lack of ambition (清高) was admired since the educated Chinese saw the hermit who renounced all connection with society as the ideal and the position of government official as much less satisfying. Chang San-Feng was born at midnight on April 9, 1247, and the anniversary of this day is now celebrated by followers of Tai-Chi Chuan with dining, drinking and demonstrations of Tai-Chi Chuan.

To the ancient Chinese, physical appearance reflected one's level of intelligence and character. This method of evaluation is similar to the more familiar art of palmistry, but the Chinese looked at not only the hand, but the whole body. According to legend, Chang San-Feng was born a wise man because he had the arched back of a tortoise and the figure of a crane. His large round eyes were considered a symbol of intelligence and longevity. At twelve years of age he began studying the Chinese classics. Because of his good memory and keen perception, he was eventually able to become a government official. Chang San-Feng spent some time meditating and planning his future during a visit to Ko-Hung Mountain (葛洪山), where Ko-Hung (See Figure 1-1a), a minister in the reign of Emperor Yuan (290-370 A.D.), was said to have become immortal. After the death of his parents, he resigned from his government position and returned to his birthplace long enough to give his property away to relatives. Then accompanied by two young boys, he set out to wander the mountains for thirty years visiting old temples in the hope of meeting a wise man. Finally, he settled in midwestern China in the beautiful, green Pao-Gi (寶雞) Mountains which have three pointed peaks, or San-Feng (三峯) in Chinese. It is said he mastered the well-known Shao-Lin Chuan (少林拳) during that time.

Shao-Lin Chuan is an exercise invented in the famous Shao-Lin Buddhist temple in Ho-Nan (河南), a northern province of China. The temple was built in the Shiao-Si (少室) Mountains during the Wei (魏) Dynasty in the third century A.D. Ta-Mo (達摩), an Indian Bodhidarma master who came to China in 527 A.D., lectured there for many years during the Liang (梁) Dynasty, sixth century A.D. Finding many of the monks weak, unhealthy and even prone to fall asleep during sermons and meditation, Ta-Mo pointed out the importance of having a sound body in the effort to develop a strong inner spirit. Before Ta-Mo had emphasized the need for strength, physical energy and proper body posture in effective concentration, Buddhist theory had stressed development of the soul and neglected that of the body. Ta-Mo, who encouraged the monks to exercise in the early morning for their health, created several systems of exercise: the *Yin-Gin Ching* (易筋經), or "the change of tendons," *Hsi-Swi Ching* (洗髓經), or "the marrow washing," and eighteen Buddha's hands (十八羅漢手). Thus he founded Shao-Lin Boxing.

After Ta-Mo died, his followers left Shao-Lin and boxing was abandoned until several hundred years later when Joy-Yuang (覺遠上人), a master monk who was proficient in boxing and fencing, began to teach at the temple. He learned of the eighteen Buddha's hands and decided to improve the system by adding his own skills. Thus, Shao-Lin Chuan was developed into seventy-two

In his efforts to prolong life indefinitely, a minister by the name of Ko-Hung refined "the pill of immortality" at the Ko-Hung mountain. The result of his study was the development of Taoist magic.

Figure 1-1a

hands and earned a better reputation. One of the many followers it attracted was Chang San-Feng, who stayed at the temple for about ten years and mastered all the Shao-Lin exercises.

The treasures of the Shao-Lin Temple were called the five Chuans (五拳). Each Chuan was named for the animal best exemplifying its attributes. The Chuans originally had only six postures each. At the present time, however, each Chuan has over one hundred postures. Having mastered these five Chuans, a player can develop many variations. The original Chuans are: 1. Dragon Chuan—training attention and spirit; emphasizing lightness, stillness and change. 2. Tiger Chuan—strengthening the bones, emphasizing jumping up and down. 3. Leopard Chuan—practicing the application of force; emphasizing jumping and fighting. 4. Snake Chuan—practicing inner breathing, prolonging the body; becoming very sensitive and active. 5. Crane Chuan—training concentration, stability, accuracy and determination to defeat the opponent.

All the styles, names and clans of Chinese martial arts are generated from Shao-Lin Chuan, the prototypical Chinese martial art. However, Tai-Chi Chuan differs from other martial arts because Chang San-Feng added the theory of the *I Ching* and Taoist breathing techniques, or Chi-Kung (氣功), to Shao-Lin Chuan. Therefore, the way of practice transcends martial art towards will, mind, body and nature—very close to the practice of Tao (道) itself, or the way of Nature.

Now let us return to Chang San-Feng's life. In 1314, at the age of sixty-seven he finally met a Taoist, Ho-Lung (火龍), whose name means "fire dragon." This hermit taught Chang the method of being immortal, but Chang practiced in the high mountains for four years with very little achievement. He then moved to Wu-Tang Mountain (武當山) and finally, after staying there for nine years, became aware of the truth and Tao. Again he started wandering from north to south. When he returned to his birthplace, he found all of his relatives had died. When the Yuan Dynasty ended in 1368 and the Ming Dynasty (明朝1368-1654) began, Chang San-Feng was afraid of being needed by the royal family since he was a well-known immortal Taoist and so pretended to be mad. Thereby, he earned another nickname of "Sloppy Taoist." In 1385, the Emperor ordered him to serve the government, but he hid himself near the border of Yun-Nan province which is in the southwest of China, until 1399. He had to go back to Wu-Tang Mountain at that time to meet his best friend, Wan Pu-Tse (完樸子). In 1407, Emperor Chen-Tzu (成祖) sent two officials to visit Chang on Wu-Tang Mountain, but they could not find him. The emperor then ordered high-ranking officials to build a big temple on Wu-Tang Mountain in Chang's honor. In 1459, Emperor Yiu-Chung bestowed a title of immortality on Chang. Thus, according to legend, Chang San-Feng was born at the end of the Sung (宋)

Dynasty and lived through the whole Yuan Dynasty to the reign of Tein-Chung (定宗) in the Ming Dynasty, a period of more than 200 years.

There are different stories as to how Chang San-Feng created Tai-Chi Chuan. One, that he created it in his dreams, may seem improbable. However, just as the French mathematician Pascal invented a geometrical theory at 16 years of age in a dream after studying the problem during the day, Chang San-Feng with his sound foundation in Shao-Lin Chuan might have used the subconscious to create Tai-Chi Chuan. According to another story, when he lived in Wu-Tang Mountain, Chang heard birds making an unusual noise and saw them all staring down at the ground where a serpent was lifting its head and watching upward. A moment later, a magpie, spreading its wings, descended to attack the serpent, which moved slightly to escape the attack, but maintained its usual circular shape. So, the contest continued, up and down, back and forth, several times till Chang stepped out of the door. Immediately the magpie flew away and the serpent disappeared. Chang then realized the truth of softness over firmness (柔能克剛) and created Tai-Chi Chuan. Another legend is that when Chang San-Feng saw the monks practicing boxing on Wu-Tang Mountain, he thought they used too much force and outer strength and therefore lacked balance. If Yin and Yang were balanced inside the body, one would be less clumsy. Accordingly, he used principles from the Tao of nature, the Tai-Chi diagram and the *I Ching* to develop Tai-Chi Chuan. The purpose of the movements in Tai-Chi is to transfer the Chi, or intrinsic energy, to the Shen, or spirit (練氣化神), and to use inner rather than outer force. After Chang San-Feng, the famous Tai-Chi masters included Wang Tsung (陝西王宗), Chen Tun-Chow (溫州陳同州), Chang Sung-Hsi (海塩張松溪), Yeh Chi-Ma (四明葉繼美), Wang Tsung-Yueh (山右王宗岳), and Chiang Fah (河北蔣發). Finally, Chiang Fah taught Tai-Chi Chuan to Chen's family.

1-2. LEGENDS ABOUT CHANG SAN-FENG

*T*ales about Chang San-Feng have been widely circulated and believed from generation to generation. Many of the stories which follow may seemed exaggerated to Westerners; in fact, there are not even many Chinese who would believe them. This disbelief results from not having been exposed to the remarkable accomplishment of a person who is even moderately skilled at Tai-Chi Chuan. In any case, serious students can use stories of Chang San-Feng's achievements to provide examples of their ultimate goals. As such, they are teaching stories which remind us that practice makes perfect.

It is said Chang San-Feng had five hobbies: (1) sword dancing in moonlight, (2) playing Tai-Chi Chuan on a dark night, (3) climbing mountains on a windy

night,   (4) reading classics on a rainy night and   (5) meditating at midnight.
He believed that sword dancing in moonlight brought energy (增神), playing
Tai-Chi Chuan on a dark night brought vigor (益精), climbing mountains on
windy nights lengthened the breath (長氣), reading classics on a rainy night
cleaned the mind (明心), and meditating at midnight brightened one's nature
(見性). These five are the Taoist's main goals, continually sought by them. If
people are able to reach these ends, then they are not far from Tao.

In bitterly cold winter, when the path in front of the temple was covered
with snow, Chang liked to go out and enjoy the snowy landscape. After he
walked on the path, no footprints remained, just as if no one had stepped there.
This phenomenon is called "stepping on snow leaving no footprints" and is
considered the highest ability. He also could melt the snow when he passed by
using his inner force, the pure "Yang" air. The heat from his body was so
incredible that the path then would appear as if it were under warm sunshine.
It is also said that as he meditated at midnight, the Chi from his body went
rustling through his robe as if the wind had blown it. Moreover, the walls
surrounding him shook. These phenomena indicated that his inner force had
reached a peak level. He had reached the stage where Chi had been transferred
to Shen; his spiritual and physical energy were in harmony. One night, a sudden
rain storm hit the mountain. Many trees fell and a huge rock weighing near a
ton rolled down toward the temple but was blocked by another huge rock on
the way. It was a critical situation during the storm, but Chang, as he had the
hobby of climbing mountains on windy nights, climbed the edge of the first
rock, lifted the second one, and threw it into a creek. His strength was truly
amazing.

Chang San-Feng was fond of apes and cranes, which were always around
him in Wu-Tang Mountain. When he forbade himself to eat cooked crops (辟穀)
for several months, the ape would go to the forests to pick wild fruits for the
master. The crane would act as a guard, driving the snakes and serpents away. If
there was a python, the crane would tell Chang San-Feng, who killed pythons
with his bare hands. When the python raised its head and struck, Chang moved
his body aside swiftly, concentrated his inner force, held his breath, and using
the Mustang Ruffling Its Mane(野馬分鬃) hold, grasped the snake's neck with
one hand and body with the other. Chang then turned his body, applying force
with his waist and legs so that the python became straight. After the snake was
stretched, Chang would throw it to the hillside breaking it into several bloody
sections. Any aged python which might feel Chang spying would do well to hide
itself in the moor or high mountains. It is also said he liked to use the Bend the
Bow to Shoot the Tiger (彎弓射虎) technique to kill tigers with his bare
hands. When a tiger jumped towards him, he stepped forward and turned his

torso a little to the right causing the tiger to miss its target. Chang would then grasp the tiger's rear paws, tearing it into two parts.

Chang raised a very big ape who was so clever that, after watching his master practice everyday for a long time, he could play Tai-Chi. Chang named this ape Hsiao-Ting (學定) which means "to learn to be stable," because the nature of the ape is fickle and Chang wanted his pet to have stability. Hsiao-Ting helped him·in many ways. It is said that Chang cut wood without an ax. As he entered the forest, he would stretch his arms using the Diagonal Flying posture (斜飛式) and, slightly separating his two palms to the right and left, broke several branches which dropped to the ground. Hsiao-Ting picked them up and carried them home as firewood. Chang never needed other help.

The Mongolian royal family of the Yuan Dynasty once were hunting in the Wu-Tang Mountain as Chang was picking herbs to be used as medicine. He was quite aware of all Mongolians being good archers, but he did not like their pompous attitude. While he stood there watching, the Mongols ordered him to walk away. This made Chang angry, but he spoke to the prince with a smile saying, "Your highness hunts with bow and arrow; I use my bare hands." Suddenly a pair of hawks flew across the woods, and Chang jumped some several feet high and caught them. He dropped to the ground like a falling leaf, without making any noise. The prince was shocked. Chang placed the birds on each of his palms. No matter how hard the birds tried to fly, they could not lift themselves. Chang then said, "I have mercy on living creatures; I do not want to hurt the birds." As soon as he withdrew his palms, the hawks flew into the sky. One of the prince's followers was angry and drew his bow to shoot an arrow at Chang. The master opened his mouth and caught the arrow with his teeth; then holding the arrow with his index and middle fingers, he threw it towards a tree. "I have no need of any violent weapons," said he. The arrow struck and was buried deep in the tree.

1-3. TAI-CHI CHUAN BEFORE CHANG SAN-FENG

𝒥 n the Tang Dynasty (唐朝 618-905 A.D.), it is said that there was a style of martial art similar to Tai-Chi Chuan, known by a different name. A hermit named Hsa Suan-Ming (許宣平), a native of An-Huei (安徽) province in southeast China, lived on Tse-Yang Mountain (紫陽山) and ate only uncooked food. Hsa was seven feet five inches tall, with a long beard flowing to his navel and extremely long hair flowing to his feet. Hsa ran as fast as a horse and often carried firewood to town to sell. He would always sing the following:

Bearing firewood to market in the morning
Bringing wine back at sunset.
Where is my home?
It is in the green woods through the clouds.

Li-Pai (李白 701-762 A.D.), one of China's greatest poets in the Tang Dynasty, made a special trip to visit Hsa, but not finding him, he left a poem on the bridge near Hsa's home.   Today the name of that bridge is Waiting Immortality Bridge (望仙橋).   Hsa's style of Tai-Chi Chuan was called *San Hsi Chi* (三世七) since there were thirty-seven movements, similar to the thirteen movements in Chen's Tai-Chi Chuan.   Some of the different names are "Shoot snow goose with a bow," "Dust pan posture," "The sparrow lifts its tail," "Flip fingers," "Tan mountain is angry," "Grind the mill," and "Hang on the tree and kick."   The training method consisted of single posture practice, i.e., finishing one movement then starting another without a standard sequence. After completing the thirty-seven postures, the player automatically put them together as a whole continuous movement, "with the eight trigrams (八卦) in the arms and five elements under the feet," which means "all the changes of movement according to the principles of the *I Ching*."   Completely identifiable with the Tai-Chi principle, the form was called Long Chuan (長拳) because of its continuity.

Li Tao Tze (李道子), another expert in the Tang dynasty also created a long Chuan called *Hsien-Tien Chuan* (先天拳).   Hsien-Tien means "the stage before the universe is created."   It is said Li lived from the Tang Dynasty through the Ming Dynasty (618-1644) — more than a thousand years.   He seldom talked to people and ate nothing but a few pounds of bran daily.   If it were necessary for him to speak, he said only, Great future (大造化), meaning "good luck."   He taught his student Yu Lieu-Chu (余蓮舟) the following about the inner experience of Long Chuan:

It is soundless and formless.
The body must be as transparent as air.
All the movements follow the way of nature,
Like the chime of a big bell
That hangs from the ceiling of an old temple.
Sometimes, like a tiger's growl or, an ape's call,
Still water runs deep.
The sea rises in waves;
There is sound in body and mind.

Yu's family carried on Li's Long Chuan from generation to generation.

These stories about Hsa Suan-Ming and Li Tao-Tze illustrate the existence of martial arts like Tai-Chi Chuan in the Tang Dynasty. In the Liang Dynasty (907-921 A.D.), Hen Kon Yu (韓拱月), an expert in the Tai-Chi martial arts, developed the Nine Little Heavens (小九天). He taught Chen Lin-Hsi (程靈洗), who taught Chen Mee (程　泌), both of whom are officially recorded in history. This Chuan has fourteen movements, including "Lift hand," "Single whip," "Big and small punch," and 'Grasp sparrow's tail" — which have the same postures in Yang's Tai-Chi Chuan. In addition, the Tai-Chi Chuan movements "Looking at fist under elbow" and "Step back to drive away monkey" are the same respectively as "Flower among the leaves" and "Cloud on Monkey's head" in Hen Kon-Yu's Chuan.

· Chen Lin-Hsi stated that no one can master Tai-Chi Chuan without studying the *I Ching*. Tai-Chi Chuan must be understood by the mind. When practicing Tai-Chi Chuan, you must know your own intentions but not allow anyone else to know them. These words thoroughly describe the practical use of Tai-Chi Chuan.

Furthermore, it is said that Hu Chin-Tze (胡鏡子) developed a Tai-Chi martial art called *Hu-Tien Fa* (後天法), but no one knows when or where he was born. Hu Tien means "the stage after the universe is created," and Fa means "method". Hu-Tien Fa, which has 17 postures emphasizes the use of various elbow movements. Its major postures are ward-off, roll-back, press, push, pull, split, elbow, and shoulder-strike. Their functions are similar to those of the corresponding moves in Yang's Tai-Chi Chuan. During Hu's trip to Yang-Chow (揚州), a famous, beautiful city on the northern shore of the lower Yangtze River, he wrote a poem which reads:

> As time goes by
> You do not care, nor I.
> Wandering everywhere without anyone's interference,
> I feel the spring breeze
> As I play the flute in the tavern pavilion.

We can imagine his carefree and open-minded attitude toward life.

In summary, while there were several Tai-Chi martial arts before Chang San-Feng, it was he who achieved their union. From Tai-Chi's narrow martial origins, Chang San-Feng added the Taoist breathing techniques or Chi-Kung and utilized the *I Ching* principles in order, as Chang himself stated, to finally broaden Tai-Chi Chuan to help all people enjoy a long, healthy life. For these reasons, people came to respect and refer to Chang San-Feng as the founder of Tai-Chi Chuan. Chang transformed Tai-Chi Chuan from a martial technique into a way of improving the body, mind and spirit, thus enabling one to progress through the stage of tranquility to ultimately enter the world of the fourth dimension (See Chapter 2-5).

1-4. THE CHEN FAMILY'S TAI-CHI CHUAN

*T*ai-Chi Chuan has been recorded in formal documents since the time of Chen Wang-Ting (陳王廷). Chen was born in Ho-Nan province in northern China during the late sixteenth century and was appointed as an army officer in San-Tung province in 1618. He returned to his birthplace at the collapse of the Ming Dynasty in 1644. At the time he began teaching Tai-Chi Chuan, it consisted of five *Lu* (路), or "routines". He also taught two additional Lu: *Pao-Twi* (砲捶), which means the punches are very fast and violent, like cannon shots; and *Long Chuan,* which has 108 postures.

From generation to generation many new teaching methods were accumulated, and many excellent boxers produced. In each of the five generations after Chen Wang-Ting there was a famous Tai-Chi expert. Chen Chang-Hsin (陳長興1771-1853)united and simplified Chen's Tai-Chi Chuan to a first routine of Tai-Chi Chuan, and a second routine of Pao-Twi. Chen Yu-Ben (陳有本) simplified the movements even further in order to meet the requirement and needs of the era; i.e., strict martial arts training was not stressed as much because the gun had been introduced into Chinese weaponry, a development which was to greatly affect all the martial arts. Another, Chen Chin-Ping (陳清萍) incorporated the Shiao-jar (小架) style for busier and tighter (緊凑) movements. He thus followed the principle of "not changing original action," by which the names of the original movements were left intact, but the postures were altered and circling movements were added to each step. Thus, Chen's Tai-Chi Chuan branched into three styles: Chen Chang-Hsin's Old Style, Chen Yu-Ben's New Style, and Chen Chin-Ping's Shiao-Jar.

The first routine of Chen Chang-Hsin's Tai-Chi Chuan is the oldest known form, from which all other forms have been derived. It has simple movements, more softness and less firmness. Ward-off (掤), roll-back (擟), press (擠) and push (按), or the four directions (四正), were practiced primarily. Elbow (肘), split (挒), pull (採), and shoulder strike (靠), which are the four corners (四隅), were practiced secondarily. Both quality and quantity of movement require softness.

For the student, the routine is like a self-teaching encyclopedia of the science of movement, and of the martial arts techniques, and also of the correct use of breathing. The key to using this tool is the regular practice of the Chan-Ssu Chin, or silk-cocoon chin, which will be described in Chapter 3. One must learn the movement of the body as a coherent unit by originating all movements from its center and by giving circularity to arm and also leg movements.

The student who regularly practices this Chin will gradually learn to follow these principles intuitively and directly, and will then be able to study how the routine explicitly and systematically works out the many possibilities that result.

A simple example of the unitary study is Posture two. King Kong Nailed Fist, where the fist hits the open palm as the foot stamps the ground. A study of complex circularity can be seen in Posture fourteen. Hidden Hand Punch. Here the wardoff arm, the torso, and the right arm and fist are all wound counterclockwise, which brings the wardoff arm out while the right fist is brought back beside the torso, 'hidden'. The coiled-up torsional energy is then released with a clockwise movement that draws the wardoff arm back while the right fist spirals forward with all the energy of the unwinding torso in it.

These possibilities are compounded through a large variety of kicks and punches that go to vigorous degrees like leaping into the air or going all the way to the ground with a leg split. Still other portions of the routine illustrate slow, moderate movements whose outer purpose seems obscure, while within the body the principles of circularity are being applied invisibly.

Coordinating breathing with the movements is a study in itself, and its basic rhythm is emphasized in Posture four. 60% Open 40% Closed, which appears 7 times in the routine. Here the hands are brought down and out from behind the ears during a slow exhalation.

Doubleweighting, or balancing the body's weight between the two legs, is avoided in T'ai Chi as it makes a quick response possible. Its correct role is repeatedly illustrated in the routine as a transitional stage between two postures.

When the routine is performed, it begins with the student facing north, and ends facing the reverse south. It is then repeated, thus finally bringing the practitioner to the north and the same starting place again.

Because of the frequent and clear shifts of movement from vigorous to soft, the routine makes it possible for a student to observe and gain awareness of many varieties of alternation between yin and yang, and how they are successfully made.

The serious student learning the form from a teacher will enhance the benefits of the learning by committing the series of pictures to memory, using them both as a standard, and as training in inner visualization of one's movement. The emphasis on inner training that is so marked in T'ai Chi is being echoed in modern scientific studies of the capabilities of the body. One study, in recent years for example, shows that an average person is capable of clear visual memory and distinction between a minimum of one quarter of a million human faces.

In the first routine's style, the body leads the hands (以身運手); one must forget one's arms and allow the hands to follow the body. In this way one attains a continuous change of moves and makes the Yin and Yang of the body more apparent.

The postures of Chen's first Lu are presented here by name and in diagrams. The numbers on the diagrams refer to the list of the postures names. The pictures of the first Lu depict Chen Fu-Ku's (陳發科 1887-1957) son, Chen Chai-Kuei. These diagrams are reproduced from the most authentic, original sources available, those written by Chen Sin (陳鑫) and Shen Chia-Jen (沈家楨).

The first Lu of Chen's Tai-Chi Chuan:

1. Beginning of Tai-Chi (抱太極)
2. King-Kong mailed fist (金剛搗碓)
3. Grasp sparrow's tail (懶扎衣)
4. 40% open and 60% closed (六封四閉)
5. Single whip (單鞭)
6. King-Kong nailed fist (金剛搗碓)
7. White crane spreads wings (白鶴涼翅)
8. First side walk and twist step (斜行拗步)
9. First conclusion (初收)
10. Kick forward and twist step (前蹚拗步)
11. Second side walk and twist step (斜行拗步)
12. Second conclusion (再收)
13. Kick forward and twist step (摟膝拗步)
14. Hidden hand punch (掩手紅捶)
15. King-Kong nailed fist (金剛搗碓)
16. Chop opponent with fist (披身捶)
17. Bending back and shoulder-strike (背折靠)
18. Blue dragon flies up from water (青龍出水)
19. Push with both hands (雙推手)
20. Three changes of palm (三變掌)
21. Fist under elbow (肘底看拳)
22. Upper arm rolls (倒捲肱)

23. Backward and press elbow (退步壓肘)
24. Middle stage (中盤)
25. White crane spreads wings (白鶴涼翅)
26. Side walk and twist step (斜行拗步)
27. Fan through the back (閃通背)
28. Hidden hand punch (掩手紅捶)
29. 60% open and 40% closed (六封四閉)
30. Single whip (單鞭)
31. Waving hands like clouds (雲手)
32. High pat on horse (高探馬)
33. Rub right foot (右擦腳)
34. Rub left foot (左擦腳)
35. Turn body and kick (左蹬一根)
36. Kick forward and twist step (前蹚拗步)
37. Hit ground with fist (舖地捶)
38. Jump and kick twice (踢二起)
39. Animal head posture (獸頭勢)
40. Hurricane kick (旋風腳)
41. Turn body and kick (右蹬一根)
42. Hidden hand punch (掩手紅捶)
43. Small grasp and hit (小擒拿)
44. Embrace head and push mountain (抱頭推山)
45. Three changes of palm (三變掌)
46. 60% open and 40% closed (六封四閉)
47. Single whip (單鞭)
48. Front posture (前招)
49. Back posture (後招)
50. Mustang ruffling its mane (野馬分鬃)
51. 60% open and 40% closed (六封四閉)
52. Single whip (單鞭)
53. Shake foot twice (雙震腳)
54. Fair lady works at shuttles (玉女穿梭)
55. Grasp sparrow's tail (懶扎衣)

56.   60% open & 40% closed（六封四閉）

57.   Single whip（單鞭）

58.   Waving hands like clouds（雲手）

59.   Sweep leg and cross kick（擺腳跌岔）

60.   Golden pheasant stands on one leg（金雞獨立）

61.   Upper arm rolls（倒捲肱）

62.   Withdraw and press elbow（退步壓肘）

63.   Middle posture（中盤）

64.   White crane spreads wings（白鶴涼翅）

65.   Side walk & twist step（斜行拗步）

66.   Fan through the back（閃通背）

67.   Hidden hand punch（掩手紅捶）

68.   60% open and 40% closed（六封四閉）

69.   Single whip（單鞭）

70.   Waving hands like clouds（雲手）

71.   High pat on horse（高探馬）

72.   Cross hands and sweep lotus with one leg（擺蓮腿）

73.   Punch opponent's groin（指膛捶）

74.   White ape offers fruits（白猿獻菓）

75.   60% open and 40% closed（六封四閉）

76.   Single whip（單鞭）

77.   Sparrow ground dragon（雀地龍）

78.   Step up to form seven stars of the dipper（上步摘星）

79.   Step back to ride tiger（退步跨虎）

80.   Turn around and sweep lotus（轉身擺腳）

81.   Face opponent cannon（當頭砲）

82.   King-Kong nailed fist（金剛搗碓）

83.   Conclusion of Tai-Chi（合太極）

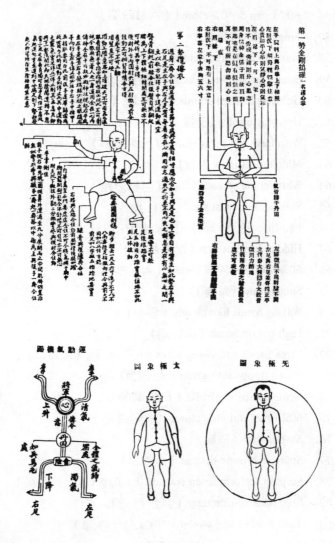

These pictures are from Chen-Sin's (1849-1929) book, *Chen's Tai-Chi Chuan*, published in 1933. The figure demonstrates how one should pay attention during the practice of Tai-Chi Chuan. All of these concepts are very difficult to translate into English.

Figure 1-4a

1

2

3

4

5

6 7

8

9

10

11   12

13

14

15

16

17

18

19

20   **21**

22

23

24   ### 25

26

27

28

29

30

31

32

33

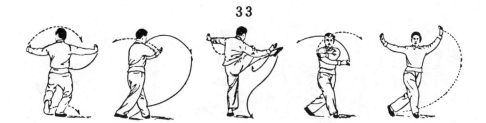

34   **35**

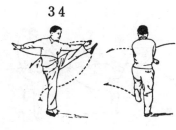

36   **37**

38

39

40

41

42

43

44

45   **46**

47

48   **49**

50   51

52

53   54

5 5

5 6

5 7

5 8

59

60

61

62

63

64

65

66

67

68

69

70

71

72

74

73

75

76

78

77

79

80

81

82

83

Pao-Twi (砲捶), Chen's second routine, is a more complicated set of movements with more firmness and less softness than the first routine. Its form of
attack emphasizes elbow, split, pull, shoulder-strike and the four corners. The
four directions, or ward-off, roll-back, press and push, play supplemental roles.
Thus the relative emphasis on the practice of the four corners and four
directions is reversed from that in the first Lu. Quality and quantity of
movement require solidity and firmness, and fast action is important. The style
of Pao-Twi, the second Lu, emphasizes hands leading the body (以手運身);
i.e., when you punch forward, your body has to follow the direction of your
hand or fist, or in other words, the attacking motion, which is usually
accompanied by a jump, pulls your body forward. In terms of physical
appearance, the first Lu possesses slowness, softness, and stability; the second Lu
possesses swiftness, hardness, and high-jumping. As for quality and quantity of
movement, in both the first and second Lu Chen's Tai-Chi Chuan harmonizes
softness and firmness. Its movements alternate speed with slowness to form the
Tai-Chi inner strength which allows fast responses to fast actions and slow
responses to slow actions.

Pao-Twi, now almost extinct, is shown here in diagrams keyed by numbers
to the names of the postures on the accompanying list. Most of the diagrams
portray Chen Fu-Ku (See Figure 1-4b), the grandson of Chen Chang-Hsin
(陳長興). Chen Fu-Ku carried on the Chen family legacy and developed his
own skill by practicing the Tai-Chi Chuan solo exercise twenty times every day.
Even after he was sixty, he performed it ten times daily. Many other
well-known Tai-Chi specialists studied under him when he came to Peking.

Chen Fu-Ku （1887-1957)

Figure 1-4b

Chen's Second Lu, or Pao-Twi:

1. Beginning of Pao-Twi（砲捶起勢）
2. King-Kong nailed fist（金剛搗碓）
3. Grasp sparrow's tail（懶扎衣）
4. 60% open and 40% closed（六卦四閉）
5. Single whip（單鞭）
6. Deflect downward, intercept, and punch（搬攔捶）
7. Guard the heart punch（護心捶）
8. Side walk and twist step（斜行拗步）
9. Attack waist, press elbow and punch（煞腰壓肘拳）
10. Wells down punch（井攬直入）
11. Plum flowers swept by wind（風掃梅花）
12. King-Kong mailed fist（金剛搗碓）
13. Hidden body punch（庇身捶）
14. Chop opponent with fist（披身捶）
15. Cut hand（斬手）
16. Sleeves dance like turning flowers（翻花舞袖）
17. Hidden hand punch（掩手紅捶）
18. Flying step and elbow（飛步拗鸞肘）
19. Waving hands like clouds（雲手 3 times）
20. High pat on horse（高探馬）
21. Waving hands like clouds（雲手 3 times）
22. High pat on horse（高探馬）
23. Machine cannon 1（連珠砲一）
24. Machine cannon 2（連珠砲二）
25. Machine cannon 3（連珠砲三）
26. Ride unicorn and face back（倒騎麟）
27. White snake sticks out tongue 1（白蛇吐信一）
28. White snake sticks out tongue 2（白蛇吐信二）
29. White snake sticks out tongue 3（白蛇吐信三）
30. Turn flower under sea bottom（海底翻花）
31. Hidden hand punch（掩手紅捶）

32. Turn body and six coincides (轉身六合)
33. Left firecraker 1 (左裹鞭炮一)
34. Left firecraker 2 (左裹鞭炮二)
35. Right firecraker 1 (右裹鞭炮一)
36. Right firecraker 2 (右裹鞭炮二)
37. Animal head posture (獸頭勢)
38. Cut frame (劈架子)
39. Sleeves dance like turning flowers (翻花舞袖)
40. Hidden hand posture (掩手紅捶)
41. Subdued tiger (伏虎勢)
42. Color eyebrow red (抹眉紅拳)
43. Yellow dragon plays water right (右黃龍出水)
44. Yellow dragon plays water left (左黃龍出水)
45. Turn body and kick left (左蹬一根)
46. Turn body and kick right (右蹬一根)
47. Turn flower under sea bottom (海底翻花)
48. Hidden hand punch (掩手紅捶)
49. Sweep ground with leg (掃地腿)
50. Hidden hand punch (掩手紅捶)
51. Left rush (左冲)
52. Right rush (右冲)
53. Insert on opposite direction (倒插)
54. Turn flower under sea bottom (海底翻花)
55. Hidden hand punch (掩手紅捶)
56. Seize upper arm 1 (奪二肱一)
57. Seize upper arm 2 (奪二肱二)
58. Machine cannon (連珠砲)
59. Fair lady works at shuttles (玉女穿梭)
60. Four heads cannon (四頭砲)
61. Fair lady works at shuttles (玉女穿梭)
62. Four heads cannon (四頭砲)
63. Chop opponent with fist (披身捶)
64. Twist elbow (拗鸞肘)

1

2

3

4

5

6

7

8   **9**   **10**   **11**

12   **13**   **14**   **15**

16   **17**

18   **19**

20   **21**   **22**

23   **24**

25   **26**   **27**

28   **29**   **30**   **31**

3 2   **3 3**

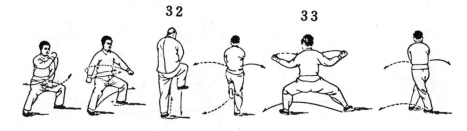

3 4   **3 5**

3 6   **3 7**   **3 8**

3 9   **4 0**   **4 1**   **4 2**

44 **45**

46 **47** **48**

49 **50**

51 **52** **53**

54   55   56

57   58

59   60   61   62

63   64   65   66   67

68   69   70   71

1-5. THE YANG FAMILY'S TAI-CHI CHUAN

*T*ai-Chi Chuan was considered a family treasure of the Chen's and was kept secret, rarely being shown to people outside the family. For instance, Chen Chang-Hsin taught his son and his relatives, but only two persons with other family names: Yang Lew-Shan (楊露禪) and Li Pei-Kuei (李伯魁). Yang, especially, learned this extraordinary skill with extreme patience and effort.

Yang Lew-Shan (1799-1872) was born in Ho-Pei Province (河北省) in northern China. His ancestors were farmers. He was small and thin but fond of the martial arts. At first, he learned the thirty-three long-form movements of a hard boxing style from Shao-Lin, an old boxer, who felt that Yang had great boxing talent and was capable of high achievement if he had the right guidance from a superior master. The old man then told him of the Chens, and Yang went to them in hopes of becoming a student. However, as he had a family name other than Chen, he was refused. He stayed on as a farm worker to wait for any chance to learn Tai-Chi Chuan. Finally, Chen Chang-Hsin discovered Yang's intention and, deeply impressed by Yang's sincerity, Chen accepted him as a student. The story goes that Yang had worked there for several years without learning anything about Tai-Chi Chuan. Then one night, awakening from his sleep, Yang heard the Heng-Haah (哼哈) sound from the next house. Peeping through the fence, he saw Chen Chang-Hsin teaching his students Tai-Chi Chuan. From then on, he watched and practiced right away before returning to his bedroom. Yang concentrated on these daily lessons, made surprising progress, and on occasion was even able to beat Chen's advanced students. Chen realized Yang's talent and potential and taught him all the skills, techniques and secrets of Tai-Chi Chuan.

After learning Tai-Chi Chuan from Chen Chang-Hsin, Yang Lew-Shan returned to his birthplace and gave Tai-Chi lessons to his neighbors. He had many students. At that time, Tai-Chi Chuan was called *Hua* (化), or "neutralizing", Chuan and *Mein* (綿), or "soft", Chuan because it turned defense to attack and was as soft as cotton. Years later, Yang left for Beijing, the capital, to teach Tai-Chi to the royal family, and Yang's Tai-Chi became quite well known.

Yang, who had a strong character, was very fond of contests of strength with other boxers. He traveled throughout northern China with his luggage and spear on his back. Hearing of any excellent fighters, he would visit them and match skills. Although he was skilled, he never in his life hurt anyone seriously. His enthusiasm for pugilistic art and his sense of honor won people's respect.

Because he never lost a contest and had no rival, he earned the title Yang Wu-Ti (*Wu-Ti* 無敵 means no enemy and no rival). Yang did not look like a boxer; however, he often lifted and flung his opponents even though they weighed twice as much as he. Nobody knew the source of his strength. The following are some of the many legends about him.

A rich man called Chang, who lived in Beijing, was fond of boxing and had over thirty fighters as escorts. He admired Yang and invited him to his house. When the weak-looking Yang arrived, Chang misjudged him and indifferently treated him to a very plain dinner. Yang was well aware of the meal's meaning, but pretended that he did not care how he was treated, drinking and eating happily by himself. Chang rudely said to Yang, "I have heard your honorable name as well as of the renowned softness of Tai-Chi Chuan. But, I wonder if you and your Tai-Chi can defeat people."

"There are three kinds of people that I cannot beat," Yang quickly replied.

Chang asked, "What three kinds of people are they?"

"They are made of brass, iron, or wood. The rest I can defeat," said Yang.

"I have an escort of thirty people. The best is Liu (劉) who can lift three hundred pounds. Would you like to compete with him?"

"Of course," answered Yang.

The contest began. Liu's entrance "sounded windy," which means he came in like the rushing wind, and he looked as violent as a tiger. As he approached Yang, Yang led him to emptiness with his right hand and pushed him gently with his left. Immediately Liu was thrown ten feet across the yard, like a flying kite with a suddenly broken string. Chang clapped his hands and laughed, "Tai-Chi is indeed a wonderful art." Chang ordered his servant to prepare a luxurious dinner, and Yang was respected as a Grand Master.

Yang was also master of the spear. He could gracefully lift light articles by touching them with his spear, thus utilizing his sticking energy —he never failed. If there was a fire, he tore down the wall with his spear to stop the fire from spreading. He shot arrows not with a bow but with his fingers, and he always hit the targets with one hundred percent accuracy.

In Kwang-Pin (廣平) city, Yang engaged in a contest high on top of the city wall. His opponent retreated to the edge of the city wall and finally fell, losing his balance. At this very critical moment, Yang jumped forward from five yards away and held this man's foot, saving his life.

His agility was shown in other ways. One rainy day, Yang was sitting in the living room when his daughter stepped on the porch with a brass basin in her hands. Before entering the door, she slipped and Yang rushed out to hold her arm so that she avoided a fall. Even the water in the basin did not spill.

During Yang's stay in Beijing, another boxer was jealous of Yang's title "No

Rival" and challenged Yang. Yang said with a smile, "Since you insist upon battling, I will let you hit me three times." The challenger then struck Yang's stomach with great force. Yang laughed aloud, using the force in his abdomen to throw his opponent to the ground. Another day, Yang was fishing at the riverside when two boxers passed by on the bank behind and above him. These two men were afraid of Yang and wanted to dampen Yang's reputation by pushing him into the river. They approached stealthily. Yang, having special hearing ability, realized they were behind him and prepared himself. Using the posture High pat on horse (高探馬), Yang raised his back, bowed his head, and flung the two men into the river.

Yang Lew-Shan had three sons. The eldest died in childhood. The second son was named Yang-Yu (楊鈺 1837-1892); the third Yang-Chian (楊鑑 1839-1917, See Figure 1-5a). Both were famous Tai-Chi experts. When Yang Lew-Shan was very old, and people still begged to be his students, Yang-Yu took over the role as their real teacher even though later many people said they were students of Yang Lew-Shan. Yang-Yu learned Tai-Chi Chuan from his father, practicing all day, every day, without stop, no matter how cold the winter or how hot the summer. Yang Lew-Shan never let his son Yang-Yu have a rest and often punished him with a whip. This harshness almost caused Yang-Yu to run away from home. Like his father Yang-Yu had a strong character and liked to attack others. Those attacked by him were often hurt by being thrown almost ten feet away. When Yang-Yu was young, he had a contest with a strong fighter who grasped Yang-Yu's wrist. Yang-Yu used Tai-Chi's cool strength (冷勁), a sudden attack without warning, so that the fighter was beaten. When Yang-Yu proudly told his father he had won, his father laughed at him and criticized, "It is good news; however, because your sleeve was torn, you did not have, Tai-Chi strength. The theory of Tai-Chi is that nobody knows you, only you know them." Then Yang-Yu looked at his sleeve which was torn from using too much force. Although he was discouraged by his father's remark, he was also challenged. Practicing and studying twice as hard as before, he reached a very high level; however, he did not like to teach students. He liked to test his inner force by putting a few grains of rice on his abdomen, and while he was saying "Haah," the grains were launched to the ceiling.

Yang-Chian was called "Mr. Number Three." His father was so strict with his sons that Yang-Chian felt extremely exhausted and desperate. Yang-Chian planned several times to cut his hair and become a Buddhist monk, but he never succeeded because he was stopped by other family members. From this example, it can be imagined how much the students suffered during the learning of Yang's Tai-Chi Chuan. It was almost beyond normal tolerance. Yang-Chian, who was good-natured, had many students. He taught three styles: large,

楊健侯先生遺像

Yang Chian
(1839-1917)

Figure 1-5a

楊少侯先生遺像

Yang Chao-Hsiung
(1862-1930)

Figure 1-5b

medium and small. His achievement, harmony of firmness and softness, reached a high level. He often held a duster to practice Tai-Chi while his followers used swords. His opponents were often caught in a passive position, unable to approach him. He was an expert at playing with spears and sticks. Any strength and force he applied with spears or sticks would knock the other man down. Also, he was an expert in throwing bullet balls. He was able to shoot three flying birds with three bullet balls at one time. Moreover, he could fix birds in his palm so that they could not fly away. When the birds attempted to sink down before flying, he let his palm sink so that they could not prepare to ascend. In his old age, he would practice his inner force in bed at midnight, and a strange rumbling noise could be heard. He died in 1917, a natural death without illness. It is said that since he dreamed his death a few hours before it came, he had his students and family come to bid him farewell. He took a bath, put on new clothes, and then passed away with a smile. He had three sons: the eldest was Chao-Hsiung, the second died young, and the third was named Chao-Chin.

Chao-Hsiung (兆熊 1862 - 1930, See Figure 1-5b) played Tai-Chi at age seven. Just like his uncle, Yang-Yu, Chao-Hsiung had a strong character and liked to attack first. He mastered the application in Tai-Chi. His style was small but firm; his action fast and sinking, continuous and tight. He taught aggressively and had only a few students because few people could bear his beatings. He reached high levels in Tai-Chi technique, but very few people now know his methods because he rarely taught. It is said that in Nanking a boxer, who once failed in a contest with him, wanted to get revenge. This man threw lime powder in Yang Chao-Hsiung's eyes so he could not see, and then attacked

Yang's face with his fists. Depending on his hearing ability, Yang escaped the thrusts and with light returns of his hands threw the attacker to the ground several feet away. Later it was said that "to beat the enemy with closed eyes is Yang's Tai-Chi." It is also said that once when he met a mad dog who ran to bite him, he raised his foot, throwing the dog yards away to its death. He could draw a candle flame close to him and push it away again, thus putting the fire out. This provides an example of so-called "spiritual force," but the secret to this was lost.

Chao-Chin (兆清 1883 - 1936, See Figures 1-5c and d) was also named Chen-Fu (澄甫). He had a kind nature but was not fond of Tai-Chi Chuan as a child. It was his philosophy that "It is not worth learning to be one man's enemy (as in Tai-Chi fighting); it is worth learning to be the enemy of a thousand men." However, with his grandfather's instruction and advice, he realized that Tai-Chi Chuan could not only improve his health, but also cultivate the whole nation's physical condition and awaken the spirit of the entire country. He began to practice Tai-Chi Chuan at twenty but did not perceive its significance until his father's death. He then practiced and studied day and night to attain the skills of Tai-Chi Chuan, and succeeding to such an extent as to have a soft outer appearance like cotton with an iron inner firmness. He exemplifies the highest natural talent and achievement in Tai-Chi Chuan since he was entirely self-taught after his father died. His great example encourages us that even if excellent teachers are hard to find, we can develop by ourselves if we really understand and apply the theories and principles of Tai-Chi Chuan. The current forms of so-called Yang's Tai-Chi were defined and regulated by him. Yang's style, which is comfortable, generous, light and stable, has been recognized as the easiest and most popular one.

楊澄甫先生五十四歲時像

Yang Chen-Fu

Figure 1-5c

楊 澄 甫 先 生

Figure 1-5d

Yang Chao-Chin had four sons.   They are teaching Tai-Chi in either Hong Kong or Hawaii.   While their skills are comparatively good today, in relation to their ancestors they can evoke only a deep sigh.   As you can see, there is also a life cycle in Tai-Chi Chuan.   Fortunately, however, one of his students, Cheng Man-Ching (鄭曼青 1901-1975), reached the highest level of achievement in our present time.   Cheng would often remind his students that as great as his skill was to them, so was his teacher's skill to him.   He would demonstrate how none could lay a hand on him.   Yet, he himself could not escape one finger of Yang Chen-Fu, or remove it, once it had touched him.

Yang's Tai-Chi Chuan became very popular and was taught to a large number of people.   As a result, there are many variations, in which the number and names of the postures are the same, although the movements are executed differently.   One of these variations is Wu Chian-chyan's (吳鑑泉)form.   This "Wu form," which is popular in Southern China and Hong Kong, is well known in the United States.   It is a branch of the Yang School, however, and must not be confused with the third main branch of Tai-Chi Chuan, to be discussed later.   Ultimately, Yang Chen-Fu, Yang Lew-Shan's grandson, standardized the original large, high style as Yang's long Tai-Chi Chuan.

Wu Chian-Chyan had two sons, Wu Kung Yi, and Wu Kung Tsao.   The latter published a book in 1980 giving a definitive description of the Wu variation, using photos of his brother.

A student who is able to obtain the work will observe a stilted, wooden look in the photos contrasted with the balanced and alert appearance of the pictures of their father on Figure 1-5f of this book.

Also seen will be major changes from the traditional practices: frequent tilting of the torso front and back, bending of the head, frequent appearance of locking of the knee joints.   As to whether these changes are useful, it can be said with regret that Wu Kung-Yi does not have the reputation of the father.   Students who practice the Wu-variation of the Yang Form are recommended to seek out the original pictures of Master Wu Chian-Chyan performing the postures.   One can see from observing his pictures on Figure 1-5f and comparing them with those of Master Yang Chen-Fu on Figure 1-5e that both these great masters in practicing different variations had the same grasp of the Chan-Ssu Chin.

If you have not yet begun studying with a teacher, try the first paragraph of Yang's Tai-Chi Chuan (from movements 1 to 19) using the following illustrations.   The pictures of Yang's long Tai-Chi Chuan depict Yang Chen-Fu himself. Pictures of Yang Chen-Fu, Wu Chian-Chyan and Cheng Man-Ching are shown below (Figures 1-5e, 1-5f, 1-5g).   Students will plainly see that except for slight individual differences, the postures of the two great masters, Yang and Wu, are essentially the same.

Figure 1-5e   Master Yang Chen-Fu's postures.

Figure 1-5f   Master Wu Chian-Chyan's postures.

Figure 1-5g   Master Cheng Man-Ching's postures.

Yang's Tai-Chi Chuan:

1. Beginning of Tai-Chi（太極起勢）
2. Ward-off left（左掤）
3. Ward-off right（右掤）
4. Roll-back（攦）   Grasp sparrow's tail（攬雀尾）
5. Press（擠）
6. Push（按）
7. Single whip（單鞭）
8. Lift hand（提手上勢）
9. White crane spreads wings（白鶴涼翅）
10. Brush knee and twist step, right（右摟膝拗步）
11. Playing guitar（手揮琵琶）
12. Brush knee and twist step, right（右摟膝拗步）
13. Brush knee and twist step, left（左摟膝拗步）
14. Brush knee and twist step, right（右摟膝拗步）
15. Playing guitar（手揮琵琶）
16. Brush knee and twist step, right（右摟膝拗步）
17. Step forward, deflect downward, intercept and punch（搬攔捶）
18. Withdraw and push（如封似閉）
19. Cross hands（十字手）
20. Embrace tiger return to the mountain（抱虎歸山）
21. Grasp sparrow's tail（攬雀尾）
22. Diagonal single whip（斜單鞭）
23. Fist under elbow（肘底看捶）
24. Step back to drive away monkey, right（右倒攆猴）
25. Step back to drive away monkey, left（左倒攆猴）
26. Step back to drive away monkey, right（右倒攆猴）
27. Diagonal flying posture（斜飛式）
28. Lift hand（提手上勢）
29. White crane spreads wings（白鶴涼翅）
30. Brush knee and twist step（摟膝拗步）
31. Needle at sea bottom（海底針）

32. Fan through the back（扇通背）

33. Turn around and chop（轉身撇身捶 ）

34. Step forward, deflect downward, intercept and punch（搬攔捶）

35. Step forward, grasp sparrow's tail（上步 攬雀尾）

36. Single whip（單鞭）

37. Waving hands like clouds (three times)（雲手）

38. Single whip（單鞭）

39. High pat on horse（高探馬）

40. Separate right foot（右分腳）

41. Separate left foot（左分腳 ）

42. Turn around and kick with left sole（ 轉身蹬腳）

43. Brush knee and twist step, right（右摟膝拗步 ）

44. Brush knee and twist step, left（左摟膝拗步 ）

45. Step up and punch downward（進步栽捶）

46. Turn around and chop（ 轉身撇身捶）

47. Step forward, deflect downward, intercept and punch（搬攔捶）

48. Kick right foot（右踢腳）

49. Hit tiger at left（左打虎）

50. Hit tiger at right（右打虎）

51. Kick right foot（右踢腳）

52. Strike opponent's ears with fists（雙風貫耳）

53. Kick left foot（左踢腳）

54. Turn around and kick with right sole（轉身蹬腳）

55. Step forward, deflect downward, intercept and punch（搬攔捶）

56. Withdraw and push（如封似閉）

57. Cross hands（十字手）

58. Embrace tiger return to mountain（抱虎歸山）

59. Grasp sparrow's tail（攬雀尾）

60. Diagonal single whip（斜單鞭）

61. Mustang ruffling its mane, right（右野馬分鬃）

62. Mustang ruffling its mane, left（左野馬分鬃 ）

63. Mustang ruffling its mane, right（右野馬分鬃 ）

64. Grasp sparrow's tail（攬雀尾）

65. Single whip （單　鞭）

66. Fair lady works at shuttles (1) （玉女穿梭一）

67. Fair lady works at shuttles (2) （玉女穿梭二）

68. Fair lady works at shuttles (3) （玉女穿梭三）

69. Fair lady works at shuttles (4) （玉女穿梭四）

70. Grasp sparrow's tail （攬雀尾）

71. Single whip （單鞭）

72. Waving hands like clouds （雲手）

73. Single whip （單鞭）

74. Snake creeps down （蛇身下勢）

75. Golden pheasant stands with one leg, right （右金雞獨立）

76. Golden pheasant stands with one leg, left （左金雞獨立）

77. Step back to drive away monkey, right （右倒攆猴）

78. Step back to drive away monkey, left （左倒攆猴）

79. Step back to drive away monkey, right （右倒攆猴）

80. Diagonal flying posture （斜飛式）

81. Lift hand （提手上勢）

82. White crane spreads wings （白鶴涼翅）

83. Brush knee and twist step （摟膝拗步）

84. Needle at sea bottom （海底針）

85. Fan through the back （扇通背）

86. White snake turns body and sticks out tongue （轉身白蛇吐信）

87. Step forward, deflect downward, intercept and punch （撇攔捶）

88. Step forward and grasp sparrow's tail （上步攔雀尾）

89. Single whip （單鞭）

90. Waving hands like clouds （雲手）

91. Single whip （單鞭）

92. High pat on horse （高探馬）

93. Crossing palm （穿身十字掌）

94. Turn around and kick with right sole （轉身十字腿）

95. Punch the opponent's groin （摟膝指膛捶）

96. Step forward and grasp sparrow's tail （上步攬雀尾）

97. Single whip （單鞭）

98. Snake creeps down （蛇身下勢）

99. Step up to form seven stars of the dipper （上步七星）

100. Step back to ride tiger （轉身跨虎）

101. Turn around and sweep lotus with one leg （轉身攞蓮腿 ）

102. Shoot tiger with bow （彎弓射虎）

103. Step forward, deflect downward, intercept and punch（搬攔捶）

104. Withdraw and push （如封似閉）

105. Conclusion of Tai-Chi （合太極）

1

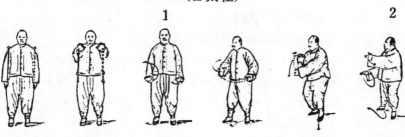

2

3

4

5

6

7

8

9

10   11

12

13   14

15   16

17

18   **19**

20

21

22

23

24

25  **26**

27  **28**

29

30     **31** **32**

33

34

35

36

41   42

43   44

45   46

47   48

49

50

51

52

53

54

55

56

57

5 8

5 9

6 0 **6 1**

6 2 **6 3**

64

65

66

67   68

69

70

71

72

73

74

75

76

77

78

79

80

81

82

83

84   **85**

86

87

88

89

90   **91**

92

93

94

95

96

97

98

99

100  101

102

103

104

105

1-6. THE WU FAMILY'S TAI-CHI CHUAN

*Y*ang Lew-Shan had a student, Wu Yu-Hsing (武禹襄 1812-1880), whose brother was a government official in Ho-Nang Province (河南省) Once, when Wu was on the way to visit his brother, he intended to see Chen Chang-Hsin (陳長興) in order to learn the first Lu Tai-Chi Chuan and the second Lu Pao-Twi. When he arrived in Chao-Pao (趙堡), midway to Chen's residence, he heard that Chen Chin-Ping (陳清萍), a man of very great achievement, taught Shiao-Jar (小架) there. He then remained there and learned Shiao-Jar from Chen Chin-Ping. Wu's Tai-Chi Chuan was called Shiao-Jar; *Shiao* means 'small" and Jar means "form;" thus it is the small style of Chen's Tai-Chi Chuan. In the meantime, Wu's brother happened on Wang Tsung-Yueh's "The Classics of Tai-Chi Chuan" in a salt store, and immediately sent the document to Wu. By practicing and researching it very thoroughly, Wu Yu-Hsing obtained more knowledge of Tai-Chi Chuan than anyone had had before. Later, his own experience and knowledge enabled him to write a famous treatise, "The Theories of Thirteen Postures," which explains the practice and secrets of Tai-Chi Chuan. He sent copies of these two treatises to his former teacher, Yang Lew-Shan, who was teaching Tai-Chi Chuan in Beijing. Yang revealed the secrets and published the papers, and from that time on, the secrets and principles of Tai-Chi Chuan were accessible to greater numbers of people. Though Wu did not have many students, one of them, his nephew Li Yi-Yu (李亦畬 1833-1892) became very famous. Li wrote many papers on Tai-Chi Chuan, and since his time its theories have been recorded systematically.

Hay Way Jen had a student, Sun Lu Tang, who had previously learned the internal martial arts schools of Pa Kua and Hsiung-I. Sun Lu Tang added these non-Tai Chi elements to the Wu form to create a new form. In my opinion the only possible evolution of the Wu School is towards formlessness, and Sun Lu Tang's achievement must be regarded as a variation, not as a new school.

Every posture of the Wu style has four states: start, connect, open and close (See Figure 1-6a). Each of them exemplifies a particular stage of the Tai-Chi principle. (1) Start — describes the change from Wu-Chi to Tai-Chi when one's thought or intention is about to be actualized; (2) Connect — describes moving from Tai-Chi to Yin-Yang in order to differentiate every part of the body into solid (substantial) and empty (insubstantial); (3) Open — describes initiating attack or retreat; and (4) Closed — describes the action of attacking or retreating. The concepts of open and closed are very complicated and much harder than their short descriptions might indicate. (See Chapter Four).

The following illustrations depict Hay Shao-Ju (郝少如), grandson of Hay Way-Jen (郝爲眞1849-1920), who was a famous master of the Wu style. When he died in 1920, his son and grandson continued in the Wu tradition.

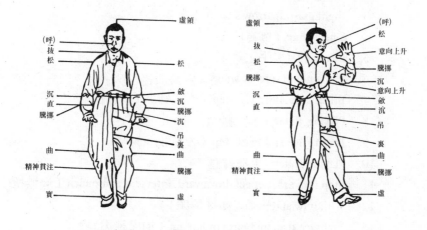

Start   Connect

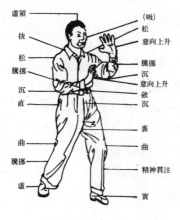

Open   Closed

Figure 1-6a

Wu's Tai-Chi Chuan

1. Beginning of Tai-Chi（太極起式）
2. Left grasp sparrow's tail（左攬雀尾）
3. Right grasp sparrow's tail（右攬雀尾）
4. Single whip（單鞭）
5. Lift hand（提手上勢）
6. White goose spreads wings（白鵝涼翅）
7. Brush knee and twist step（摟膝拗步）
8. Playing guitar（手揮琵琶）
9. Brush knee and twist step（摟膝拗步）
10. Playing guitar（手揮琵琶）
11. Step forward, deflect downward, intercept and punch（搬攔捶）
12. Withdraw and push（如封似閉）
13. Embrace tiger and push mountain（抱虎推山）
14. Playing guitar（手揮琵琶）
15. Right grasp sparrow's tail（右攬雀尾）
16. Single whip（單鞭）
17. Lift hand（提手上勢）
18. Fist under elbow（肘底看捶）
19. Step back to drive away monkey, right（右倒攆猴）
20. Step back to drive away monkey, left（左倒攆猴）
21. Step back to drive away monkey, right（右倒攆猴）
22. Step back to drive away monkey, left（左倒攆猴）
23. Playing guitar（手揮琵琶）
24. White goose spreads wings（白鵝涼翅）
25. Brush knee and twist step（摟膝拗步）
26. Playing guitar（手揮琵琶）
27. Push posture（按勢）
28. Blue dragon flies out from water（青龍出水勢）
29. Turn over the body（披身勢）
30. Three changes of the back（三甬背）
31. Single whip（單鞭）

32. Downward posture（下勢）

33. Waving hands like clouds（雲手）

34. Single whip（單鞭）

35. Lift hand（提手上勢）

36. High pat on horse（高探馬）

37. Submissive tiger posture, left（左伏虎式）

38. Separate right foot（右分腳）

39. Submissive tiger posture, right（右伏虎式）

40. Separate left foot（左分腳）

41. Turn over body and kick right foot（轉身右踢腳）

42. Single whip（單鞭）

43. Jump forward and punch downward（踐身打捶）

44. Jump high and kick twice（翻身二起）

45. Turn body posture（轉身式）

46. Withdraw and kick（退步踢腿）

47. Turn over body and kick right foot（轉身蹬腳）

48. Step forward, deflect downward, intercept and punch（搬攔捶）

49. Withdraw and push（如封似閉）

50. Embrace tiger and push mountain（抱虎推山）

51. Playing guitar（手揮琵琶）

52. Grasp sparrow's tail, right（右攬雀尾）

53. Diagonal single whip（斜單鞭）

54. Downward posture（下勢）

55. Mustang ruffling its mane（野馬分鬃）

56. Single whip（單鞭）

57. Fair lady works at shuttles（玉女穿梭）

58. Playing guitar（手揮琵琶）

59. Grasp sparrow's tail, right（右攬雀尾）

60. Single whip（單鞭）

61. Downward posture（下勢）

62. Waving hands like clouds（紜手）

63. Single whip（單鞭）

64. Downward posture（下勢）

65. Golden chicken stands with one leg（更雞獨立）

66. Step back to drive away monkey, left（左倒攆猴）

67. Step back to drive away monkey, right（右倒攆猴）

68. Step back to drive away monkey, left（左倒攆猴）

69. Step back to drive away monkey, right（右倒攆猴）

70. Playing guitar（手揮琵琶）

71. White goose spreads wings（白鵝涼翅）

72. Brush knee and twist step（摟膝拗步）

73. Playing guitar（手揮琵琶）

74. Push posture（按勢）

75. Blue dragon flies out from water（青龍出水勢）

76. Turn over the body（轉身式）

77. Three changes of the`back（三甬背）

78. Single whip（單鞭）

79. Downward posture（下勢）

80. Waving hand like clouds（紜手）

81. Single whip（單鞭）

82. Lift hand（提手上勢）

83. High pat on horse（高探馬）

84. Heart to heart palm（對心掌）

85. Turn around and sweep lotus with one leg（轉身擺蓮腿）

86. Step forward and punch opponent's groin（上步指擋捶   ）

87. Grasp sparrow's tail, right（右攬雀尾）

88. Single whip（單鞭）

89. Downward posture（下勢）

90. Step up to form seven stars of the dipper（上步七星）

91. Step back to ride tiger（退步跨虎）

92. Sweep lotus with one leg（攏蓮腿）

93. Shoot tiger with bow（彎弓射虎）

94. Double cannon punch（雙炮捶）

95. Playing guitar（手揮琵琶）

96. Conclusion of Tai-Chi（合太極）

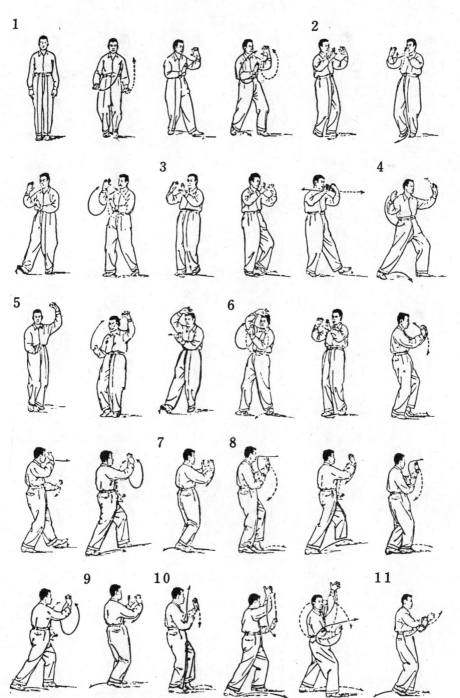

1 2

1 3   **1 4**   **1 5**

1 6   **1 7**

1 8   **1 9**

2 0

21   22

23  24

25   26 27 28  29

30

31 32 33

34

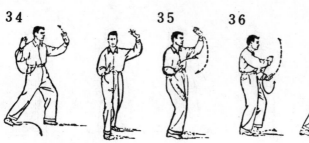

35   **36**   **37**

38   **39**   **40**

41   **42**   **43**

44   **45**

46   **47**   **48**

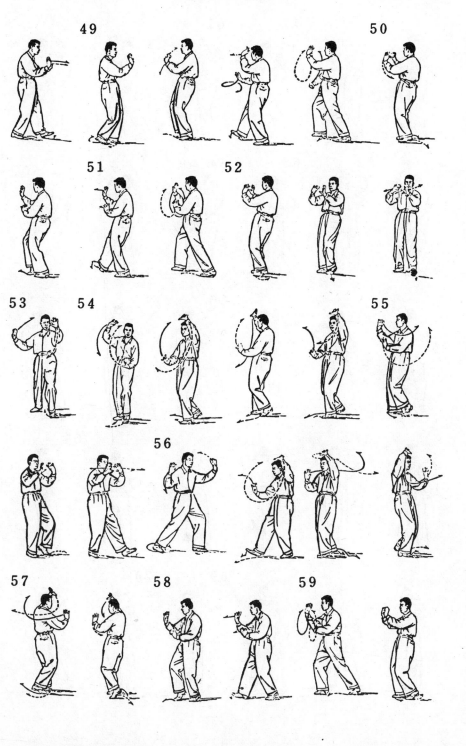

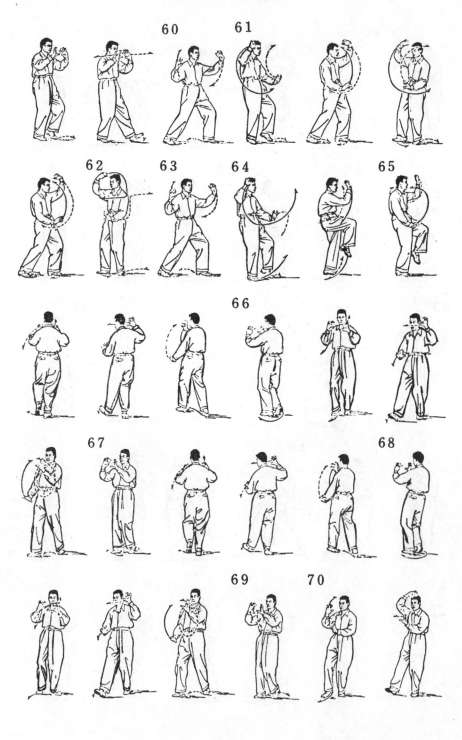

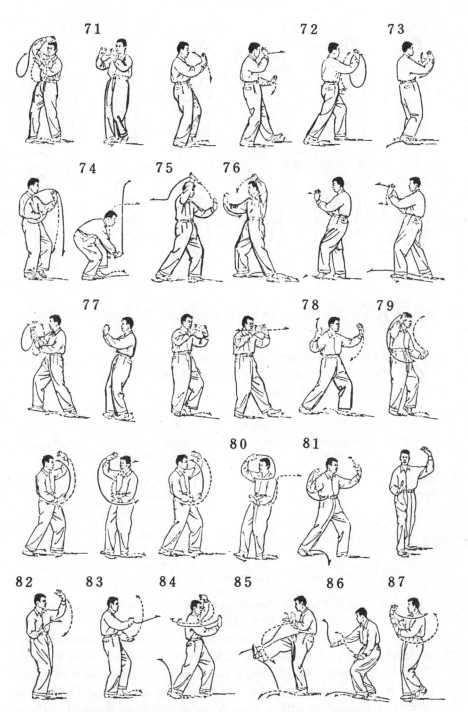

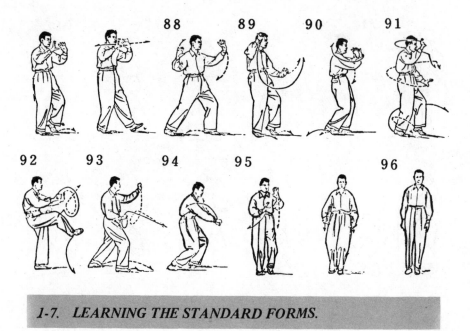

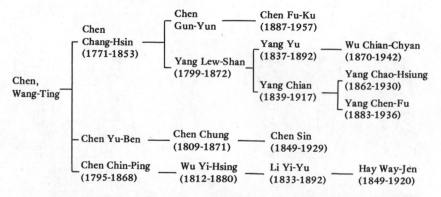

1-7.   LEARNING THE STANDARD FORMS.

*B*ecause of differences in individual styles, Tai-Chi Chuan developed three main branches: Chen's, Yang's and Wu's, the genealogy of which is indicated briefly below:

		Chen Gun-Yun	Chen Fu-Ku (1887-1957)	
	Chen Chang-Hsin (1771-1853)		Yang Yu (1837-1892)	Wu Chian-Chyan (1870-1942)
Chen, Wang-Ting		Yang Lew-Shan (1799-1872)	Yang Chian (1839-1917)	Yang Chao-Hsiung (1862-1930)
				Yang Chen-Fu (1883-1936)
	Chen Yu-Ben	Chen Chung (1809-1871)	Chen Sin (1849-1929)	
	Chen Chin-Ping (1795-1868)	Wu Yi-Hsing (1812-1880)	Li Yi-Yu (1833-1892)	Hay Way-Jen (1849-1920)

Since Tai-Chi Chuan is based upon flowing movements, it is the most important that the beginner learn the proper way to move from posture to posture. These transitions, which are part of a continuum, are too complicated to describe clearly. For this reason it is exceedingly difficult to learn Tai-Chi Chuan from a book. Nonetheless, a Tai-Chi book supplemented with photographs is a valuable reference for one who has concluded the Tai-Chi solo exercise in conjunction with a teacher. Accordingly, the above illustrations demonstrate the most important characteristics of each of the three main branches of Tai-Chi Chuan. These illustrations, along with complete lists of the postures, will give an experienced student a basis for comparing the different styles. Clearly, without a masterful teacher, these illustrations alone are patently insufficient for learning Tai-Chi. Such instruction could best be accomplished through films rather than merely with still photos, and it is the intent of the author to make such supplemental films in the future.

The uses of the three forms clearly derive from their individual histories. The Chen is really the original form, and its completeness comes from this. It is superior for martial arts and the healing arts, and sports as well. The Chan Ssu Chin is shown clearly in its movements, as well as the breathing, and other subtleties.

The Yang family did the most to popularize the previously secret discipline by taking their form to Beijing and teaching to the members of the royal family and court of the Ching dynasty. They also began giving lessons to nonroyalty.

These two factors had to be taken into account with the form that was taught. The members of the court tended to be people who led an 'easy' life. They would have reacted negatively to a form that contained the rigors of the Chen. In addition, the Manchu dynasty was a racial minority; racial prejudices existed just as in South Africa today, and the teaching of a form that was obviously highly developed as a martial art could have caused fear and anxiety to the rulers.

The result of all this was the graceful and even form present today, and a form that is many times more popular than Chen and Wu.

The highest use of the Yang form is in the cultivation of health. However, its martial arts aspects are revealed in the practice of applying each posture as a means of self-defense. For many years, these martial arts applications were hidden from Tai Chi practitioners.

Chao Chin (1883-1936), also named Chen-Fu, defined and regulated the form of Yang Tai Chi popular today. However, Chen-Fu did not reveal the highly effective martial arts application techniques or sparring, his family devised to accompany the practice of the soft, comfortable Yang postures.

Legend has it that Chen-Fu kept the secrets of the Yang form application or sparring locked in a drawer. According to this legend, Chen Yen-Lin (1906-), who tutored the children of Chen-Fu, once discovered the drawer unlocked and learned of the Yang form application. In the 1920's, Chen Yen-Lin wrote a book called Tai Chi Chuan, and using pictures and explanations, revealed the Tai Chi application or sparring system devised by Yang's family.

In 1980 I met with Chen Yen-Lin in Shanghai, China, and he told me that, contrary to legend, he had learned of the Tai Chi application or sparring directly from Chen-Fu's uncle Yang-Yu.

The Yang form application is both beautiful and deadly. The flowing motions of two partners performing the application is almost like a dance, with its precise timing and coordinated movements. Yet, at the same time, each movement is designed for self-defense, and if applied, could break a limb or even kill an opponent.

The practice of application requires a great deal of practice. First, one must learn two different sequences of 44 postures each, typically referred to as the "A" side and the "B" side. These postures are taken directly from the Yang form, but their sequence is ingeniously devised so that each posture of A can be matched with each posture of B. Once the sequence is learned, two partners, one performing A and the other B, can match together for a flowing exercise of Tai Chi sparring. Each posture of A is matched by a posture of B, which in turn is followed by a posture of A, and so on, through the 44 postures on each side.

The matching together of the 88 postures is so intricate and effective, that one marvels at the cleverness of Yang's family in developing such an effective system of application.

By means of precise timing, and a perfect matching together of the movements, Tai Chi application teaches one to neutralize or Hwa (化) your partner's force, control or Na (拿) and attack or Da (打).

To learn Yang Tai Chi without learning Tai Chi application or sparring can be compared to going to a shoe store to buy a pair of shoes, and bringing home only the empty shoe box. The practice of the application gives one the ability to use the Yang postures with great awareness and effectiveness. With continued practice of Tai Chi application, Yang's Tai Chi can be effective as a martial arts system as well as a system for maintaining good health.

But the student seeking the highest achievement, whether in martial arts or healing, should turn to the Wu form after a strong groundwork in the Chen or Yang. With the Wu Form, formal exterior movements ultimately disappear into formlessness that can appear like ordinary movements, while inside there is an intense practice of the discipline equalling those of the other forms. That's why the Wu is called Shiao-jar.

The three main branches of Tai-Chi Chuan differ in style but remain within the framework of basic Tai-Chi principles and the *I-Ching* theory. It is important not to change these basic styles of Tai-Chi Chuan because to do so upsets a complicated and carefully balanced system. Great skill, talent and the practical and theoretical mastery of these principles, plus generations of refinement were all necessary to develop these three diverse styles, without violating the fundamental principles.

Some people may think that modifying Tai-Chi Chuan is simple and attempt to do so.   Since Tai-Chi Chuan is really an art, changing it is like editing a Beethoven symphony.   Omitting any part of the three main styles of Tai-Chi Chuan is also like chopping words out of a poem; to do so destroys its meter, rhyme and meaning.   One who has not devoted many years of study to such an art should avoid introducing personal variations into the form, especially when teaching beginners.   The situation is the same as teaching handwriting to children. Whatever one's own personal style of calligraphy, in the classroom the standard form of the letter is taught and no matter what school you may go to, the standard written or printed alphabet is the same.   In the same way we have our alphabets of Tai-Chi Chuan, which are the postures of the standard Chen, Wu and Yang styles of Tai-Chi Chuan.   It is the duty of Tai-Chi teachers to teach their students one of these standard forms, just as it is the duty of handwriting teachers to teach their students the standard alphabet.   To do this, one uses a text showing the standard letters, and in Tai-Chi Chuan we have such standards since there are photographs of the great masters of the Chen, Wu and Yang schools.   For example, if one wishes to teach the Yang style, one should use the available pictures of Yang Chen-Fu in executing the forms.

If one wants to save time in learning or practicing Tai-Chi Chuan, it's better to practice only a part of a routine than to alter or simplify its basic form.   When one does not have time to read a whole book, it is better to read only a chapter or so and return later to where one has left off.   To leave out chapters would cause one to lose important parts of the story and interrupt the book's continuity.   If one objects that the form is not balanced, the solution is simply to do both the right and left forms, not to add some postures from the left form to the right form.

Therefore, a beginner of Tai-Chi Chuan should study Chen's, Wu's or Yang's style diligently, progressing with each step in the proper sequence.   In this way the full value of Tai-Chi Chuan is gained and its profound principles are better understood.   Moreover, it is the duty of anyone intending to study Tai-Chi Chuan to determine if a teacher does in fact teach one of the three standard styles, as well as his or her own personal variations.   Personal creativity is necessary but never to the exclusion of the original standard form.   Remember! Without a standard alphabet and standard spelling it would not be possible for me to write these words, or for you, the reader, to understand them.   The illustrations are intended to serve as standards to judge against, and as a device to provide for better communication among all students of Tai-Chi Chuan. It is my purpose to encourage communication between all students and teachers of Tai-Chi Chuan, so I have provided illustrations of teachers and practitioners who best exemplify a particular style.

CHAPTER
TWO

PHILOSOPHY

Tai-Chi Chuan can be compared to a window with the curtains drawn. The onlooker cannot judge what is inside by looking through the window because the curtains prevent a clear view. Likewise, one cannot judge Tai-Chi Chuan by its appearance. One person may say it's a form of healthful exercise, another a martial art and so on. These are only outside perceptions of the Tai-Chi movements. More importantly, the core of Tai-Chi Chuan is its philosophy; every Tai-Chi movement involves the Tai-Chi philosophy of time and space. To understand Tai-Chi Chuan by only watching the outer movements is like trying to look inside a room through drawn curtains. One must go into the room to see clearly; one must understand Tai-Chi philosophy to view the full picture of Tai-Chi Chuan.

The profound philosophy of Tai-Chi Chuan brings into harmony Western scientific knowledge and ancient Chinese wisdom. Traditionally, these two areas of study have remained quite separate. In reality, the two actually are closely related. Tai-Chi is both scientific and philosophical. In this chapter, I will explain Tai-Chi philosophy in a scientific manner which the Western mind can readily understand.

2-1. YIN-YANG AND TAI-CHI

*A*ncient Chinese philosophers called the void and boundless state which prevailed before the world was created and from which the universe was formed Wu-Chi (無極) or the ultimate nothingness. Before creation, it is said there is nothing, yet certainly there is something. We do not know what that something is, nor do we know what that something comes from; but certainly something is there. This something cannot be comprehended rationally; its existence is only implied, like an object one almost catches sight of in a fog. Ancient Chinese philosophers described it as the phenomenon of nothingness (無物之物) or "thing of none". That is to say, that it has form, yet is unformed; it has shape that is still without shape; or , one could say, it is vagueness confused. One meets it, and it has no front; one follows, and there is no rear. This phenomenon of nothingness was the source of movement and stillness. Everything in the universe, including Yin and Yang, is believed to evolve continually from this unperceivable source. Lao Tzu (老子) called it Tao (道), the *I Ching* named it Tai-Chi (太極) and Wang Tsung-Yueh (王宗岳) who lived in Ching Dynasty in his theory of Tai-Chi Chuan commented:

> Tai-Chi is born of Wu-Chi or the ultimate nothingness. It is origin of dynamic and static states and the mother of Yin and Yang. If they move, they separate. If they remain static, they combine.

Generally speaking, the concepts of Wu-Chi and Tai-Chi describe not only the aspects of creation of the universe, but also stages of all relationships between people, between objects or between people and objects. For example, a room before people enter it is in the Wu-Chi stage; when people go into the room they bring movements and Tai-Chi begins. Tai-Chi is, thus, the source of Yin and Yang. The relationship between a person and a piano is Wu-Chi if the person has no intention to play it. When the person starts to play the piano or even has the intention to play, the relationship becomes Tai-Chi. Wu-Chi then exists before anything happens, for even the intention to act arises from Wu-Chi.

When something arises from Wu-Chi, the original state of nothingness no longer exists. At this point, the state of Tai-Chi begins. The situation then has two aspects. The voidness of Wu-Chi is Yin (陰) and the something originating from Wu-Chi is Yang (陽). In general, Yin and Yang are complementary opposites which unite to form a whole. Although they are opposite in nature, there is a harmonious relationship between them. For example, where there is day, there must be night and where there is night, there must be day. Day is Yang, night is Yin. The relatonship of day and night is that of opposites. Nevertheless, they are mutually coexisting and inseparable just like two sides of a coin. Another example of Yin and Yang complementarity is the relationship between the sky and the earth. The sky is Yang and the earth is Yin. Among human beings, man is Yang and woman is Yin.

The characteristics of Yang are heat, motion and outward centrifugal force; whereas cold, stillness and inward centripetal force are the characteristics of Yin. The idea of Yin and Yang can be illustrated by the various stages of an object's movement. The beginning of the motion is the birth of Yang and the end of the motion is the birth of Yin. The beginning of stillness is the birth of mildness, and the end of stillness is the birth of rigidity. Aspects of Yin and Yang changes may be likened to the various forms of water. At the boiling point, water becomes steam and produces tremendous power. This is Yang. At the freezing point, water becomes ice and enters its still, but no less powerful, stage. This is Yin.

In prime condition, a man is full of energy. He has a strong mind, warmth in his limbs and an active and ambitious spirit. At this point, the function of Yang has reached its peak and excellent opportunities are within his grasp. He is like a river which has swelled to the edge of its banks. It has no way to flow but outward.   At the opposite end of this spectrum is a man lacking energy. His mind is unsound, his limbs are cold, his movements and temper are uneven and his attitude towards life is pessimistic. The function of Yang is at its lowest point, and the function of Yin is high. At this stage, one should confine oneself and stay with the present situation. An attempt to advance would invite only failure. This withdrawal need not be negative or permanent. By retreating with Yin's character as a guideline, one can cultivate the positive side.

Faced with a slight failure, some people complain of having bad luck. They feel lost and confused because they do not understand the process of Yin-Yang theory. If there is sunshine, there will be rain. After the rain, sunshine follows.

Yin-Yang theory has many direct applications to Tai-Chi Chuan. For example, the Push-hands practice trains one to relax oneself for defense and to move to a better position, but never to abandon one's place and to retreat. Just as the tree dropping its leaves in winter waits for spring to leaf and grow again, one must utilize the character of Yin to cultivate a turning point for progress. When one reaches the extreme of Yin, one will find the beginning of Yang and have the chance to counter the opponent.

Up to this point, the Yin-Yang interaction theory has been explained with examples from human behavior and natural phenomena, but it can also be explained in a graphic method called the Fu Sze Tai-Chi diagram (伏羲太極圖), ancient Tai-Chi diagram or diagram of the natural universe (See Figure 2-1a).

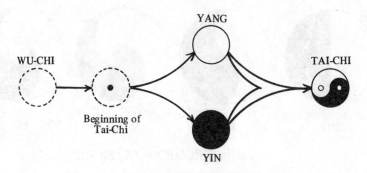

Figure 2-1a

There are several basic principles that should be discussed about the Tai-Chi diagram:

1.   The dividing line for Yin and Yang in the diagram is curved and not straight.

If the dividing line were straight, it would indicate that Tai-Chi is in a motionless state. The curved line shows Tai-Chi is in a state of dynamic circular movement. Variations in the curvature of the line represent different speeds of movement. A small curvature means slow motion. This phenomenon can be demonstrated in the two ways described below.

First, divide a circle into eight equal segments by using four diameters. Color one half of the circle black and the other white. Because the diameters are straight lines, the circle looks motionless; but, if the four straight diameters are replaced with four curved lines passing through the center, the circle appears to be moving. As the curvature of the lines increases, so does the apparent speed of the movement. Different curvatures of the lines are illustrated in Figure 2-1b.

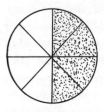 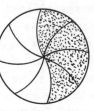 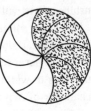

Silent	Slow	Moving	Fast
(not moving)	(moving slightly)	(not fast, not slow)	(moving quickly)

Figure 2-1b

CLOCKWISE (YIN)

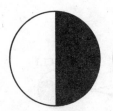   

Still	Slow	Moving	Fast

COUNTERCLOCKWISE (YANG)

Figure 2-1c

For the second example, black and white paint are placed in a shallow pan. Each color should occupy one half of the pan. When the pan is spun, the dividing line for the black and white paint will change from a straight to a curved line. The faster the pan spins, the greater the curvature will be. Finally, a small circle appears in the center. Figure 2-1c illustrates changes with movement.

From the two examples explained above, one can easily see that the Tai-Chi is not only a circular plane figure in a still condition, but also a moving object like a rotating globe. This type of rotation affects the speed (fast or slow) as well as the direction (clockwise or counterclockwise) of the motion. One may observe that the Tai-Chi diagram accurately represents the circular motion of various objects, from whirlpools to spiral nebulae.

The continuous practice of Tai-Chi Chuan enables a master to develop a fast internal energy called silk-cocoon *chin* or Chan-Ssu Chin (纏絲勁). The theory and practice of the silk-cocoon chin will be described further in Chapter 3. Just as the turning wheel throws off objects which come into contact with it, so can a Tai-Chi expert throw opponents outward along the tangential direction. A true expert in Tai-Chi Chuan can show tremendous power just by standing still. When others only touch his or her body, they are thrown a few feet away.

2. The equally large black and white areas inside a Tai-Chi diagram represent Yin and Yang, respectively. Because each is shaped like a fish, they are called the Yin-Yang two fishes (陰陽雙魚). They are continually moving and changing, mutually integrating and restraining and yet, maintain their continuous balance and harmony.

Both Western-style athletics and Chinese arts, such as boxing, have, as their primary purpose, the strengthening of body muscles. Young people with large, strong muscles look very healthy, but after the approach of middle age, the amount of exercise done is usually quite limited. Then, the muscles become fatty tissue and one is likely to become weaker and weaker. Many years ago, it was important for people to have large, strong muscles in order to do heavy work. In modern times, people have less need for large muscles because there are machines to do most of the heavy work.

If the outside of the human body is Yang and the internal organs are Yin, one can see how overdeveloped body muscles will cause an imbalance. The internal organs, such as the heart and kidneys, have to do extra work and will gradually weaken. Overwhelming Yang causes the retreat of Yin. Strong Yang, weak Yin (陽盛陰衰), as this condition is called, is abnormal. Strong Yin, weak Yang (陰盛陽衰) is also abnormal. The only normal and desirable condition is Yin-Yang balance. These conditions are shown in Figure 2-1d.

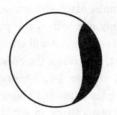

Ying-Yang Balance   Strong Yang, Weak Yin   Strong Yin, Weak Yang
(Normal)   (Abnormal)   (Abnormal)

Figure 2-1d

Unlike most other exercises, the exercises performed in the practice of Tai-Chi Chuan do not require awkward force or posture. Instead, complete relaxation is required. One practices the postures of Tai-Chi Chuan, imagining the purpose of each one and using the full concentration of the internal spirit. With persistent practice, one can eventually obtain Yin-Yang balance. Then, the outside appearance is soft like cotton while the inside is strong like steel. This level of achievement is called the "needle inside the cotton". In this condition, youth and good health are maintained and prolonged. It is believed that if one can reach this acme of perfection, one can bring one's body to eternal existence like gold or diamonds.

3. The white portion of the Tai-Chi diagram contains a black dot, whereas inside the black portion is a white dot. Thus, inside Yin there is Yang and inside Yang there is Yin. Similarly, males (Yang) have a small amount of female hormones (Yin), and females (Yin) have a small amount of male hormones (Yang).

This interrelationship of Yin and Yang is well shown in Tai-Chi Chuan. The Tai-Chi postures are to be neither totally relaxed (Yin) nor totally tense (Yang). Tai-Chi aims to combine relaxation with awareness for Yin-Yang balance. In addition, a step forward always contains the intention to withdraw, and a step backwards always includes the intention to advance. When a person who has had advanced Tai-Chi Chuan training practices the Push-hands exercise with another, a small step forward with a slight withdrawal of the body will throw an opponent several feet away.

4. The amount of white in the Tai-Chi diagram changes gradually from the top to the bottom. It begins at the top of the circle and reaches its maximum size at the base. Where the white part of the diagram is largest, the black portion starts to emerge. The point where the black portion reaches its maximum size is the beginning of the white portion. Thus, the extreme of Yang is the creation of

Yin, and the extreme of Yin is the creation of Yang. The daily changes in the position of the sun illustrate this principle. When it is high noon, the sun is in its most powerful stage; but, at the same time, it is the beginning of sunset. The transportation system in the United States is another example. Americans now have super highways, mass production automobiles and one or more cars for each family. The result of this extreme convenience is inconvenience, traffic jams, a lack of parking spaces, air pollution and the high cost of cars and gasoline. If convenience is Yang, inconvenience is Yin. The extreme of Yang is the creation of Yin in this situation, just as it is in all others. Several European countries, for example, the Netherlands, have begun to use bicycles to replace the troublesome autombile. In doing so, they free themselves from the high price of gasoline and problems with traffic and parking. In this case, the extreme of Yin leads to the creation of Yang.

According to the principles of Tai-Chi Chuan, extreme softness is followed by extreme hardness. Thus, in the practice of Tai-Chi Chuan, awkward force must be given up completely. The body should appear to have total softness, while the inner spirit is concentrated with strength. The longer Tai-Chi Chuan is practiced, the better the results. At the highest level of achievement, one's great strength is not outwardly visible. One's movement is unpredictable at this stage. A slight raising and shifting of the hands and legs will appear soft, graceful and powerless; yet, this ultimate strength of Tai-chi Chuan can defeat every other kind of strength that exists.

5.   Lao-Tzu said in the *Tao Te Ching* (道德經): "The way begot one, the one became two, then the two begot three. From three came everything else." "The way begot one" describes Wu-Chi's generation of Tai-Chi. Even though Wu-Chi, which existed before the universe formed, was intangible and immaterial, it was the source of creation. At the beginning of movement, Tai-Chi, which is "one", evolved. Next the "two" were created, as motion caused the Yin and Yang to separate. Since Yin always contains some Yang and Yang always contains some Yin, the Yang could combine with the Yin again to form three. Thus, the two created three just as a married couple have a child. After the two changed to three, a cycle had begun; production and reproduction continued ceaselessly, as more and more was endlessly created.

Lao-Tzu concluded, "From what-is all the world of things was born, but what-is sprang in turn from what-is-not." Everything evolved through a cycle which began from nothing, then moved to an unexplainable something which was the source of everything; everything came from the three, three came from two, two came from one, one came from nothing. Thus, everything comes from nothing. For example, first there was no civilization, then it began with the stone age and evolved gradually into our atomic age. Now humanity has progressed to the point of landing on the moon and leaving footprints in the moon dust. Such elaborate technology developed from no technology. Our technology has become so complex that we use a computer to control it, yet the computer is run on a binary system which uses two numbers, a zero and a one. Zero and one are only the mathematical symbols for "yes" and "no", essentially a return to Yin and Yang. So, our technological process is a cycle from the Tai-Chi to everything else and then back from everything to Tai-Chi again.

6. What is the meaning of the entire Tai-Chi diagram? The Tai-Chi diagram illustrates how two opposites can be harmonized into a whole interrelated unit. Like other principles of Tai-Chi, this one can apply to natural as well as human relationships.

For example, positive and negative polarities in electricity can be seen in terms of Yin and Yang harmony. Neither a positive electric charge nor a negative one can separately produce light or heat. These opposites need each other to become electricity, just as both Yin and Yang are necessary to form a Tai-Chi unity.

In working out the proper combinations of yin and yang in T'ai Chi, the student will find a guide in Confucianism and Taoism, the two major schools of Chinese philosophy. Confucian philsophy emphasizes moderation and standards of proportion, so-called 'golden mean philosophy' (中庸之道) that can be seen in Western thought in the development of notions of proportion. Taoism emphasizes the continuous importance of changes, which can make any rigid standard for behaviour inappropriate.

We can see the two approaches at work in an example of a man who earns $100. How much ought he spend and how much save? The Confucian approach might say "Save $50, spend $50." The Taoist might reply "If he doesn't need any money at the moment, he cannot spend a penny. But if he truly needs to, he may spend the whole $100."

In T'ai Chi, the hard tenseness or soft suppleness with which the hands are held, shows an application of these two concepts. First, the hand is never held 'totally' soft, for then it is outside the useful proportions of movement and is called 'dead'. Similarly, it is never held totally rigidly in an outward attack gesture; this would also develop poor balance. Studying the hands of Masters Yang Chen-Fu and Wu Chian-Chyan on pages 48 and 49 will give a feeling for the proper amounts of softness and hardness.

The beginner may practice a yin-yang cycle of making the palm hard at the full extension of a gesture and soft at its complete retraction. He will study the yin-yang changes by making the transition back and forth as smooth and even as possible.

After long practice, he may then practice the " belly of the fingers" that is used to express hardness in the Chen Form. Here, instead of making the whole palm hard, the force is applied only to the third segment, or the belly of finger, of the four fingers, while the rest of the hand remains supple.

Finally, he will evolve to a practice in which the 'hard' palm remains completely soft in appearance outside, yet inside it is completely energized with a force that is not manifested, yet is ready to be called upon at any time.

The Tai-Chi diagram can also illustrate the relationship of a married couple. By complementing each other in spite of emotional and physiological differences, a husband and wife will live in harmony. Instead of fighting, they can help each other to create a peaceful family unit. Although traditional interpretations of Yin-Yang relationships considered women naturally more passive and subordinate to men, various aspects of a marital system may be stable in one of three general ways: the submission of a wife to her husband, the submission of a husband to his wife, and equal cooperation between the two partners. In reality, any relationship combines these three general attributes with varying degrees of emphasis. The same principles can apply to the reconciliation of opposites for any one person or human interaction.

In Tai-Chi Chuan itself, the highest achievement combines the attributes of both Yin and Yang. The Tai-Chi master can choose how to respond to any situation. In response to an attack, he or she can disappear like the fog, resist like a mountain or fight back like a tiger. Thus, the master understands the separation and combination of Yin and Yang.

2-2. THE FIVE ELEMENTS OR WU-HSING

*O*ver two thousand years ago, the Chinese Naturalist School (Yin-Yang Chia, 陰陽家) developed the theory of *Wu-Hsing* (五行). The five elements — water, fire, wood, metal and earth — were not considered types of inactive matter, but dynamic processes which were basic to an understanding of the natural world. ("Five elements", the usual English translation for *Wu-Hsing*, fails to convey the idea of movement implied in the Chinese term *hsing*.) The characteristic qualities of each of the *hsing* (行) was derived from the careful observation of natural events. Thus water has the properties of soaking and descending (since water flows downward). Fire both heats and moves upward (since flames rise into the air). Wood allows its form to be shaped into straight or curved pieces. Metal can be melted, molded, and then hardened. Earth's properties include the provision of nourishment through sowing and reaping. These elements have been used both as categories in the classification of many different phenomena and as images of the agents in a variety of dynamically interrelated systems. Four major principles describing changes in and interrelationships among the five elements were also developed: mutual creation, mutual closeness, mutual destruction and mutual fear.

According to the principle of mutual creation (相生), the five elements produce each other: "Wood creates fire, fire creates earth, earth creates metal, metal creates water, and water creates wood". Wood creates fire since fire results from rubbing two pieces of wood together, and wood burns easily. In leaving ashes which become part of the soil, fire creates earth. Observations that metallic ores are found in the earth led to the conclusion that earth creates metal. Metal creates water because metal mirrors exposed at night (a ritual practice) collect dew, or because metal when heated becomes liquid. Finally, water creates wood by nourishing the growth of plants.

The same pairs of elements are related to each other by the *principle of mutual closeness* (相親). Each element is considered attracted to its source. Thus wood is close to water, water to metal, metal to earth, earth to fire, and fire to wood. The close relationship between these pairs of elements is like that between a mother and child. An element becomes close to its creator in much the same way that a child is close to its mother.

The *principle of mutual destruction* (相尅) describes the series of conflicts between pairs of elements. Wood weakens earth by removing nutrients from the soil. Earth limits water by natural bodies of water, such as lakes and rivers, and man-made dams. (According to a well-known Chinese proverb, "When water comes it must be stopped by earth".) Water extinguishes fire. Fire conquers metal by melting it. Metal, in the form of axes and knives, can cut down trees and carve wood. Conversely, by the *principle of mutual fear* (相懼), an element respects or fears the element which could destroy it. Wood fears metal, metal fire, fire water, water earth, and earth fears wood.

The cycles involving the four principles of mutuality are given diagramatic representation in Figure 2-2a. The similarities and differences among the principles can be analyzed in terms of Yin and Yang. Creation and closeness, both constructive principles, are considered Yang; whereas, destruction and fearfulness, their opposites, are viewed as Yin.

In addition to representing forces in the natural world, the five elements provide guiding principles for physiology, pathology, diagnosis, and therapy in traditional Chinese medicine. In the human body, the internal organs are divided into two groups: the five *Tsuan* (五臟), Yin or solid organs, and the six *Fu* (六腑), Yang or hollow organs. Each of the Yin and Yang organs are identified with one of the elements. The heart (Yin) and small intestine (Yang) are associated with fire, the spleen (Yin) and stomach (Yang) with earth, the

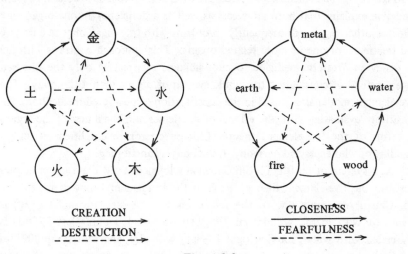

Figure 2-2a

lungs (Yin) and large intestine (Yang) with metal, the kidney (Yin) and bladder (Yang) with water, and the liver (Yin) and gallbladder (Yang) with wood (See Table 2-2a).

Table 2-2a

Five Elements	Wood	Fire	Earth	Metal	Water
Directions	East	South	Center	West	North
Seasons	Spring	Summer	Long Summer	Fall	Winter
Colors	Blue	Red	Yellow	White	Black
Flavors	Sour	Bitter	Sweet	Acid	Salt
Organs	Liver	Heart	Spleen	Lung	Kidney
Sense Organs	Eye	Tongue	Mouth	Nose	Ear

Chinese Physicians began applying the theory of the five elements to the maintenance of health and the cure of illness thousands of years ago. In time, clinical experience led to the development of sophisticated theories based on the five elements. For example, the five-element medical model stresses interrelationships among the internal organs rather than their individual functioning. Using the principles of mutual creation and mutual destruction, Chinese medicine explains that both an excess as well as a deficiency in one organ may affect another organ. Consequently, problems with one organ may be cured by the treatment of one or more related organs. This approach contrasts with the tendency in Western medicine to cure sickness by treating only the diseased organ instead of considering the whole system of organs within the body. The five-element model also is used in the classification of powdered medications. In sensitively evaluating both the effects of medicines and the illness of the organs in terms of the five-element theory, Chinese doctors exemplified an understanding of wholeness and harmony in the body's functioning.

As a system of health, Tai-Chi Chuan employs not only Yin-Yang principles but also the five-element theory. Each of the fundamental movements in Tai-Chi Chuan represents one of the five elements. A step forward (前進) is identified with metal, withdrawal (後退) with wood, looking left (左顧) is associated with water, looking right (右盼) with fire, and central equilibrium (中定) is connected to earth. Thus in addition to developing a healthy Yin-Yang relationship between mental activity and physical movement, Tai-Chi is designed to balance the internal organs and promote harmony in the entire body. Maintaining a dynamically balanced system preserves health by preventing illness and improves the quality as well as the length of life.

2-3.   THE EIGHT TRIGRAMS

The *I Ching*, also called the *Book of Changes,* tells of the formation of the eight trigrams, or Pa-Kua (八卦). According to *Ta-Chuan* (大篆):

> In the system of the I Ching, there is the Tai-Chi, or the Grand Terminus, which generated the two forms or Liung-Yi. Those two forms generated four symbols or Ssu-Hsiang. Those four symbols divided further to generate the eight trigrams or Pa-Kua.

The Tai-Chi is the very first dot which emerges from the emptiness of the Wu-Chi. It contains the moving power of both dynamic and static states and is the source of Yin and Yang. In the static state, Yin and Yang are combined to form a whole, but in a state of motion they separate, generating the two forms or Liung-Yi (兩儀).

Yang is often represented by a line segment or a small white circle. Yin is usually represented by two broken line segments or by a small black circle. Different symbols for Yin and Yang are shown in Figure 2-3a.

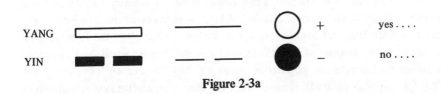

Figure 2-3a

The properties of the two forms can be explained with the use of a straight directional line. Assuming that the point of origin is the Tai-Chi, Yin and Yang indicate negative and positive direction. Figure 2-3b shows that Yang can be represented by the positive direction, and Yin by the negative direction.

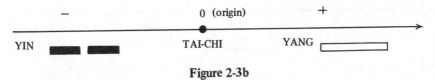

Figure 2-3b

Using numerical symbols, the ancient *I Ching* considered Tai-Chi as zero, Yang as one (an odd number), and Yin as two (an even number). It is more effective, however, to use the binary system to illustrate the properties of Yin and Yang. By defining Yang as zero and Yin as one, or Yin as zero and Yang as one, we can further explain the development of the Tai-Chi theory in terms of the two forms and the four symbols or Ssu-Hsiang (四象).

The four symbols are the result of the combination of the two forms. Two Yang symbols placed together, one above the other, are called the great Yang (太 陽). A Yin sign placed above a Yang sign is called the lesser Yin (少陰). One Yin sign placed above another is called the great Yin (太陰). A Yang sign placed above a Yin sign is called the lesser Yang (少陽). Pictures of the four symbols are shown in Figure 2-3c.

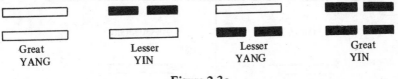

| Great
YANG | Lesser
YIN | Lesser
YANG | Great
YIN |

Figure 2-3c

The principle of the four symbols can be applied to every object or situation. Based upon its characteristics, principle and quantity, everything can be divided into four mutually related subdivisions. For a simple example, we can use Yin and Yang symbols to describe the relationships among several different nations in terms of population and land. Nations like the United States and China have a lot of land and large populations. Some nations, like Canada and Australia, have a lot of land but relatively small populations. A country like Japan has a dense population and a small amount of land, whereas countries like Iceland are small in both land and population. Using the lower position of the four symbols to indicate the amount of land (Yang for large, and Yin for small) and the upper position to indicate the population density (Yang for densely populated, and Yin for thinly populated), we can make the four comparative symbols shown in Figure 2-3d. From the diagram we can see that China and the United States would be considered countries of great Yang, while a country like Iceland would be considered one of great Yin.

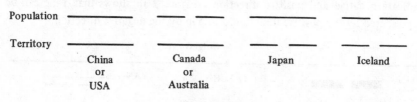

Population

Territory

China · or · USA   Canada · or · Australia   Japan   Iceland

Figure 2-3d

The geometric equivalent of the four symbols are the four quadrants of a rectangular coordinate plane. As in the two forms, Yang would represent positive direction and Yin would represent negative direction. Figure 2-3e demonstrates the relationships between the four symbols and the four quadrants.

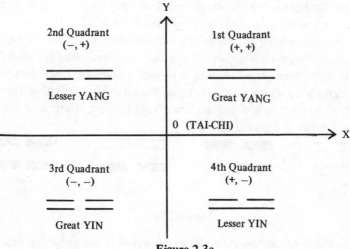

Y

2nd Quadrant
(−, +)

1st Quadrant
(+, +)

Lesser YANG

Great YANG

0   (TAI-CHI)   X

3rd Quadrant
(−, −)

4th Quadrant
(+, −)

Great YIN

Lesser YIN

Figure 2-3e

If zero represents Yang and one represents Yin, the properties of the four symbols, taken in order, can be explained from the numerical point of view (See Table 2-3a).

Table 2-3a

Numerical Properties of the Four Symbols

Four Symbols	Symbol	Binary System	Decimal System	Order	Odd/Even
Great Yang	══════	00	0	1	Even
Lesser Yin	══ ══	01	1	2	Odd
Lesser Yang	══ ══	10	2	3	Even
Great Yin	══ ══	11	3	4	Odd

Just as in analytical geometry, where a graphic method is used to explain equations, three layers of Yin-Yang symbols are used to represent each category in the Tai-Chi system. These symbols are called the eight trigrams (八卦). They can be used to classify all the phenomena of the universe into eight categories and to analyze natural and social events with a scientific method that searches for the mutual relationships of their principles, phenomena and quantities. The Tai-Chi system can be widely applied and is not limited to the analysis of one particular object or event.

An ancient mnemonic for remembering the formation of the eight trigrams has the following lyrics:

Chien	乾三連	Three continuous	══════
Kun	坤六斷	Six broken	══ ══
Chen	震仰杯	Upwards cup	══ ══
Ken	艮覆碗	Overturned bowl	══ ══
Li	離中斷	Empty middle	══ ══
Kan	坎中滿	Full middle	══ ══
Tui	兌上缺	Deficient Top	══ ══
Sun	巽下斷	Broken bottom	══ ══

These eight trigrams are the maximum number of figures which can be formed from two kinds of lines in groups of three. It was the Emperor Fu Hsi (2852-2738 B.C.), the first ruler in Chinese history, who applied the eight trigrams to the Tai-Chi diagram in order to demonstrate how Yin and Yang interact with each other. Fu Hsi's circular arrangement of the eight trigrams is called the Fu Hsi or Hsien-Tien eight trigrams (先天八卦, See Figure 2-3f). *Hsien-Tien* means "the stage before the universe is created".

Figure 2-3f

Along with the Hsien-Tien eight trigrams just described, there is another method of arrangement called the Hu-Tien eight trigrams (後天八卦). According to legend, it was drawn by Chou Wen-Wang (文王), the founder of the Chou Dynasty at about 1143 B.C., and is based upon the *I Ching* which says:

> The ruler comes forth in *Chen* to start his creation. He completes everything in *Sun*. He manifests things to see one another in *Li* and causes them to serve each other in *Kun*. He rejoices in *Tui* and battles in *Chien*. He is comforted and takes rest in *Kan* and finishes his work of the year in *Ken*.

Starting from the east, the order of the Hu-Tien eight trigrams is in a clockwise sequence of Chen, Sun, Li, Kun, Tui, Chien, Kan and Ken. This sequence is used to explain the principle of the motion of the universe and was the basis for the development of the Chinese calendar. Figure 2-3g below shows the movement of the Hu-Tien cycle.

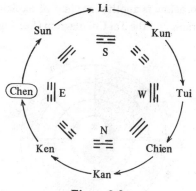

Figure 2-3g

Diagrams on the development of the Tai-Chi system help to demonstrate how the Tai-Chi produced the two forms and the two forms produced the four symbols, which produced the eight trigrams. Two different methods are used to explain this process. One uses a rectangular form (See Figure 2-3h), and the other uses a tree diagram (See Figure 2-3i).

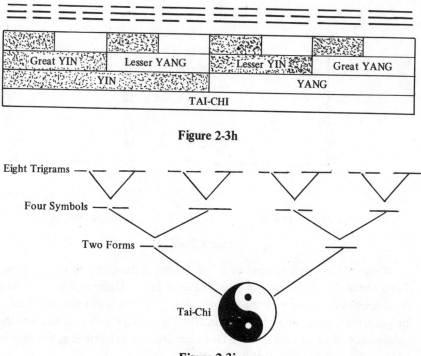

Figure 2-3h

Figure 2-3i

The circular form below is another method of explaining the relationships between the eight trigrams and the Tai-Chi diagram (See Figure 2-3j).

Figure 2-3j

Principles from the Tai-Chi system also lend themselves to describing relationships in geometry. Figure 2-3k uses three-dimensional space coordinates to show the difference between the right-handed and the left-handed systems.

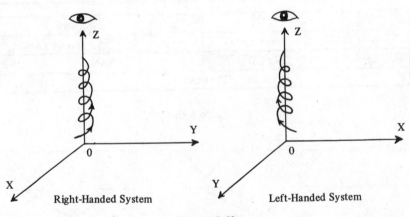

Figure 2-3k

Whether in a right-handed or a left-handed system, the three coordinate planes divide the space into eight parts called octants. Mathematicians still have not determined the order of the octants. However, if one assumes that Yang is the positive direction and Yin is the negative direction of each axis, and uses the arrangement of Hsien-Tien and Hu-Tien eight trigrams as references, it is easy to determine the order of the octants (See Table 2-3b).

Table 2-3b

Trigrams	Symbol	Octant	Order
Chien	☰	$(+,+,+)$	1
Tui	☱	$(+,+,-)$	2
Li	☲	$(+,-,+)$	3
Chen	☳	$(+,-,-)$	4
Sun	☴	$(-,+,+)$	5
Kan	☵	$(-,+,-)$	6
Ken	☶	$(-,-,+)$	7
Kun	☷	$(-,-,-)$	8

As explained in the previous passage on the four symbols, Yang represents zero and Yin is one. A trigram is read from the bottom to the top. It progresses in the same manner as the binary system. For example, Kan ☵ is 101 in the binary system, or five in the decimal system. If n is used for a base, then Kan represents n^2+1. Similarly, Chen ☳ when translated to the binary system becomes 011 which is the equivalent of three in the decimal system and can change to the n base of n+1. Table 2-3c shows these relationships.

Table 2-3c

Trigram	Symbol	Binary System	Decimal System	Order	Base of n
Chien	☰	000	0	1	0
Tui	☱	001	1	2	1
Li	☲	010	2	3	n
Chen	☳	011	3	4	n+1
Sun	☴	100	4	5	n^2

Kan		101	5	6	n^2+1
Ken		110	6	7	n^2+n
Kun		111	7	8	n^2+n+1

The binary system was developed by the German mathematician Leibnitz in the nineteenth century. However, the ancient Chinese were familiar with the idea of the binary system through the eight trigrams five thousand years ago. Furthermore, each of the eight trigrams represents both a numerical concept and suggests the nature of the object it symbolizes. The relationships between the trigrams and other categories shown in Table 2-3d were created thousands of years ago.

Table 2-3d

Trigram	Symbol	Image	Family Relative	Body	Animal	Characteristic
Chien		heaven	father	head	horse	strength
Tui		lake	youngest daughter	mouth	sheep	pleasure
Li		fire	midle daughter	eye	pheasant	clinging
Chen		thunder	oldest son	foot	dragon	shaking
Sun		wind	oldest daughter	thigh	rooster	gentle
Kan		water	middle son	ear	hawk	abysmal
Ken		mountain	youngest son	hand	dog	stillness
Kun		earth	mother	belly	cow	accepting

Tai-Chi Chuan has eight basic postures which are symbolized by the eight trigrams: ward-off (掤), roll-back (擠), press (擠), push (按), pull-down (採), split (挒), elbow (肘) and shoulder-strike (靠). Each is related to Chien, Kun, Kan, Li, Sun, Chen, Tui and Ken, respectively. These postures are explained in Chapter Six.

2-4. *INTRODUCTION TO THE* I CHING

*T*he text of the *I Ching* (易經), or as it is usually called in English, the *Book of Changes*, seems to have been prepared before 1000 B.C., some time during the last days of the Shang Dynasty (商朝1766-1150 B.C.) and the beginning of the Chou Dynasty (周朝1150-249 B.C.), It was one of the five classics (五經) edited by Confucius (孔子 551-479 B.C.), who is reported to have wished he had fifty more years to study it. Ever since the time of Confucius it has not lost its enormous significance. Representatives from every segment of Chinese society – Confucianists and Taoists, learned literary scholars and street shamans, the official state cult and private individuals – have at one time or another consulted the *I Ching*.

The Chinese character for the letter *I* was created by combining symbols for the sun (日) and the moon (月). The sun symbol representing the Yang force was placed on top of the moon symbol indicating the Yin force. Just as the appearance of the sun and moon alternate, so the two fundamental forces, Yin and Yang, complement each other. Based on the principles manifested in such natural phenomena, *I* has three meanings: the easy, the changing, and the constant.

The book starts with the observation of natural events and daily life. These primary data of life are simple and easy to understand, e.g. a decayed willow sprouting flowers. *The Great Treatise*, or *Ta Chuan* (大篆), one of the oldest commentaries on the *I Ching*, describes the results of following the way of the easy and simple.

> Chien knows through the easy.
> Kun does things simply.
> What is easy is easy to know.
> What is simple is simple to follow.
> He who is easy to know makes friends.
> He who is simple to follow attains good works.
> He who possesses friends can endure forever.
> He who performs good works can become great.

What is the nature of the changing and the constant according to the *I Ching*? The wind may change the mirror image of a white cloud reflected in a stream, but the substance (i.e., the white cloud itself) is still unchanged. Although this change looks natural and simple, it is complicated in meaning. In order to understand the concept of change, one must first consider the opposite of change. One might think that the opposite of change is rest or standstill; however, these are but aspects of change. In Chinese thought the opposite of change is perceived as the growth of what ought to decrease, the downfall of what ought to rule. Change, then, is not an external principle that imprints itself upon phenomena; it is an inner tendency according to which development naturally takes place. Although the phenomena of the universe are continually changing, underlying their changes is the principle of constancy. For example, if there is lightning, thunder must follow; after the moon is full, it must wane; if a decayed willow produces flowers, they will not last long.

The *I Ching* is not a religious book but rather a book of profound wisdom which describes nature in terms of linear symbols. The method used in the *I Ching* analyzes every phenomenon into six stages. The symbols of Yin and Yang indicate the process of change. No matter how complex the event, the *I Ching* can trace the past, explain the present and predict the future. *Ta Chuan* describes the wide applicability of the *I Ching*.

> The use of the *I* is wide and great! If we speak of what is far, no limit can be set to it; if we speak of what is near, it is still and correct; if we speak of what is between heaven and earth, it embraces everything.

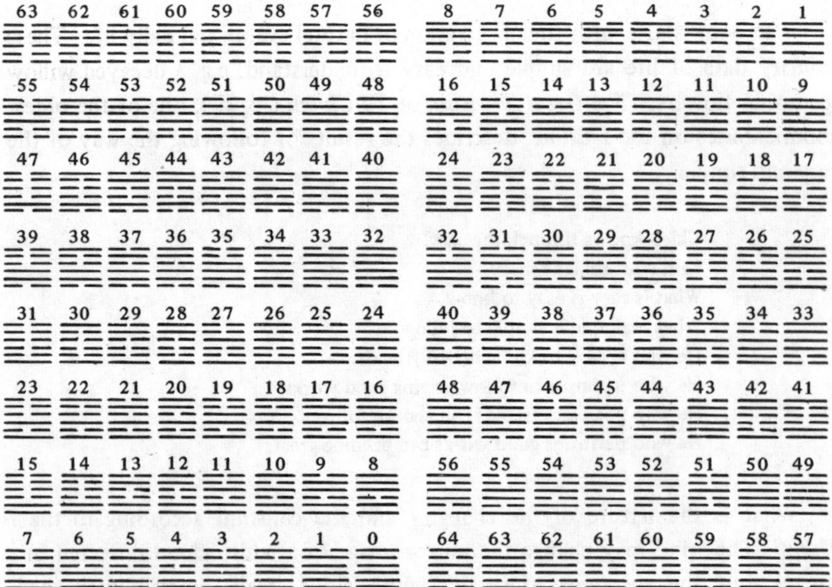

63	62	61	60	59	58	57	56		8	7	6	5	4	3	2	1
55	54	53	52	51	50	49	48		16	15	14	13	12	11	10	9
47	46	45	44	43	42	41	40		24	23	22	21	20	19	18	17
39	38	37	36	35	34	33	32		32	31	30	29	28	27	26	25
31	30	29	28	27	26	25	24		40	39	38	37	36	35	34	33
23	22	21	20	19	18	17	16		48	47	46	45	44	43	42	41
15	14	13	12	11	10	9	8		56	55	54	53	52	51	50	49
7	6	5	4	3	2	1	0		64	63	62	61	60	59	58	57

Figure 2-4a

From the above comments we can see that the domain of the *I Ching* is as profound and all encompassing as the universe. Not only can it explain the relationships among people in society, but it also can provide an explanation for the ever-changing phenomena of the natural world. Within the changing processes of the universe, the *I Ching* searches for the unchanging truth of the entire process of origin, development and outcome.

The conceptual system in the I Ching is based on the Tai-Chi, which develops into the two forms. The two forms lead to the four symbols which precede the eight trigrams. From the eight trigrams the 64 hexagrams are formed, as shown in Figure 2-4a.

Every pair of trigrams has its mutual relationship and purpose; put together, the two trigrams become a hexagram, forming a logical unit or whole, with a changed meaning and developmental process. For example, if earth (≡≡ ≡≡) is below and heaven (≡≡≡≡) is above, the proper balance is symbolized. Should the position of the two trigrams be reversed, the opposite of the natural order, the meaning attached to the hexagram would be weakness (See Figure 2-4b).

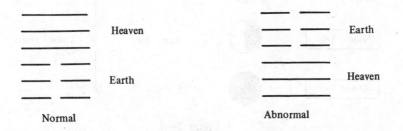

Heaven	Earth
Earth	Heaven
Normal	Abnormal

Figure 2-4b

As illustrated in Figure 2-4c, the name for the lower trigram is the inner trigram (內卦), while the upper one is called the outer trigram (外卦).

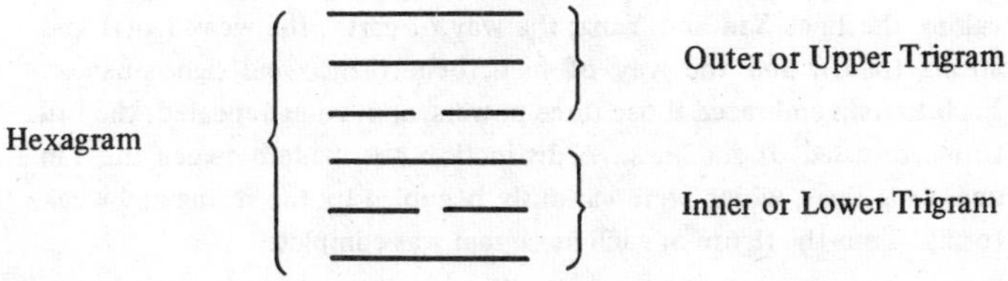

Hexagram {
    } Outer or Upper Trigram

    } Inner or Lower Trigram

Figure 2-4c

The inner and outer trigrams can be understood in terms of the development of a particular phenomenon. For example, when a stone is thrown into the water, ripples of concentric circles spread outward from the point of contact. The force of the throw determines the speed and extent of this spreading. Like the stone in this example, the inner trigram represents the basic foundation of a particular phenomenon. Like the ripples, the outer trigram illustrates the outward development of an event. The way in which an outside situation develops depends on its basic inner foundation. The inner trigram then is the subjective condition, and the outer trigram the objective condition of a particular phenomenon.

Each trigram has three positions, called Yao (爻), for the arrangement of Yin or Yang lines. The upper Yao contains the image of heaven or sky, the lower Yao the image of earth, and the middle Yao the image of the humanity or man. These three images are called the three powers (三才), as indicated in Figure 2-4d.

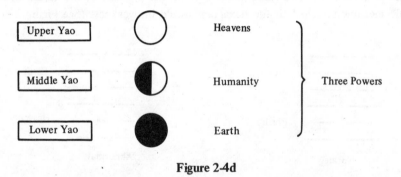

Figure 2-4d

The Treatise of Remarks on the Trigrams, or *Shuo Kua* (少康), explains the development of the trigrams and hexagrams in the following way:

> When the ancient sages designed the *I*, its figures conformed with the principles underlying the nature of men and things, and the ordinances appointed for them by Heaven. They exhibited the way of Heaven, calling the lines Yin and Yang; the way of earth, the weak (soft) and strong (hard); and the way of men, benevolence and righteousness. Each trigram embraced those three powers, and, being repeated, the full form consisted of six lines. A distinction was made between the Yin and Yang lines, which were variously occupied by the strong and weak forms. Thus the figure of each hexagram was completed.

Each hexagram, having six positions, has six Yaos. The Yaos in a hexagram are described in order from bottom to top as first, second, third, fourth, fifth, and top Yao. The six Yaos indicate the six stages necessary for the development of a phenomenon. According to the traditional commentaries on the *I Ching*,

> The Yao speaks of the changes.
>
> The lines of Yao correspond to the movements taking place on earth. In the trigrams, these lines are in high and low positions, and we designate them from their component elements; Yang or Yin.
>
> The lines are mixed together and elegant forms arise. When such forms are not in their appropriate places, the ideas of good and bad fortune are produced.

The Yaos in a hexagram follow the same pattern as in a trigram, except that each of the three powers or images consists of two Yaos. Their positions are shown in Figure 2-4e.

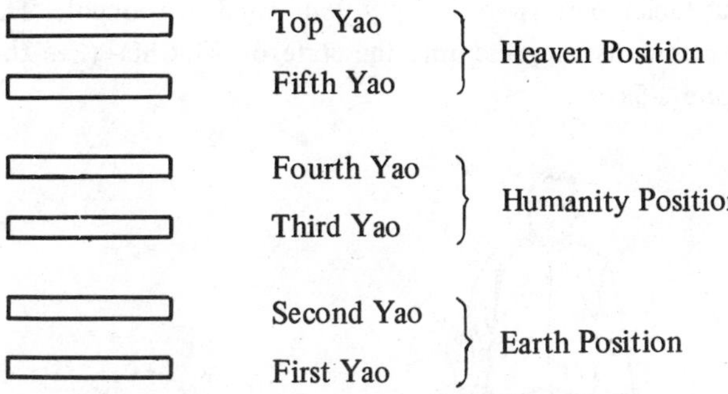

Top Yao

Fifth Yao

} Heaven Position

Fourth Yao

Third Yao

} Humanity Position

Second Yao

First Yao

} Earth Position

Figure 2-4e

Tai-Chi Chuan was developed from these basic principles of the *I Ching*. For Tai-Chi the inner trigram represents one's state of mind and the outer one the condition of one's body. These two sets of trigrams have been translated into a series of continuous movements, incorporating the constant changing between Yin and Yang. The principles of Yin-Yang changes apply to the visible outer movements as well as to the changes occurring inside the body and the mind. In addition, balanced, harmonious movements and psychological well-being are interrelated. One could compare the body to a car carrying passengers (the inner organs and the nervous system including the brain). If the driver of this car goes smoothly, the passengers will feel comfortable. Jarring movements, on the other hand, will disturb the passengers. Therefore, the mind needs to direct the body in the practice of smooth, continuous movements. At the same time, if one takes care of the outside (i.e., the movements), the outside will automatically take care of the inside. Following Tai-Chi principles in one's outside posture promotes a feeling of mental "stillness". This inner calm will facilitate dealing with one's life in general.

The principle ideas underlying Tai-Chi Chuan are easily grasped, but the movements need constant practice. Gradually, the physical and the psychological aspects of this art join in mutual harmony. One will eventually be in prefect accord with heaven and coexist peacefully with the way of nature.

2-5. THE PHILOSOPHY OF TAI-CHI CHUAN

*B*efore starting to practice Tai-Chi Chuan, stand erect facing north. Keep the head, neck and torso in one line, perpendicular to the earth, but relax as completely as possible. Avoid any nervous or muscular tension, any conscious facial expression. Empty your mind of thought. The result will be a look of serenity, representing the state of Wu-Chi. (See the beginning stance in Figure 2-5a).

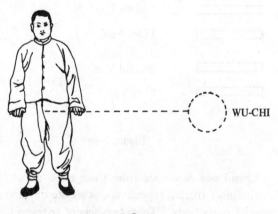

WU-CHI

Figure 2-5a

The starting stage of Tai-Chi Chuan can be compared to a seed being planted in the ground in the spring. Something inside this seed is changing to a sprout. In much the same way the concept of practicing Tai-Chi Chuan is formed in the very first moment of change; everything is mobilized in a physical as well as in a mental sense. This transition from outer stillness to readiness for movement is called going from Wu-Chi to Tai-Chi (無極而太極).

Once the stage of Tai-Chi begins, one has a strong intention to practice Tai-Chi Chuan. The weight of the body rests squarely on the feet; in other words, one must be rooted to the ground. The Chinese say, "The root of the

body is in the feet" (其 根 在 腳),this rootedness evokes the image of the earth.
One's head and spine should be straight. In order for the spirit of vitality, or
Shen (神), to ascend to the top of the head, it must be held as if suspended by
a string from the ceiling of the room. The image of the sky is evoked by the
saying, "The spirit of vitality, or Shen, reaches to the top of the head" (虛 領 頂
勁). By relaxing totally, one aims to throw open every bone and muscle of the
body. In this way one allows the intrinsic energy, or Chi, to sink to the *Tan-
Tien*, a point three fingers below the navel, and two fingers' width inside the
abdomen. This principle, represented by the image of the humanity, is described
as "the Chi sinks to the Tan-Tien" (氣沉丹田). These three images, earth, sky
and humanity, are called the three powers (See Figure 2-5b).

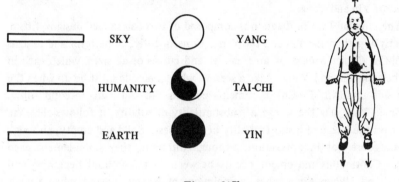

▭ SKY	◯	YANG
▭ HUMANITY	☯	TAI-CHI
▭ EARTH	●	YIN

Figure 2-5b

The idea of the three powers (三才) is very important in that it shows
humanity living between earth and sky. When one practices Tai-Chi Chuan for
years, gradually one will feel that every movement of Tai-Chi Chuan is the
movement of the universe. One's body may be perceived as moving like the
branch of a tree, blown every which way by the wind. One's breathing will be
part of the movement of the universe as well. The awareness of the environment
being engaged in a gigantic cosmic dance will suddenly dawn on you. You and
the universe will become identical, like the Tai-Chi diagram. You are then the
Tai-Chi and the Tai-Chi will be you, or you will be the universe and the universe
will be you.

The idea of identification with something else is not new. Patriotism
teaches a citizen to identify with a country; many religions teach their followers
to identify with God. These ways of identification still retain two entities, an
individual and his or her country, or an individual and God. The identification
in the Tai-Chi philosophy eliminates dualism. You are the Tai-Chi, and the Tai-
Chi is you. Now, if the universe is you, then everything the universe reveals is

you. All human beings are identified with you, and you with them. Therefore, you suffer if others suffer; you are happy if others are happy. It is not a question of seeing others as having troubles, but their problems become yours. This total identification is the foundation of universal harmony and world peace. Only after this realization can one feel that the universe is beautiful and life meaningful.

Once the Tai-Chi Chuan begins, Yin and Yang emerge from every action. Solidity and emptiness (虛實), or substantiality and insubstantiality, start to separate. Thus the stretch of the arms is Yang, the withdrawal Yin; in general the expansion in movement is Yang, the contraction Yin; forward is Yang, backward Yin, etc. Nothing exists without its opposite; there is nothing that does not change in order to be permanent. This duality is the so-called "two forms" of Yin and Yang.

The circular Tai-Chi diagram is composed of two fish-shaped designs, fitting perfectly together, the Yin and the Yang. Consequently, all patterns and designs of Tai-Chi Chuan consist of arcs, circles and curves of all sizes, which each in turn balance Yin and Yang. Like a seesaw, where one side must be up when the other side is down, Tai-Chi movements contain Yin and Yang in equilibrium.

Since Yang has the image of substantiality or solidity, it follows that Yin must have the image of insubstantiality or emptiness. Solid and empty, although opposites, are not in opposition; although different, they complement each other. Continuous movement occurs between them, without beginning and without end. When Yin reaches its final moment, Yang is created; when Yang is completed, Yin begins again.

It is important then in practicing Tai-Chi Chuan to distinguish solidity from emptiness (分清虛實). Within solidity there must be emptiness, just as there is Yin in Yang and Yang in Yin. In Figure 2-5c the relationships between solidity and emptiness are shown in terms of the four symbols.

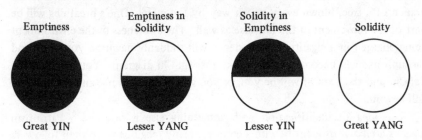

Figure 2-5c

The development from the four symbols into the eight trigrams is the next step in Tai-Chi Chuan. The eight trigrams (八卦) represent the eight basic postures of Tai-Chi Chuan, also called the Eight Gates or Pa-Men (八門): ward-off or Peng (掤), roll-back or Lu (攦), press or Chi (擠), push or An (按), pull-down or Tsai (探), split or' Lieh (挒), elbow or Chou (肘), and shoulder-strike or Kao (靠). The relationships between the Eight Gates and the eight trigrams are shown in Figure 2-5d.

Figure 2-5d

Ward-off, roll-back, press and push are located in the south, north, west and east, respectively, hence they are named the *Four Directions* or Ssa Cheng (四正). The positions of pull-down, split, elbow and shoulder-strike are in the southeast, northwest, southwest and northeast, respectively, so these are called the *Four Corners* or Ssa Yu (四隅). A more detailed explanation of the Eight Gates will be given in Chapter Six.

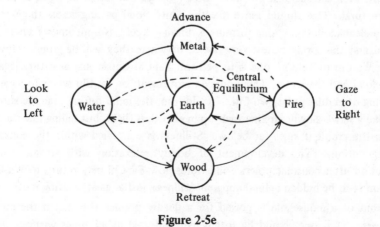

Figure 2-5e

According to Chang San-Feng's *Theory of Tai-Chi Chuan*, "The Five Steps or Wu-Pu of Tai-Chi Chuan are advance, retreat, look to the left, gaze to the right and central equilibrium". As shown in Figure 2-5e, these Five Steps can represent the five elements: metal, wood, water, fire and earth.

The Eight Gates plus the Five Steps are termed the Tai-Chi Chuan thirteen postures, (十三勢), the basis for the different styles of Tai-Chi Chuan. Thus Tai-Chi Chuan applies ideas from the Tai-Chi diagram, the five elements, and the *I Ching*. Total in concept, it is a synthesis of movement and function. The Eight Gates, constituting a regular octant, has four directions and four corners, which are both squares. This square or octant generates the hand and upper torso movements. The Five Steps form a circle, generating the leg and foot movements. The square or octant and the circle are connected by the body. One could imagine the square and the circle as cardboard figures connected in the center by a string.

In fact, the circle and the square may be interchanged. That is, the circle may generate the square and vice versa. According to the *I Ching* theory, there is unlimited interaction. Yet all these changes are confined to the domain of the changing eight trigrams, which themselves derive from the four symbols. The four symbols, however, come from the two forms which, in turn, return to the Tai-Chi. The development from nothing to something and the return from something to nothing describes a basic concept in Tai-Chi Chuan and Taoist philosophy. Everything in the world is involved in a cyclic process, from Wu-Chi to Tai-Chi and then back again to Wu-Chi.

The relationship between this cyclic process and Tai-Chi Chuan is clearly reflected in the postures themselves. While practicing Tai-Chi Chuan, one should not use even the slightest awkward force (拙力), but rather be light, or Ching, and natural. One should move like the white cloud passing across the sky, or like a clear mountain spring forming a running creek. No one knows where the cloud and the spring water come from, or where they will be going. Moving from Wu-Chi to Tai-Chi, one is to perform Tai-Chi Chuan just as nature creates the cloud and the water. One's outside movement, or Tai-Chi seems to have no starting or ending point, Wu-Chi. In addition, the mind during practice should be like a hawk slowly circling high up in effortless flight, but falling like a stone upon the rabbit it spies far below. Stillness is concealed within the constant flying action. The development of bodily relaxation with strong mental intention after constant practice illustrates how Tai-Chi may return to Wu-Chi. Action is to be hidden behind apparent stillness, just as a cat, waiting motionless in front of a mousehole is poised for a deadly pounce the instant the mouse appears. Thus one should be totally concentrated at all times without using outer force. Finally, although the movements are large and stretched at first, they become more subtle during the more advanced stages. The emphasis shifts from the outside form to the inside one. During the final stage no outward movement can be detected; yet a master, when touched, can throw one across the room.

The final result of long practice and proper execution of Tai-Chi Chuan comes into sight when the practitioner achieves an internal cleansing which is manifested as a clear flame or fire. This flame is the image of unity within the individual, resulting from disengagement from the confusing and distracting physical surroundings. Eventually, while practicing Tai-Chi Chuan time and space are no longer relevant. The practitioner does not even perceive the presence of other people. Neither sight, sound, nor the passing of time pierce concentration on the Tai-Chi Chuan. When this stage occurs, one is no longer a separate unity but mixes with the universe and becomes reconnected to the unity of everything. One has progressed from achieving personal unity, the first great achievement in the practice of Tai-Chi Chuan, to the next step of identification with the universe. Thus the environment of the fourth dimension is near.

What is the meaning of the fourth dimension? From a geometric point of view a point has no dimensions. Nevertheless, everything in the universe, even the universe itself, is a set of points. In reality, the point is Tai-Chi. A straight line has only one dimension — its length. A directed line, however, possesses positive and negative directions representing the two forms, Yin and Yang (See Figure 2-5f).

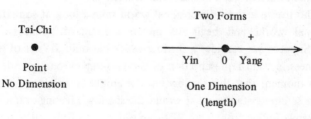

Figure 2-5f

A plane has length and width bringing us to two dimensions. If a rectangle's coordinate is set, there are four quadrants, which represent the geometric equivalent of the four symbols. A hexahedron, having length, width and height is of a three dimensional nature. If a space coordinate is set, eight octants appear, providing the geometric equivalent of the eight trigrams (See Figure 2-5g).

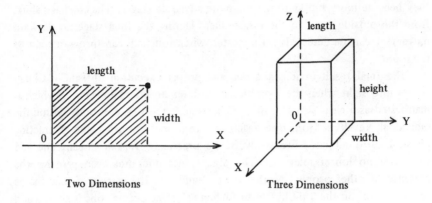

Figure 2-5g

In order to conceptualize the fourth dimension, one adds time to length, width and height.

In general, we live in a three-dimensional world but are continually in contact with the flow of time. Therefore, our domain of thinking always reaches into the four dimensional world. Einstein's theory of relativity provides us with an example of how our thinking extends into the fourth dimension. Since relativity theory deals with the discovery of secrets relating time and space, it is difficult to understand and accept for most of us. Studying the *I Ching* diligently and practicing Tai-Chi Chuan regularly will open up the essential harmony between Eastern wisdom and Western science.

Let us who live in a three-dimensional world take a look at something in a two-dimensional world and begin to understand the differences between dimensions. Suppose we consider a shadow which has only the size of its shape but no thickness, a valid representation of the two-dimensional world. Let us imagine for a moment that this shadow has the ability to think and feel as we do. Under these circumstances what would the shadow's feeling or understanding be of an apple falling from a tree? From our point of view it is so easy to describe and to talk about, but since the shadow lives in a two-dimensional world, lacking the sense of height, it will not know anything before the apple reaches or after the apple leaves the plane where the shadow exists. In other words, the shadow experiences only the intersection of the apple with the plane of its existence (See Figure 2-5h).

At first, when the apple begins to touch the plane, the shadow can see a point of contact on the plane. When the apple falls further, the shadow will see a continued series of circles which are the intersections of the plane and the bottom part of the apple. The further down the apple comes, the larger the

doesn't know anything above the plane

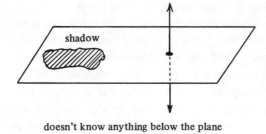

doesn't know anything below the plane

Figure 2-5h

circles will be until the maximum size is reached at the point where the middle of the apple intersects with the plane. After the intersection with the largest part of the apple, the circles seen by the shadow will steadily decrease in size. Finally, a point appears which is the intersection of the top of the apple just leaving the plane where the shadow stays. The above explanation is worthwhile since it gives us an understanding of the experience of a falling apple from a two-dimensional perspective, shown in Figure 2-5i.

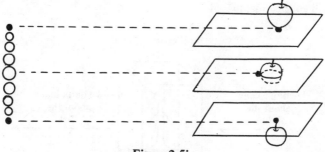

Figure 2-5i

The "real" situation, as we see it from a three-dimensional point of view is shown in Figure 2-5j.

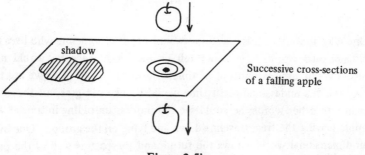

Successive cross-sections
of a falling apple

Figure 2-5j

The shadow has no way of understanding the entire process of an apple's falling from a tree the way we do, nor does the shadow realize the entire shape of an apple since it has no sense of height. Its experience is limited to the width and length of the plane. Even if it were possible to tell the shadow what the shape of an apple is, and that it first grew on a tree and then fell to the ground, it would not change the perception of the shadow towards an apple since its understanding is limited to two-dimensional concepts. For similar reasons Einstein's theory of relativity is difficult for most people to comprehend. Since we are living in a three-dimensional world of length, width and height, we are not cognizant of the dimension of time, just as the shadow is ignorant of height. No person has ever seen the future; no shadow perceives any form before the apple reaches the plane where the shadow "lives". No one has caught the past; nor is the shadow aware of how the apple came to penetrate its plane of existence. We can perceive only a continuous series of moments (the present), much as the shadow can "see" only the points and circles of the intersections of the apple with the plane of its existence. We are unable to grasp the meaning of this continuous "present", as the shadow cannot understand what the shape of the apple is like. No one knows where this continuous present came from and where it will go (See Figure 2-5k).

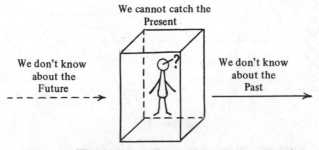

What is the meaning of this continuous present?

Figure 2-5k

One way to answer this question would be to find someone who lives in the four-dimensional world. He could tell us the truth since he would not be confined by our limited concept of time. He would be to us as we are to the shadow, and his understanding of time would be like our grasp of the concept of height. In other words, he could see the process unfolding in time as we see the apple leaving the tree, traveling down and lying on the ground. One living in a four-dimensional world knows the future and the past as well as the present. He perceives us as space travelers, being born here, moving through life and finally staying in one place at the time of death. In this sense then, one who lives in a four-dimensional world is really a god, defined in the most modern and scientific manner. Likewise, a person living in a three-dimensional world would be god for the shadow with its limited two-dimensional existence.

Time and space, which can be seen as two different systems, must be discussed in more detail. Time is one phase of universal phenomena which are changing with respect to space. Theoretically speaking, from a four-dimensional point of view, space and time are fully equivalent and unified. In our world time has three aspects: biological, psychological and physical.

Biological time is defined according to the biological changes in the human body during its life span. For instance, some people may turn gray while still in their twenties; others may not have a single gray hair even though fifty years old. Biological time then differs for each individual.

Psychological time is defined by the activity of human consciousness. Examples of this kind of time include the speed with which time seems to pass whenever one is happily employed, and the feeling of time going slowly when one is kept waiting even for a short while. Psychological time changes with one's reactions to the environment.

Physical time is shown on a clock for structure and calculations in everyday life. Modern physics knows that if a rocket is traveling near the speed of light, time will pass relatively slowly. If the rocket's speed increased to match the speed of light, time would be motionlessness. Theoretically time would flow backwards once the rocket passed the speed of light. It is interesting to think that the passengers on a rocket traveling faster than the speed of light would apparently become younger and younger. Although this theory reveals that time is changing relative to speed, in reality we have not yet been able to build a rocket capable of moving at speeds that high. Time is not something which exists objectively by itself. It is a part of the universe. Space and time form a complex continuum which is undifferentiated, just like the relationship between height and the two-dimensional world. In the undifferentiated continuum of space and time, time occurs in relation to the process of change. Once it becomes possible to change the structure of the phenomena in the universe, it will also become possible to influence the speed of time.

More than two thousand years ago, a Chinese philosopher Chuang-Tzu (莊子) discovered that the shadow of a flying bird is actually still. Few people would immediately accept such a statement. However, using present-day scientific approaches, we can explain how Chuang-Tzu's description is accurate. What happens when a bird is flying can be compared to what the human eye perceives when viewing a movie. In a movie individual still frames which differ slightly from each other are shown sequentially at the speed of 24 frames per second.   This sequence of stills is perceived by the human eye as movement. The shadow of a flying bird in one instant is actually only an image projected from the bird to the ground. In itself it is motionless, but because the bird is flying at a certain speed, these images follow each other at a rapid rate and produce the illusion of movement. A bird's flying from position A to another position B requires a certain amount of time. However, although the shadow of the bird follows the bird's movement from A to B, it has no real activity of its own. Instead, the shadow, a series of instantaneous motionless projected images, is in no way affected by time.

The most important principle in Tai-Chi Chuan is to seek stillness in movement (動中求靜). The outside appearance of Tai-Chi Chuan has soft and natural movements, like the bird flying in the sky, but the mind governs the body. When performing Tai-Chi Chuan then, one must think in terms of the projection of the series of movements, every individual quiet posture, by the mind.   Since space and motion cannot be separated from time in relativity theory, one's body while performing Tai-Chi Chuan will, like a flying bird, emerge in physical time. But like the projected image of the flying bird, one's inner body is always keeping still. Therefore, it is not influenced by the current of biological and psychological time. In other words, the speed of biological and psychological time approaches zero as a limit, creating a state of emotional stillness.   For this reason then, the persistent practice of Tai-Chi Chuan will imbue one with full spirits and rejuvenation. Tai-Chi will, in fact, become a revelation showing the relationship between time and space, creating a gate through which the four-dimensional world can be entered.

CHAPTER
THREE
FOUNDATION

*T*ai-Chi Chuan combines *To-Noa* (吐納) and *Tao-Yie* (導引) techniques developed by Taoist monks. To reach the highest level of achievement in Tai-Chi Chuan one must follow a special plan of training incorporating both these skills. Otherwise, one's achievement will be limited even after twenty or thirty years of diligent practice and the attainment of good health.

According to Chinese medical theory, special forms of exercise can both prevent and cure illness by facilitating the unobstructed circulation of Chi and blood (氣血). Perhaps the most famous of these is the five animals exercise, where one imitates the movements of the tiger, bear, ape, deer and crane. Tao-Yie, the name given to the forms developed by the Taoists, affect both the outside and the inside of the body. Outside, the movement of every joint promotes good blood circulation. Inside, the Chi and breathing are eventually brought to every part of the body. Tai-Chi Chuan shows all these benefits.

To-Noa, the complement of Tao-Yie, refers to breathing exercises, or Chi-Kung. Literally translated, *To* is "the exhalation of carbon dioxide", and *Noa* is "the inhalation of fresh air". To-Noa encompasses two major areas; the practice of the training itself, and the method of letting the breath penetrate into every part of the entire body.

3-1. TAI-CHI CHI-KUNG

*C*hi-Kung (氣功) signifies "the use of the breathing to develop the Chi for special purposes, such as fighting or healing". Eight major breathing methods, some of which occur in combination with others, can be differentiated. Some of these happen spontaneously: natural breathing, natural deep breathing, sighing (a type of cleansing breath) and inhaling extra air for more energy (a type of tonic breath). Other methods require special practice: alternate breathing, postbirth abdominal breathing and prebirth breathing. In addition to occurring spontaneously, the cleansing or tonic breath may be practiced voluntarily in combination with pre- or postbirth breathing. The ultimate stage in breathing is called the tortoise breath. Each of these methods will be described in more detail below.

1. Natural Breathing: The regular breath one takes constantly without thinking about it.

2. Cleansing (瀉) Breath: Inhaling through the nose and exhaling through the mouth.

This kind of breathing emphasizes exhalation. Expelling the air takes longer than inhaling. The purpose of this type of breathing is to relax inner tension or to lower a fever. Sighing is a spontaneous manifestation of the cleansing breath.

3. Tonic (補) Breath: Inhaling through the mouth and exhaling through the nose.

This kind of breathing emphasizes inhalation, which is longer than exhalation. Through this method one can gain energy and improve blood circulation.

Examples where tonic breathing is appropriate and tends to occur spontaneously are in lifting heavy weights, preparing to dive into a swimming pool.

4. Alternate Breathing: Inhaling through one nostril and exhaling through the other.

At first this technique can be practiced with the aid of both index fingers. The right index finger closes the right nostril as one inhales through the left nostril. Then the left index finger closes the left nostril, and one exhales from the opened right nostril. Later one practices without using the fingers. Eventually the breath, controlled by this method, becomes long, slow and deep. Achieving such control is easier said than done.

Alternate breathing might be used in relieving the pain of a headache. If the pain is on the right side of the head, inhale through the right nostril, hold and imagine the air mixing with the pain, then exhale the mixture through the left nostril, for example. This breathing may also be used to relieve dizziness or states of emotional worriedness.

5. Natural Deep Breath.

One does not need anyone to explain what a deep breath is. Wherever one finds fresh air and open space, one automatically stretches one's arms wide open and takes a deep breath, be it on the top of a mountain or at the seashore.

6. Long Breath: Abdominal Postbirth Breathing (後天呼吸).

The long breath is a form of abdominal breathing. On inhaling the lower abdomen expands because of the air coming in; during exhalation the lower abdomen contracts.

7. Prebirth or Prenatal Breathing (先天呼吸).

This form of breathing is also called "reverse breathing", since the type of abdominal breathing used reverses the method of the long breath. The lower abdomen contracts as one inhales, and it expands with air on exhalation. According to traditional Taoist theory, prebirth breathing imitates the general breathing pattern of the fetus in its mother's womb (胎息). Through the umbilical cord the fetus receives oxygen and food and eliminates carbon dioxide and other waste products. In order to take in oxygen, the fetus must *draw in* the lower abdomen; in order to eliminate carbon dioxide, the fetus must *push out* the lower abdomen. When the umbilical cord is cut, prebirth breathing ceases and postbirth breathing, from the mouth and nose, begins.

The progress of our lives in time can be compared to a boat floating on a river. If no special methods of locomotion, such as oars or motors, are used, the boat will follow the river's current downstream until the end of the river, just as our lives naturally follow the path from birth to death. If we can row the boat, we may be able to slow the boat's movement, but the current is too strong for us to move the boat upstream. A more powerful kind of energy, such as that of a motor, is needed before the boat can progress against the river's current. In Tai-Chi Chuan prebirth breathing is designed to provide the special kind of energy required for rejuvenation. According to Taoist theory, a number of different methods, such as diet, exercise, and special breathing techniques, can slow down the natural progress of life from birth to death. However, postbirth breathing cannot change the direction of this natural current. Only when the prebirth breathing becomes the normal breathing pattern can the aging process actually be reversed.

8. Tortoise Breath.

Even prebirth breathing alone will not enable one to reach the ultimate breathing stage. Forgetting the prebirth method after its mastery over many years leads one to the so-called tortoise breath (龜息).

Even the writer did not believe that the Tortise Breath was a meaningful development when he began the study of T'ai Chi. After 17 years he has not reached this stage yet, but has found profound changes and improvements he did not expect. Normal breathing is slow and calm, like that of an athlete: 3 to 4 breaths a minute, as contrasted with 16 to 18 breaths for the average person. When there is very hard work for one or two hours or occasional very strenuous work, shortness of breath does not occur.

As mentioned above, Tai-Chi Chuan uses the prebirth breathing method. The atmospheric pressure and gases present in the abdominal cavity and inner

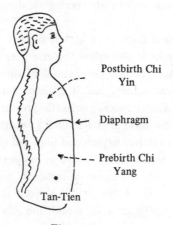

Postbirth Chi
Yin

Diaphragm

Prebirth Chi
Yang

Tan-Tien

Figure 3-1a

organs of a fetus are known as the prebirth Chi, or *Hsien-Tien Chi* (先天氣), which is Yang. The air which the lungs bring into the chest cavity once the child is born is called the postbirth Chi, or *Hu-Tuin Chi* (後天氣), which is Yin. The diaphragm becomes the divider between the two above-mentioned layers of Chi as shown in Figure 3-1a.

The prebirth breathing method can be described in terms of the combination and separation of Yin and Yang. On inhalation, the postbirth Chi, which begins to fill the lungs, gradually approaches the diaphragm, at the same time as the lower abdomen contracts and the prebirth Chi pushes up towards the diaphragm. Thus this type of inhalation combines the two Chis into a whole, or Tai-Chi, which is represented by the Tai-Chi diagram (see Figure 3-1b, left side). During exhalation, the two Chis separate; the postbirth Chi leaves the body through the nose, while the prebirth Chi sinks to the *Tan-Tien* (丹田), a point found three finger-widths below the navel and two finger-widths inside, causing the lower abdomen to expand (see Figure 3-1b, right side).

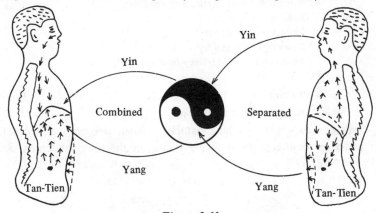

Yin · Combined · Yang · Tan-Tien · Yin · Separated · Yang · Tan-Tien

Figure 3-1b

The Taoist technical term for this kind of breathing is *Chi-Ton* (氣通). Ton means "to permeate and mix". Thus Chi-Ton describes the diffusion and mixture of the prebirth and postbirth Chi. In addition to facilitating voluntary control of the breathing, Chi-Ton benefits the internal organs, alternately squeezing and releasing them. This inner form of exercise differentiates Tai-Chi from most other exercise systems, which emphasize strengthening and developing the external musculature.

After long practice of the prebirth Chi-Kung (先天氣功), a tremendous energy called Chin is produced by the reservoir of prebirth Chi in the lower abdomen. This energy is the source of force for the *Shen-Kung* (身弓) or "torso-bow", which will be explained in Chapter Four. The development of

Chin is shown by a condition described by the Taoist technical term *Nau-Ta* (內丹), or "inner ball"; when pushed or punched, the abdomen of a person with Nau-Ta feels like an elastic ball. After long and diligent practice, conscious control of this inner ball will lead to extremely strong, possibly unlimited Chin. An example of Chin's power can be seen in Yang Lew-Shan, who, with a minute swelling of the abdomen at the instant he was hit, could throw the strongest boxer across the room.

Two sounds are incorporated in the practice of the prebirth breathing: *Heng* (哼) and *Haah* (哈). These sounds were kept secret for many years, appearing only in an old song on Tai-Chi Chuan from the reign of Chien-Lung (乾隆 1736-1795). Here is the translation:

> Hold your Tan-Tien to practice Chi-Kung.
> Heng-Haah – the two Chis are very wonderful.
> When they are in motion, they separate.
> When they remain static, they combine.
> Bend and stretch.
> Let nature take its course.
> Respond slowly and follow quickly.
> Then you know everything from the truth.

The song also emphasized that this secret must be taught orally; however, I wish to write an explanation at this point. The first step is to practice the Heng-Haah sounds while breathing naturally. When Heng is sounded, let the lower abdomen contract; when saying Haah, let the lower abdomen expand (see Figure 3-1c).

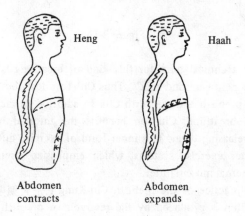

Heng   Haah

Abdomen   Abdomen
contracts   expands

Figure 3-1c

Practice three to five minutes at a time, at least three times a day. After approximately two weeks, one can start the second step. The procedure is as follows:

1. Hold your Tan-Tien lightly with your hands.

2. When saying Heng, contract the lower abdomen to let the prebirth Chi move upward from the Tan-Tien to the diaphragm.

3. Inhale through the nose, letting the postbirth Chi fill the chest. Then hold the breath a few seconds, but naturally, without straining. This process enhances the tonic effect and lets the prebirth Chi and postbirth Chi mix together to form a Tai-Chi diagram.

4. On exhaling through the mouth, say Haah, thus enabling the postbirth Chi to exit, while the prebirth Chi sinks to the Tan-Tien. The lower abdomen will expand, and Yin and Yang are separated.

The goal of the first stage of the Tai-Chi Chi-Kung is to be able to use the prebirth breathing automatically. As the foundation of Tai-Chi Chi-Kung, this method must become an integral part of your life; you can take advantage of countless moments during each day to practice it. After about one year of practice you will find the Chi beginning to accumulate in the Tan-Tien, very much like brooks, rivers and streams collect in the ocean.

The second part of the breathing method consists of letting the breath penetrate every part of the body. The Taoist term for this technique is Tao-Yie, which literally translated means "to lead out". Like a small pilot boat guiding a larger ship into or out of a harbor, Tao-Yie embodies the process of moving the breath both from the outside to the inside and from the inside to the outside. In the former, one inhales, stretches the inner organs and leads the movement of the Chi by one's outer movement, such as opening out the arms. In the latter, the will and the movement send the Chi from the inside of the body to the outside through, for example, the hands and arms. In meditation one practices controlling the Chi by using the will without body movement. But if meditation and movement are combined, as in Tai-Chi Chuan, it will be much easier to control the Chi.

3-2. THE PRACTICE OF TAI-CHI CHI-KUNG

*O*nce the foundation for correct Tai-Chi breathing is established by practicing the Heng-Haah sounds, and synchronizing them with the appropriate abdominal movements, one is ready to learn the Tai-Chi Chi-Kung itself.

The type of breathing in the Tai-Chi Chi-Kung is practically identical to that in Tai-Chi Chuan. In both, the breathing rhythmically combines the To-Noa and the Tao-Yie so that the body's movement guides the breathing. In the Tai-Chi Chi-Kung, however, one concentrates solely on the breathing, whereas the breathing is only one of several equally important elements in Tai-Chi Chuan.

Learning the Tai-Chi Chi-Kung will facilitate learning Tai-Chi Chuan. For one who has already practiced Tai-Chi Chuan, the diligent practice of the corresponding Chi-Kung may transform one into a tiger with wings (如虎添翼), that is, into one who not only can run and jump like a tiger, but also has achieved the skill of flying. By practicing the Tai-Chi Chi-Kung, the student of Tai-Chi Chuan will progress more rapidly. In addition, he or she will gain greater understanding of the three ingredients necessary for the mastery of this art: balancing the Chi and the blood, building up inner energy and knowing the secret of Tai-Chi Chuan, which is the Tai-Chi Chi-Kung.

The Tai-Chi Chi-Kung, unlike purely physical exercise, is specifically designed to invigorate every internal organ of the body as well as to strengthen the general musculature. For the elderly, and even the infirm, the Tai-Chi Chi-Kung holds the promise of great reward, even when done only by itself. The exercise has the power to improve and fully rejuvenate one's general state of health, and furthermore, to arrest the aging process. In short, benefits from its regular practice are valuable beyond description; it can truly transform one's experience of aliveness to that of joyful self-expression.

Before learning the specific movements and their sequence, the student is well-advised to observe and to cultivate each of the following principles of the Tai-Chi Chi-Kung.

1. Be natural, quiet and relaxed.

In the usual waking state, both body and mind are generally more or less active. The relationship between activity and relaxation is reflected in the Yin and Yang of the Tai-Chi diagram. One cannot be fully relaxed while even partially active. Relaxation requires stilling both the body and the conscious mind; one must learn to relax the body and allow the conscious mind to assume a state of relaxed alertness. In the Tai-Chi Chi-Kung, the spirit of vitality, or Shen, is also stilled. Thus one can avoid becoming tired, achieve a sense of well-being, and conserve energy.

2. Combine the will and the Chi.

The Chi is released through combining the prebirth and postbirth Chi, a process developed by visualization and practice. Control over the Chi is achieved by the practice of consciously leading the Chi so that eventually the conscious mind will automatically control the Chi's movement within the body. When the internal and external breathing become fully integrated, the breath becomes slow, soft and deep.

3. Establish solidity in the lower body and legs.

"If you empty people's hearts and minds, and also fill their bellies, you weaken their ambition" (虛心實腹). This pronouncement by Lao-Tzu applies to the prebirth breathing's effect on the body and spirit. According to the Chinese medical tradition, the prebirth Chi is the source of all vital activities. It has important functions both in the creative processes of birth and growth and in the destructive processes of sickness, aging, and death. When an infant is born, the lower body is quite solid, or full, in relation to the upper body. As the child grows to maturity, this fullness becomes displaced to the upper torso and arms. The instability exhibited by many older people while walking illustrates the weakness of their legs and feet supporting a relatively solid upper body. Practicing the Tai-Chi Chi-Kung will slow, and even reverse this aging process, making the lower body more solid and stable, and reserving more Chi in the Tan-Tien.

4. Move slowly and cultivate stability.

All movement in the Tai-Chi Chi-Kung must be deliberate, slow and even-paced. Such control allows the breathing to become long, soft and deep. One must learn to inhale and exhale without conscious effort. During practice, the mind moves the limbs with minimal internal exertion and minimal externally visible force.

5. Practice diligently and regularly.

Mental concentration on physical movement is necessary throughout the exercise. The mind must be disciplined to focus on the activity at hand and thereby to exclude other thoughts. The deliberate cultivation of the virtues of patience, perseverence and regular daily practice are essential to achieving the goal of conscious control of the Chi.

6. Observe moderation in the extent of movement.

Limit the extent of individual movements so that no excessive strain is felt. Otherwise the gradual increase in range of motion to its natural limit ultimately will be retarded. For example, when bending forward at the waist, it is wise not to let your arms hang any lower than feels natural at the moment. Persistent practice without straining will soon enough allow for your hands to reach the floor. Since the time needed varies greatly among individuals, it is not wise to attempt to compete with others in this respect. In the effort to achieve the purpose of the Tai-Chi Chi-Kung, such variations among individuals are irrelevant. What really matters is perseverence with intent toward mastery.

The following describes how to practice the movements in the Tai-Chi Chi-Kung.

POSTURE 1

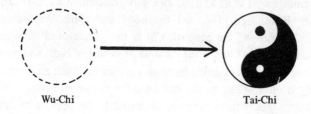

Wu-Chi   Tai-Chi

1. Place feet shoulder-width apart with knees naturally straight, arms at the sides. The body is relaxed; the head and spine are straight. Breathe evenly, and concentrate on the Tan-Tien.

POSTURE 2

1. While you say the sound Heng, slowly raise the arms, palms facing down, fingers pointing down and wrists limp. As the arms move upward, you are

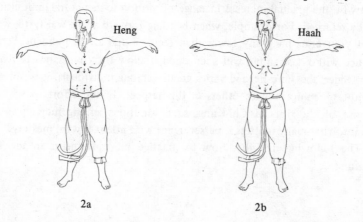

Heng   Haah

2a   2b

inhaling the postbirth Chi (air) through the nose. The prebirth Chi moves upward from the Tan-Tien to the diaphragm as the lower abdomen contracts (Posture 2a).

2. As you say Haah, exhale through the mouth, straightening your hands at the wrists, fingers pointing out and palms facing the earth. The prebirth Chi sinks back to the Tan-Tien as the lower abdomen relaxes and expands to its natural position (Posture 2b).

POSTURE 3

1. While you say the sound Heng, the lower abdomen contracts. Gradually move the hands horizontally to the front of the body as you cross the right wrist over the left, palms down. Inhale the postbirth Chi through the nose. The prebirth Chi moves from the Tan-Tien to the diaphragm (Posture 3a).

2. As you say Haah, allow the hands to drop at the wrists, palms facing the body. The postbirth Chi is exhaled from the mouth, the prebirth Chi sinks to the Tan-Tien and the lower abdomen expands (Posture 3b).

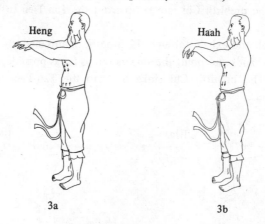

Heng

Haah

3a

3b

POSTURE 4

1. While you say the sound Heng and contract the lower abdomen, lower the hands and turn them inward, keeping the wrists crossed (Posture 4a). Simultaneously bend the knees as if to sit, but keep the spine straight. Breathe naturally. As the arms are unfolding and moving to the sides, gradually straighten the knees (Posture 4b). At the same time, inhale the postbirth Chi through the nose and send the prebirth Chi up from the Tan-Tien to the diaphragm.

2. Say Haah, sit down slightly and lift the palms upward and outward extending the arms to the front of the body. The postbirth Chi is exhaled from the mouth and the prebirth Chi sinks back to the Tan-Tien. The lower abdomen expands (Posture 4c).

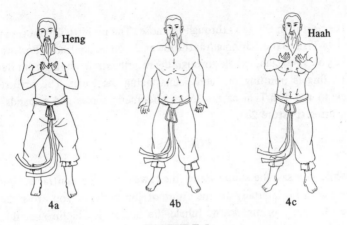

4a   4b   4c

POSTURE 5

1. Say Heng and contract the lower abdomen. Hollow the chest and inhale as the arms are moved apart horizontally 180 degrees, palms up, and the legs are straightened. The prebirth Chi moves up from the Tan-Tien to the diaphragm (Posture 5a).

2. Say Haah and exhale through the mouth. Simultaneously straighten the arms, open the hands and point the fingers out as far as possible, with palms up (Posture 5b). The prebirth Chi sinks back to the Tan-Tien and the lower abdomen expands.

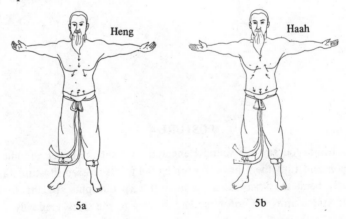

5a   5b

POSTURE 6

1. Say Heng, contract the lower abdomen and bend the knees as if to sit, keeping the spine and head straight as you inhale through the nose and move the prebirth Chi up to the diaphragm. The loose fists are brought next to the head,

palms first facing towards the ears and then turned gradually to the front (Posture 6a).

2. Say Haah, exhale through the mouth and send the prebirth Chi back to the Tan-Tien as you relax and your lower abdomen expands. At the same time, straighten the legs and lower the arms to shoulder level, opening the fists and extending the fingers, palms down (Posture 6b).

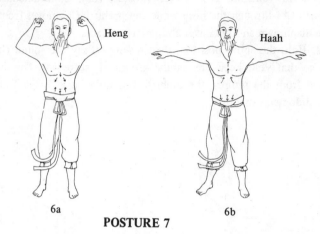

Heng

Haah

6a

6b

POSTURE 7

1. Say Heng and contract the lower abdomen. Repeat Posture 6, except that as you inhale, bring the fists first next to your ears and then straight above the head (Posture 7a).

2. Say Haah, open the fists, extend the legs, standing on your toes and raising the arms and hands. Cross the hands over the head with palms facing forward (Posture 7b). The postbirth Chi is exhaled from the mouth, prebirth Chi sinks to the Tan-Tien and the lower abdomen expands.

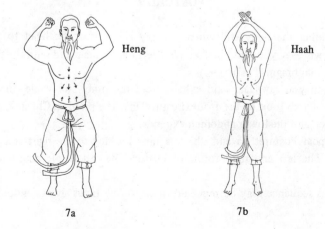

Heng

Haah

7a

7b

POSTURE 8

1. Remain on your toes as you say the sound Heng and gradually lower the arms describing a circle so that they come naturally together with the hands in front of the lower abdomen, the back of the left hand on the right palm with the thumbs touching each other (Posture 8a). Simultaneously inhale the postbirth Chi through the nose while the prebirth Chi moves from the Tan-Tien to the diaphragm and the lower abdomen contracts.

2. Hold the above position, then when you say the sound Haah, lower the body so that your heels are on the ground (Posture 8b). The postbirth Chi is exhaled from the mouth, the prebirth Chi sinks back to the Tan-Tien and the lower abdomen expands.

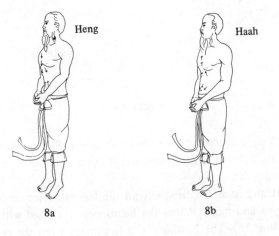

Heng

Haah

8a   8b

POSTURE 9

1. Holding the body still when you say Heng, turn the head to the left looking down over your shoulder at your left heel. Inhale and send the prebirth Chi to the diaphragm (Posture 9a).

2. When you say Haah and exhale, hold the body still while turning the head gradually to look to the front (Posture 9b). The prebirth Chi sinks back to the Tan-Tien and the lower abdomen expands.

3. Repeat Postures 9a and 9b, this time looking to the right and then to the front. The left and right forms of Postures 9a and 9b are counted as one sequence.

4. This sequence may be repeated three to five times always ending on the right.

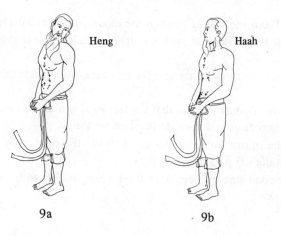

Heng   Haah

9a   9b

POSTURE 10

1. Hold your position while you say Heng and contract the abdomen. Inhale through the nose while lifting the joined palms to chest height (Postures 10a and 10b).

2. Say Haah and exhale through the mouth while you turn the palms face down and bring them to the floor, bending at the waist and keeping the knees straight, but not locked. (Posture 10c).

3. This up-and-down series may be repeated three to five times. Ideally, the palms should be touching the floor in the last posture of the series.

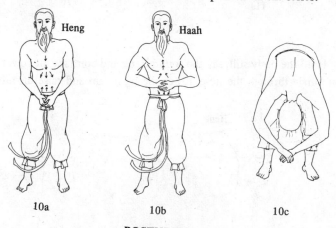

Heng   Haah

10a   10b   10c

POSTURE 11

1. Say Heng and contract the abdomen. Inhale through the nose while rising from the floor. Bend the knees as if to sit, crossing the wrists in front of the chest (right over left), palms facing the body (Posture 11a).

2. Say Haah and exhale through the mouth, straighten the legs, lift the left (inside) palm to the sky and push the right (outside) palm to the earth (Posture 11b).

3. Repeat Postures 11a and 11b, this time using their mirror images, as follows:

    a. Reverse Posture 11a, so that the left wrist is over the right, the left hand on the outside and the right hand on the inside.

    b. In the mirror image of Posture 11b lift the right palm to the sky and push the left palm down to the earth.

4. This combination is repeated three times, ending with the right palm to the sky.

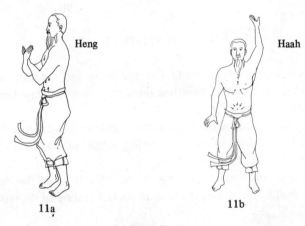

Heng   Haah

11a   11b

POSTURE 12

1. Hold the body still, say the sound Heng and contract the lower abdomen. As you inhale through the nose, lower the right arm and raise the left, bringing

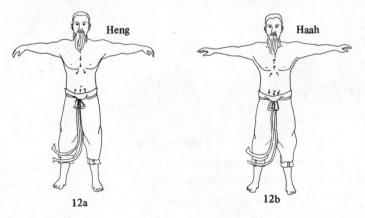

Heng   Haah

12a   12b

the arms to shoulder-height with the palms facing down and the wrists bent (Posture 12a).

2. Say Haah and exhale through the mouth. Extend the hands and fingers, palms down (Posture 12b).

POSTURE 13

1. Say Heng and contract the abdomen. As you inhale through the nose, gradually move the arms to the front of the body with the right wrist crossed over the left, palms facing down (Posture 13a — same as Posture 3a).

2. Say Haah and exhale through the mouth, letting the hands drop at the wrists, with the palms facing the body. The prebirth Chi sinks as the abdomen relaxes and expands (Posture 13b — same as Posture 3b).

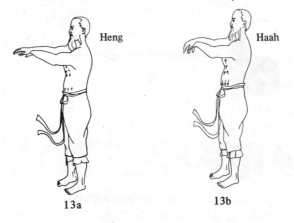

Heng   Haah

13a   13b

POSTURE 14

1. Say Heng and contract the abdomen. As you inhale through the nose, lower the hands and fold them inward, simultaneously bending the knees as if to sit but keeping the spine straight. After the arms have dropped and unfolded in front of the thighs, the left palm lays on the right palm, the thumbs touching each other (Posture 14a — same as Posture 8a). While straightening the legs, gradually move the joined palms up to the chest (Posture 14b — same as Posture 10a).

2. Say Haah and exhale through the mouth, as you turn the joined palms downward. Separate them and allow them to float down, ending with the arms at the sides (Posture 14c).

3. Hold the body at rest for a couple of minutes and feel the whole body gradually calm down. This is Tai-Chi returning to Wu-Chi. ·

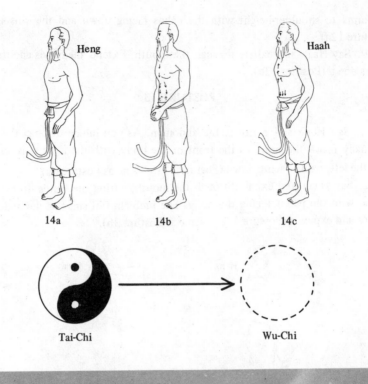

Heng   Haah

14a   14b   14c

Tai-Chi   Wu-Chi

3-3. TAI-CHI MEDITATION

The main purpose of practicing Tai-Chi meditation, or *Ching-Tso* (靜坐), and Chi-Kung, is to "cultivate Chi" (練 氣), or prebirth Chi in the Tan-Tien. If one can persist in practicing meditation and Chi-Kung two or three times a day, the prebirth Chi will fill to overflowing in one's abdomen. The Chi will then heave and subside with one's breathing like waves beating against the shore. For this reason, the Taoists called the lower abdomen "the ocean of Chi", or *Chi-Hai* (氣海). When one reaches this stage, the abdomen becomes very pliable, yet though like a balloon filled with air tending to expand. One then will have great vitality and should learn meditation to let the prebirth Chi circulate to every part of the body. If one learns Chi-Kung and meditation at the same time, they will complement each other.

Like Tai-Chi Chuan and other exercises or sports, meditation requires not only an understanding of basic principles and methods, but, more importantly, energetic practice. One's own body is the laboratory to be used for investigating and researching meditation. The purpose is to cultivate one's physical and mental abilities according to meditation techniques. As a result, the prebirth Chi flows to every part of the body, improving one's health and sense of vitality.

Furthermore, with the help of natural ability to elevate one's awareness and wisdom, meditation, like Tai-Chi Chuan, can lead one to the world of the fourth dimension and ultimate enlightenment. Although one begins meditation from the most elementary level, one must not forget its ultimate objective.

Meditation has different branches, each with its own special method of practice. Since Tai-Chi Chuan is a fruit of Taoism, elementary Taoist meditation methods will be introduced in this chapter. Both standing and sitting meditation techniques will be discussed.

The Chinese term for standing meditation is *Jan-Chung* (站椿); "to stand" (Jan) like a "stake" (Chung). One should use one's consciousness rather than one's strength to let the soles of the feet softly touch the ground. One must imagine that the foot or feet bearing one's weight sink into the ground and connect to the center of the earth. Stand twenty to thirty minutes at a time every day.

In *Hun-Yuan Kung* (渾元功), or "the Beginning Posture" of Tai-Chi Chuan, stand straight, placing the feet parallel and shoulder-width apart. Feel comfortable and easy without tension or strain. The head is held as if suspended by a string from above. Keep the shoulders low and loose so that the neck and back are free of tension. The chest is neither pushed up nor hollowed out. The abdomen must not protrude or overcontract. The arms hang naturally with the elbows loose and the palms facing downward. The legs are straight with flexible knee joints. In short, no joint is stiffened, or locked (see Figure 3-3a).

Figure 3-3a

Breathe naturally through the nose, and keep the lips and teeth lightly shut. The tip of the tongue touches the upper palate just behind the teeth. The eyes are to look forward and focus with a quiet and steady gaze on something green, such as a tree or hill. To help eliminate thoughts of out side problems and facilitate concentration, think of how firmly you are standing. After a long period of practice, one will gradually feel the prebirth Chi starting to flow. Experiencing this process — the development of nonaction, or Wu-Chi, into action, or Tai-Chi — is the purpose of Hun-Yuan Kung standing meditation.

The posture "Single Whip" is called *Kai-Chan* (開 展), or "expanding", *Kung*. Its practice can expand the joints of the whole body and let the prebirth Chi flow to the limbs. In the right form eighty percent of the weight is shifted onto the left leg; the knee does not extend beyond the toes. The eyes are focused on the left hand and the right hand is hooked to the rear. The left form is the mirror image of the right. One should practice both the right and left forms (see Figure 3-3b).

Figure 3-3b

One also can use the posture "Lift Hands" for standing meditation. In fighting with an opponent, one always uses this posture for readiness; therefore,

Figure 3-3c

it is very important in Tai-Chi Chuan. Rest the weight totally on the left leg with the right heel touching the ground in front. The right hand should coincide with the right foot, the elbow with the knee, and the shoulder with the thigh. These correspondences are called *Wai-San-Ho* (外三合), or the "Three Outside Coordinations". In addition, one's awareness should be coordinated with one's intention, one's intention with one's Chi, and one's Chi with one's active use of energy. These correspondences are called *Nei-San-Ho* (內三合), or the "Three Inside Coordinations". One should practice these lift hands in both right and left forms (see Figure 3-3c).

Practicing the posture "Holding a Jug", or *Pao-Kang* (抱缸), develops one's sense of stillness within motion. In this posture, as in lift hands, one places the weight on the left leg. The shoulders, however, are turned forward, and the arms held out as if wrapped around a very large jug. One moves forward slowly until about eighty percent of the weight falls on the front leg. The left heel or toe should remain on the ground. One then returns slowly to the original position. This sequence is repeated for about five minutes in the left form and then five minutes in the right form (see Figure 3-3d).

Figure 3-3d

The sitting form of meditation, usually just called meditation, has three different postures:

1. *San-Pan* (散盤), or "loosely sitting with the legs crossed", involves crossing the calves of the leg and placing the heels under the middle of the thighs. Either the right calf is placed outside of the left, or vice versa. When one meditates, the body should be held erect, the shoulders relaxed, the elbows dropped naturally downward and the palms placed lightly on the knees as shown in Figure 3-3e.

Figure 3-3e

2. In *Tan-Pan* (單盤), or "half-lotus", one usually crosses the left leg over the right with the left toes placed on top of the right knee and the right heel under the left thigh. With practice and increased flexibility one can tuck the left heel into the right thigh. To avoid numbness when sitting a long time, one can alternate the position of the legs. The hands should be formed into a Tai-Chi knot and placed on the leg nearest the abdomen (see Figure 3-3f).

Figure 3-3f

The way to make a Tai-Chi knot is as follows:
   a. Put the tip of the left thumb at the second joint of the fourth finger; form a hollow fist with the other four fingers.
   b. Put the right thumb into the hollow fist of the left hand so that the tips of the two thumbs touch together.
   c. Cup the right hand over the left so that the fingers of the right hand wrap around the hollow left fist and each finger of the right hand lies on top of and in line with the left fingers in one-to-one correspondence.

3. In *Shuang-Pan* (雙盤), or "full-lotus", one crosses both thighs and places the heels on the knees of the opposite legs so the soles of both feet face upward. Advanced students may be able to tuck the heels into the thighs of the opposite legs. One then places the right hand above the left hand, palms upward with the two thumbs connected, on the legs near the abdomen. In this posture, the centers of the feet, hands, and tongue, which touches the roof of the mouth, total five, and are called "Five Centers Face the Sky", or *Wu Hsin Chao Tien* (五心朝天 , See Figure 3-3g).

Figure 3-3g

Nearly everyone knows how to best drive a car. It should be accelerated slowly, kept at a constant speed, and finally, brought gradually to a stop. This way of driving is good for the car and makes the passengers feel calm and comfortable. Meditation is similar. It needs the "Three Steadinesses", or *San-Wen* (三穩). That is to say, when one meditates, the start of the meditation and the finish should be slow and steady. Before meditation one should give up all thoughts. If one cannot do so, take a walk in some quiet place, such as a park, seashore, or the backyard, until one feels nothing in his or her mind and reaches the stage of Wu-Chi. Then one can come indoors to meditate. Exhale through the mouth gently and continuously a couple of times. Toward the end of each exhalation, one should bend the body forward and downward slightly to drive out more air. One may exhale either when sitting with legs crossed while pressing the lower abdomen with one's hands, or when standing with the arms hanging down naturally. If standing, one shakes the arms and hands as fast as possible, relaxes the shoulders and, with awareness, sinks the weight to the feet.

One may sit with San-Pan, Tan-Pan or Shuang-Pan, choosing the sitting position most comfortable for oneself. The posture of the hands needs to match the sitting position. If one sits outdoors, use a towel to warm the shoulders and knees, which are the places most sensitive to chill. If one doesn't have a special meditation stool, which is designed to keep one's buttocks about three inches higher than the place touched by the calves, one sits on a thin cushion to keep the spine straight. Keeping the tip of the nose and the navel on a vertical line will release the tension and pressure on one's central nervous system. The mouth should be closed with the tongue touching the roof of the mouth lightly. One breathes through the nose. The breathing naturally tends to become slower, deeper and lighter as practice progresses.

During meditation it does not matter whether the eyes are kept open or closed. For those who fall asleep easily, it is usually helpful to keep the eyes open; but visual distractions make it difficult for most people to concentrate.

It is helpful to have a Tai-Chi diagram on the wall at eye level. If one opens the eyes, one can look at the diagram in order to understand how Yin and Yang blend harmoniously. If one closes the eyes, one can concentrate on an image of the Tai-Chi diagram in the Tan-Tien. (Women who are menstruating should focus on the point centered between the breasts instead of the Tan-Tien.) Burning incense during meditation can help to purify one's mind.

It is not advisable to practice meditation when one is tired. The best time for meditation is in the early morning after one has had a good sleep, or before one goes to bed. If one has spare time, an extra meditation can take place in the afternoon. It doesn't matter how long one meditates — fifteen minutes, half an hour, or more than one hour.

Reaching the state of mind called *Ju-Ting* (入定) is a wonderful experience but very hard to describe. One feels nothing in the mind, like blankness; the whole body seems to be in a vacuum, and the breathing almost stops (息住). Both the outside and inside of the body feel very comfortable. This state could be described as a small amount of Yang within Yin. There is no response to sound, or other distractions, but one is not asleep and still knows a little about onself. For an approximate comparison, imagine what it's like to concentrate so deeply on reading an interesting book that the outside world is forgotten.

When one reaches a meditative state (before Ju-Ting) the mouth secretes more and sweeter tasting saliva. The Taoists felt the emergence of this saliva, or sweet-dew (甘露), resulted from the Chi produced by the combination of water, or energy, with fire, or awareness. This phenomenon itself was described as "water and fire already present", or *Chi-Jii* (既濟). Chi-Jii, a hexagram in the *I Ching*, represents fire below and water above, symbolizing what is already present (see Figure 3-3h). The following is the *I Ching's* explanation:

> " 'CHI—JII' intimates progress and success in small matters. There will
> be advantage in being firm and correct. There has been good fortune
> in the beginning, but there may be disorder in the end."

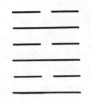

Figure 3-3h

Chi-Jii implies that while one has progressed to a certain level of achievement, one cannot stay there permanently. Like fire's changing water into vapor, one continually develops towards Ju-Ting, although it comes to one as if a sudden realization. This experience is a big step towards entering the door of meditation, reserving prebirth Chi in the Tan-Tien and increasing one's inner energy. All of these events are very important in Tai-Chi Chuan. But if one confines oneself to this stage there may be disorder in the end, as is explained in the *I Ching*, because the water, or energy, will dry up and be exhausted. The next step is to channel the prebirth Chi and reserve it in the Tan-Tien. The path, termed *Hsiao-Chou-Tien* (小周天), or "Small Heavenly Circle", is composed of ten points. Since each point has a Chinese name that is difficult to say in English, we will substitute the numbers shown in Figure 3-3i for the original Chinese words.

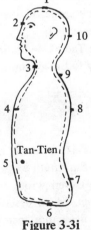

Figure 3-3i

It is advisable to learn this method in person from an experienced teacher because it is too complex to explain completely in words. Otherwise, some adverse reactions may occur. In short, one can reach a certain level of achievement with the basic Tai-Chi Chuan form, but especially to pursue *Hsu-Jing* (虚靜), (explained in Chapter 5), one needs to start meditation. Once one elevates one's pure awareness, i.e., awareness without thought, during Ju-Ting, one can finally come to the threshold of the four-dimensional world. This process depends on diligent and correct practice. It is also important to observe certain points after meditation:

1. Stop and stand up slowly, avoiding any vigorous physical or mental activities immediately after meditation.

2. Rub one's hands until very hot, cover the eyes with them and then gently open the eyes.

3. Shake the body, knocking the teeth, and massage parts of the body which feel stiff or tingling, such as the palms and the arches of the feet.

4. Since meditation improves the circulation of the Chi and blood, the body temperature may rise higher than usual, and one may even sweat. If this happens, rest awhile until returning to one's normal condition.

5. After meditating we recommend doing Tai-Chi Chuan as a continuation of the practice of meditation.

If one neglects the points mentioned above, adverse reactions may occur and affect one's next meditation. One may feel anxious and impatient and either not be able to sit as long, or feel as good as the previous time. One must also remind the beginner about another important point; when one meditates during the first stage, the legs become numb easily and one's thoughts will wander. These phenomena are unavoidable for the beginner. Only practice can make perfect. The Taoists have additional methods to deal with these kinds of conditions, but they are beyond the scope of this book. I wrote about them in another book on meditation to be called:

The Tao of Meditation
Way to Enlightenment

3-4. CHAN-SSU CHIN

O f the three schools of Tai-Chi Chuan, only the Chen School discusses how to apply the *Chan-Ssu Chin* (纏絲勁), or silk-cocoon chin. Chen Hsin (陳 鑫 1849-1929) even wrote an excellent book, *Theory and pictures of Chen's Tai-Chi Chuan*, which describes the Chan-Ssu Chin's basic principles. In order to explain the importance of this exercise, we will refer extensively to Chen's work in this chapter.

One of the classical theories on Tai-Chi Chuan (see Chapter 4-3) mentions that the manipulation of Chin (勁), or the flow of inner energy, is like the movement of a silk thread when pulled from a cocoon. As the thread is pulled, the cocoon turns. Thus the thread's movement can be analyzed from two points of view: its translation by the pulling force and its rotation by the revolving cocoon (see also Chapter 3-7). In much the same way, the Chan-Ssu Chin seeks to unify the curved and the straight (曲中求直), which are opposites. Like a bullet which revolves on its own axis and simultaneously follows a parabolic trajectory, or the earth, which turns both around the sun and on its axis, the Chan-Ssu Chin operates by forming a spiral line in space.

The flow of movement characteristic of the Chan-Ssu Chin is to be applied to Tai-Chi Chuan as a whole. People are generally aware only that Tai-Chi Chuan is comprised of circular movement. More than that, Tai-Chi appears to be propelled by a big moving screw inside of the body. Cheng Man-Ching (鄭曼青 1901-1975), perhaps the greatest Tai-Chi Chuan master known by Westerners, always reminded his students to make their hands and head move as part of the body and not independently. Sometimes he said with utmost emphasis, "If you move your hands arbitrarily, not following the body, well, you are just doing exercise, not really practicing Tai-Chi Chuan." It should further be understood that even if the hands move as part of the body, but without changing the orientation of the palm and rotating the arm, transferring the weight from one leg to the other and matching the spiral movements made by the heel, ankle, knee and every joint of the leg, well, it is still just "doing exercise", not practicing Tai-Chi Chuan. But what do we mean by "doing exercise"? Since exercises such as dance, sports, and other martial arts do not talk about the principle of the Chan-Ssu Chin, practicing Tai-Chi Chuan without using this principle is the same as doing other exercises. In addition, the Chan-Ssu Chin works like a screw, which transforms the motion from any force acting on its thread into a spiral pattern, because of the change in the radius of curvature at any place. This transformation makes it easy for one who has mastered the Chan-Ssu Chin to avoid and neutralize a force acting from the outside.

Early in 500 B.C., Sun-Tzu (孫子) said in his book *The Art of War:* "To fight and conquer in all battles is not supreme excellence; supreme excellence consists in breaking the enemy's resistance without fighting." Tai-Chi Chuan uses the same principle, i.e., to break the opponent's resistance with wit and skill, not by comparing one's strength. The Chan-Ssu Chin teaches one the application of this principle.

Basically, there are two main kinds of Chan-Ssu Chin: *Shun-Chan* (順纏), or "clockwise Chan-Ssu Chin", and *Ni-Chan* (逆纏), or "counter-clockwise Chan-Ssu Chin". The Shun-Chan is related to the arm in the following way: Starting from the Tan-Tien the Shun-Chan ascends to the shoulder, winds around the arm clockwise by going over the right shoulder from the outside of the shoulder to the inside, passes the elbow and is transmitted to the fingers with the palm turned out. For the left arm and side of the body, the movement of the Shun-Chan is a complementing counter-clockwise. The Shun-Chan, which is used for attack, is a kind of *Peng-Chin* (掤勁), or "energy of ward-off". The Ni-Chan, opposite of Shun-Chan, starts from the fingers, winds spirally along the right arm, passes over the elbow, ascends to the shoulder and returns to the Tan-Tien. The Ni-Chan, which is used to neutralize, is a kind of *Lu-Chin* (攦 勁), or "energy of roll-back". As far as the legs are concerned, the Chin starts out from the Tan-Tien and comes to point six, which has been mentioned in Chapter 3-3; it then moves along both thighs toward the inside of the leg and circles down across the knee, around the calf, ankle, heel, the center of the foot, sole and ends up at the tip of the big toe. This whole process is called the Shun-Chan of the leg. The reverse process, starting at the big toe and circling back to the Tan-Tien is called the Ni-Chan. In general, the Ni-Chan is associated with retreating and the Shun-Chan with advancing. For example, driving a screw into wood is like the Shun-Chan, and retrieving it is like the Ni-Chan. With respect to the rotational aspect of the Chin, we know that in order to rotate the palm, one must rotate the whole arm. To rotate the foot, the calf and thigh must rotate. And to rotate the waist, the intention must originate from the Tan-Tien. When all three rotational processes take place simultaneously, the movement becomes a spiralling curve in space (see Figure 3-4a).

Figure 3-4a

According to "The Theory of Tai-Chi Chuan" (see Chapter 4-1), "The Chin is rooted in the feet, bursts out in the legs, is controlled by the waist and functions through the fingers. From the feet to the legs, legs to the waist; all should be moved as a unit." It is obvious that this principle cannot be taught to a beginner, since he or she does not yet know the basics of Tai-Chi Chuan or have a method of practice. Only when the Chan-Ssu Chin has been understood and is practiced correctly can one reach the above-mentioned unity.

3-5. THE PRACTICE OF CHAN-SSU CHIN

*A*lthough Chen's book on Tai-Chi Chuan discusses the general principles behind the Chan-Ssu Chin, he does not provide a clear explanation of the relationship between the Chan-Ssu Chin and the Tai-Chi diagram or of the method of turning the palm according to the Yin and Yang changes in the Tai-Chi diagram. It is necessary to go into this information in detail so that the beginner can know how to practice and develop the Chan-Ssu Chin. The latter part of this chapter will explore several of the philosophical implications of this exercise.

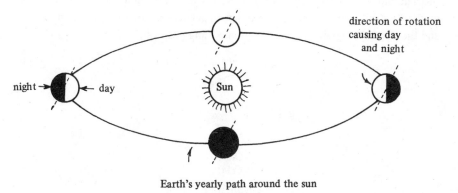

Earth's yearly path around the sun

Figure 3-5a

Figure 3-5a shows a series of relationships between the earth and the sun. One can see how the earth moves around the sun and how that movement causes daily and seasonal changes. In Chinese terms, day is Yang and night is Yin; hot weather is Yang and cold weather is Yin. These Yin and Yang changes occur gradually because of the rotation of the earth on its axis and its movement around the sun. In the practice of the Chan-Ssu Chin, it is assumed that the Tai-Chi diagram represents the sun; the black part represents Yin and the white represents Yang. With respect to one's hand which represents the earth, the palm is Yin and the back is Yang; just as the earth moves around the sun, the palm of the hand is made to trace the shape of the Tai-Chi diagram. In order for the palm to be tangential to the Tai-Chi diagram, the hand needs to rotate so that its movement matches the Yin and Yang in the Tai-Chi diagram. A plan, which involves three parts, has been designed to let the beginner understand these Yin-Yang changes and know how to practice them.

I. Fixed-Standing-Position Practice for the Hands

1. Face the wall, where a Tai-Chi diagram is fixed at about the height of one's chest. Stand erect, with head straight and shoulders slumped slightly forward. Place the feet parallel and shoulder-width apart. The elbows are bent slightly with the arms at one's side. The palms are turned down and the figner-tips are raised slightly but relaxed. One should feel comfortable and relaxed without tension or strain, but with awareness.

2. The right palm and arm are rotated counterclockwise until the arm twists and the palm is turned upward. Let the index finger aim at point A (shown in Figure 3-5b). Both the right hand and the Tai-Chi diagram are now in the ex-treme Yin position. Rotating the arm clockwise in the Shun-Chan, the index finger traces along the arc from points A to B to C. As shown in Figure 3-5b, the Yin and Yang changes of the hand vary with the proportion of Yin to Yang in the Tai-Chi diagram. When the index finger reaches point C, both the hand and the Tai-Chi diagram are in the extreme Yang position.

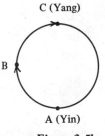

C (Yang)

B

A (Yin)

Figure 3-5b

3. Continue rotating the right arm clockwise still in the Shun-Chan with the index finger tracing along the arc from C to D. The palm, which has not changed Yang into Yin, is facing to the left just before reaching point D. Here one rotates the arm and palm clockwise to maintain the tangency of the palm to the second Ni-Chan half of the curve. The index finger trace down from D to A, moving arm and palm in a counter-clockwise direction. At point A, the palm is again facing upward, so point D is an inflection or turning point, as shown in Figure 3-5c.

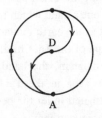

D

A

Figure 3-5c

4. Continuing the rotation of the arm counterclockwise, the index finger starts from point A and passes through points E, C, B, traveling the whole circle and returning to point A. The palm faces downward when the hand reaches the extreme Yang position at C and faces upward when the hand is at the ending point A with the arm and palm again twisted counterclockwise. This whole process is the Ni-Chan, as shown in Figure 3-5d.

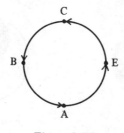

Figure 3-5d

5. In summary, start from point A, with the arm twisted counterclockwise, and the palm facing upward. Rotate the arm clockwise with the index finger tracing along the curve from points A, B, C to D. The palm faces downward at the point C and to the left at point D, moving in the Shun-Chan. Then rotate the arm clockwise 180 degrees and trace the index finger downward from point D in a slow counter-clockwise movement, go from D to A, E, C, B, and return to A, the ending point. The palm faces upward when it reaches A the first time, is downward at the point C and is upward again at the ending point A, with the arm twisted counterclockwise. This whole process constitutes one cycle (see Figure 3-5e). One should practice this sequence repeatedly.

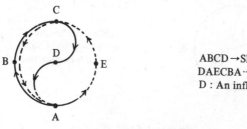

ABCD → Shun-Chan
DAECBA ---→ Ni-Chan
D : An inflection point

Figure 3-5e

6. The process of using the left hand to practice the Chan-Ssu Chin reverses the method described above. Start from point A with the left palm facing upward. Rotate the arm counterclockwise in Shun-Chan so that the index finger traces along the curve following points A,B,C (palm down) and D (an inflection

point with the palm facing right). Then rotate the arm 180 degrees counter-clockwise in Ni-Chan and begin tracing downward in a clockwise movement with the index finger from point D to A (with the arm twisted and the palm facing upward), E, C (the palm facing downward), B, and A (the palm facing upward). One can practice this cycle repeatedly.

7. The Tai-Chi diagram has two forms: clockwise and counterclockwise (see Figure 3-5f).

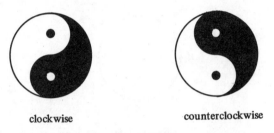

clockwise   counterclockwise

Figure 3-5f

If following the counterclockwise Tai-Chi diagram, the hand must trace the mirror image, or reverse of the clockwise Tai-Chi diagram. There are three major changes from the clockwise form:

    a. The right hand begins in the palm-up position; the left hand begins with the arm twisted and the palm up.

    b. The index finger traces the Tai-Chi diagram by first moving to the right, as the arm rotates counterclockwise.

    c. The Shun-Chan becomes the Ni-Chan and vice versa. Figure 3-5g explains the path which the index finger should trace.

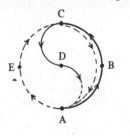

ABCD→Shun-Chan
DAECBA⋯→Ni-Chan
D : An inflection point

Figure 3-5g

    8. A most important point about the practice of this exercise is that it is so deceptively simple one might make the mistake of not spending sufficient time and energy on it. For the standing-position practice, one needs about one month of daily practice. During this time, the Tai-Chi diagram will become

etched in one's mind. As one's study progresses, the next stage involves the proper rotation of the arm so that one's hand indicates the Yin-Yang changes with a smooth, orderly flow from the Shun-Chan to the Ni-Chan and vice versa. At first the index finger should trace as large a Tai-Chi diagram as possible. Gradually, as the shoulder joint is loosened and the Yin-Yang changes are smoothly executed, the figure traced in the air becomes smaller. At this point one can then come to an understanding of how the Shun-Chan is like the rotation of a right-hand threaded screw. When one turns a screw clockwise it is driven in; with the clockwise motion in the Chan-Ssu Chin, one is screwing in forward toward the opponent, or attacking. Conversely, the Ni-Chan is similar to retrieving a screw; just as the counterclockwise turning is causing the screw to come out, so the Ni-Chan movement describes retreating from the opponent. One will also see how this motion is just like the rotation of the propeller of a ship or an airplane which turns in one direction to move the ship forward and in the other to send the ship backward. When properly executed, the tracing of the Tai-Chi diagram combines both of these directions in one complete movement. Because of this combination, one must learn the significance of the center or turning point of the Tai-Chi diagram where the arm and hand change from the Shun-Chan to the Ni-Chan and vice versa. After one month of daily practice, one may progress to the second stage where the Tai-Chi diagram is traced by the feet and legs.

II. Fixed-Standing-Position Practice for the Legs

1. Stand in the same posture as in the fixed-standing-position practice for the hands except that the hands are clasped behind the back with the forearms against each other in the small of the back. Each hand holds the opposite forearm just below the elbow.

Figure 3-5h

2. Start with the clockwise Tai-Chi diagram. Stand on the left leg and trace the diagram horizontally with the right foot and leg a few inches above the floor. The Yin-Yang changes of the foot are the same as for the palm in the hand practice. Repeat this exercise until the leg feels tired. Then change to the left leg; trace the same clockwise Tai-Chi diagram as shown in Figure 3-5h.

3. Reverse the exercise by tracing the counterclockwise Tai-Chi diagram first with the right and then with the left leg.

4. Change the orientation of the Tai-Chi diagram so that the foot traces the circle vertically in front of the body. Use the same technique of alternating right and left feet with the clockwise Tai-Chi diagram and then practicing the counterclockwise Tai-Chi diagram. These methods are shown pictorially in Figure 3-5i.

Figure 3-5i

5. One month practice of the fixed-standing-position exercise for the legs will teach one a most important fact. This exercise contains every possible kick (front, side, crescent, etc.) that can be made. By practicing this exercise over a long period of time, one will develop the ability to kick in every direction naturally and without effort.

III. Moving-Step Practice

To begin the exercise, place a picture of a clockwise Tai-Chi diagram on the wall in front of you. Starting with the feet shoulder-width apart, take a step forward with the right foot, bending the knee like a bow. Seventy percent of the weight of the body rests on this leg, and the knee should not extend beyond the toe. The left leg is straight like an arrow. This kind of step is called the bow-and-arrow step. Using this stance, the right arm is stretched and twisted counterclockwise. Using the index finger to trace the whole path, start from point A at the bottom of the Tai-Chi diagram, pass over the points B, C, D, A, E, C and return to the point A. Rather than moving only the hand and arm as one did in the standing-position practice, one has to turn the waist, adjust the legs and shift the weight of the body from one leg to another to follow the motion of the index finger. The waist and legs must move as one unit. Always keep the body and head straight. The following describes this procedure in some detail:

1. The movement of the right index finger from A (with the arm twisted, palm up) to B is caused by shifting the weight from the front right leg to the back leg while the hips are turning to the left. Turning the hips facing front without changing one's weight will then cause the index finger to trace from point B to C (with palm down). Relax the hip joints as if sitting, bend the right hip joint, turn the body somewhat to the right and the index finger will trace down from the point C through D (palm left) to A (palm up). The purpose of this body movement is to lead the index finger, which moves from the Shun-Chan to the Ni-Chan at D, the inflection point, through relaxation and a slight rightward turn of the hip joint. Then a gradual weight shift to the front leg will cause the index finger to travel from point A through E back to C (palm down).

2. Turn the right foot out to the right side (about 30 degrees) and shift one's weight onto the foot so that the index finger traces down through point B to A (with the arm twisted and palm up). Stepping forward with the left foot is a natural continuation of the previous movement and causes the left hand to move forward with palm up. Shift the weight to the right foot. The left index finger traces points A through B to C (with palm down). Relaxing the hips and turning to the right causes the index finger to travel the curve inside the Tai-Chi diagram; the movement changes from the Shun-Chan to the Ni-Chan at the inflection point D where the palm faces left. At point A, the arm is twisted and the palm up. Moving the weight from the back right foot somewhat to the left foot brings the index finger to then trace from point A through E to C (with palm down). Turn the left toe out to the left side (about 30 degrees) to move the index finger from the point C through B to A (palm up). Advancing with the right foot will bring the right arm forward with the arm twisted and palm up.

3. Continue linking these two movements and practice them without interruption. This exercise is best done outdoors since a long area is needed.

In addition to teaching one how to connect the joints and move the whole body as a single unit, the Chan-Ssu Chin exercise trains the internal organs to develop an intense inner strength, which the Chinese term *Chin*. This Chin, which is unknown in any Western form of exercise, becomes a reservoir of energy in a pure form and enables the practitioner to have seemingly endless endurance. Let us look at an example from nature to help us understand the development of this Chin, or energy source. The tornado is a vortex of energy which begins forming slowly with small whirling breezes. As the tornado develops, the winds swirl and build momentum. Obviously, as the rotation accelerates, the energy increases, and the vortex grows. Finally, the outside of the tornado looks very still as it moves in a unit, however, the whirling edge and the vacuum in the center have tremendous power. The same phenomenon occurs with the practice of the Chan-Ssu Chin. The practitioner appears very still but builds an internal rotational momentum.

To develop Tai-Chi Chuan as a martial art, one must become aware of, understand and incorporate the Chan-Ssu Chin practice. The incorporation of Chin involves two steps: (1) *Ting-Chin* (聽勁) which means "to listen" or become aware of Chin in one's own body and later, for martial arts skill, in the opponent's body, and (2) *Tong-Chin* (懂勁) which means "to understand". Actually, there does not seem to be an adequate English translation of Tong-Chin which involves realizing an experience and incorporating that understanding at a basic level. One must first know oneself and develop one's own Tong-Chin and then "understand" the Chin from one's opponent. It is therefore necessary to practice the solo exercise diligently and apply the Chan-Ssu Chin to every movement of Tai-Chi Chuan. Later one can apply the Chan-Ssu Chin to the martial arts through the practice of Push-hands, which will be discussed further in Chapter Six.

Through the practice of the Chan-Ssu Chin, one can understand and realize some of the most important Chinese philosophic concepts related to Tai-Chi, concepts not easily understood through language alone. One such concept is called "seeking stillness within motion" (動中求靜). In the standing-position practice, it appears that one traces the Tai-Chi diagram by moving only the arm. In the moving-step practice, however, the aware observer will see that the arm does not move independently. The arm is moved by the adjustments or movements of the waist and legs and, in fact, the arm remains quite still, only following the body's movement. It is important that the stillness embodied in the movement incorporates the mind as well as the body. To further elucidate the concept of inaction within action, imagine the experience of slipping on ice. When the body begins to slip on the ice, one looses one's balance, and the mind takes charge of the body almost totally on an unconscious level. The mind is cleared of all outside thoughts, and the body intrinsically tries to reestablish balance or stillness. When one practices the Chan-Ssu Chin or Tai-Chi Chuan, one must always seek this inner stillness or nonaction.

Another concept involves "seeking action within nonaction" (靜中求動). We previously noted that in the moving-step practice, the arm does not move independently of the body — an example of seeking nonaction within action. Upon further investigation, however, the arm has a very subtle, inner rotating movement which is generated again by the adjustments and movements of the waist and legs. Thus the arm is seeking action within nonaction.

The third concept to understand for progress in the practice of'the Chan-Ssu Chin is known as "Wu-Chi's generating Tai-Chi" (無極而太極) or, loosely translated, "going from nothing to something". The learning process provides an example of this concept. Students of the Chan-Ssu Chin know nothing, or Wu-Chi, before beginning to study. First, students must learn the standing-position practice. Then they begin the moving-step practice and gradually work to incorporate all of the principles previously discussed. They have moved from knowing nothing, or Wu-Chi, to knowing something, or Tai-Chi, about the Chan-Ssu Chin.

A final principle to be realized is "returning from Tai-Chi to Wu-Chi" (太極而無極), or "returning from something to nothing". This concept can be clarified by watching the development of the Chan-Ssu Chin practice. At first, practitioners trace the path of the Tai-Chi diagram with very large movements. Gradually, they internalize the Chan-Ssu Chin, thereby making the movements smaller and smaller. The final goal is reached when the action or movement continues but appears to be inactive or still. This essentially formless stage indicates that one has "returned from something to nothing", or from "Tai-Chi to Wu-Chi".

3-6. AWAKENING MENTAL POWERS

*J*t is commonly understood that to exert a large force, one needs strong muscles, or at least great physical strength. Take, for example, the process of pounding a stake into the ground with a heavy hammer. This process has basically two steps: (1) lifting the hammer as high as possible so as to maximize its potential energy, and (2) lowering the hammer as fast as possible so as to increase its speed of falling, or maximize its kinetic energy. Both of these steps require physical strength, and physical strength depends on muscles; so, as it is commonly understood, to develop a great physical force one must exercise and develop strong muscles. Yet, when one plays Tai-Chi Chuan, one is advised to use little physical strength, to relax and to be soft. How can this result in the great strength and force apparently shown by the Tai-Chi masters? What these masters possessed was Chin (勁), the special kind of internal energy developed through practice and accomplishment in Tai-Chi Chuan.

It is known that by relaxing and being soft one trains the muscles to act only as a balancing and supporting mechanism, so that the whole body becomes poised and ready to act instantaneously. But what is it that is used to power actions? It cannot be physical force as one understands it, since that would violate all of the principles of Tai-Chi Chuan. What it is, is a type of energy. Everyday we use many kinds of energy which were only suspected or imagined a hundred years ago. Electricity and its accompanying force magnetism are the most basic types of invisible energy used daily in machines. The liberation of energy by the fission of an atom, or by the fusion of hydrogen, is becoming more common as more nuclear power stations are built. One can definitely infer that there are many more forms of energy with which one is much less familiar, or which at this point in time are merely unknown.

For 1,000 years or more the Chinese Taoists have experimented and concluded that the body is a most wonderful machine, which may act as a generator of many types of energy and force. To the Taoists, however, the primary generator is the mind (心) since the mind generates consciousness (意), and with direction and exercise consciousness can develop and create. This power of consciousness, a form of concentration, is the primary goal in the practice of the Tai-Chi Chuan. As, an example, when one practices the posture push, one is instructed to imagine that one is actually pushing an opponent, but without force. One is taught to develop the energy or Chin from the feet, through the legs, the waist, the arms and finally to the hands. If a student persists in such concentration, perhaps after a year or two, he or she will notice heat or vibration in the palm during the practice of push. When this kind of concentration is developed and practiced throughout the whole Tai-Chi solo exercise and combined with daily practice of the Tai-Chi Chi-Kung, Tai-Chi meditation and Chan-Ssu Chin, after five or ten years the practitioner manifests an energy perceived as great strength and power. This energy is called *Chin* in Chinese, or "spiritual or psychic energy" in English. Whereas muscular energy is definitely limited, both as to one's strength and endurance, no such limit is imposed upon Chin, or psychic energy. In fact, the power of this form of energy increases with practice and, furthermore, does so without limit.

So the question arises: How does one develop this Chin? More than just concentration is required. Observe the difference in behavior between a young kitten and an old mother cat. Even though she has the benefit of experience to carry out her intention more efficiently and effectively, the mother cat has to some extent lost her former drive to respond and react to a stimulus. The young kitten, in contrast, is ever-ready to act and does so synchronously with its intention; its nervous energy is available for action, even without a stimulus. Human beings have the same problem; young children have a spirit, or Shen (神), which tends to diminish with age. Therefore, developing this Chin is a matter of Shen, or motivation to act immediately according to intention. Furthermore, one needs to feed one's progress back to the mind which monitors the intended action to completion.

To develop the spiritual energy or Chin, one must practice both its internal and external aspects in such a way that they complement each other and become one harmonious whole, as indicated in the dynamic movement represented by the Tai-Chi diagram. This principle applies not only to the performance of Tai-Chi, but also to walking, driving a car or riding a bicycle, as well as to waiting for a bus, sitting at the dinner table, or even sleeping and simple activities. A state of relaxed alertness should be maintained at all times, just as is the case with the young kitten. Only when one learns to feel at home with such a state is one ready to develop the Chin to reach ever higher levels of awareness and effectiveness.

It is a simple enough matter to understand what is presented here. However, to be useful, relaxed awareness must be practiced. Succeeding is a question of the will. One starts to feel alert, but soon tires, and forgets. This response is natural enough. However, it is important to renew the effort every time it occurs to you to do so. With diligent practice, one can make progress toward maintaining a state of relaxed alertness all the time. Such a state is a prerequisite for the further development of one's psychic energy, and especially for middle-aged and older persons, for becoming once again "like a young kitten".

In the Single Whip posture, the right hand forms a hook with all four fingers touching the thumb. This configuration which, according to the Chinese represents the crane's beak, has a variety of effective applications in the martial arts. One can peck at an eye or other vulnerable spot on an adversary, or grasp open-handed, etc. The following is a translation of an old Chinese song about this posture:

> Putting the five fingertips together,
> Create the image of a mountain peak,
> The culmination point of the prebirth Chi,
> Especially when total awareness is concentrated there.

Meditating on this image is valuable in developing the Chin. Hold the crane's bill about ten inches away from the body with the fingertips pointing toward one's face. Relax the elbow joint and the arm. With the fierce look of a soaring falcon, fix both eyes on the crane's beak; concentrate intently on the fingers as long as possible without blinking the eyes. At the same time imagine the Chin, stored in the Tan-Tien, rising from the lower torso through the back to the eyes as well as to the shoulder, arm and finally to the hand. Like a magnetic field between two opposite poles, the Chin connects the eyes and the crane's bill formed by the fingertips. This method of sitting meditation is to be done three times a day, alternating the hands each time. After much practice, one can meditate up to ten or more minutes for each hand. Eventually the fingertips can be felt as definitely warmer than normal, following some novel or unique feeling.

One can also practice enhancing one's spiritual force during the Chan-Ssu Chin exercise. Instead of using an open palm in the arm movement, switch to the crane's bill configuration. As the crane's bill moves clockwise to trace the Tai-Chi diagram, imagine that energy is sent forth to the fingertips from the Tan-Tien, as if advancing a right-hand-threaded screw. With counterclockwise motion, energy is absorbed in the body to be stored in the Tan-Tien, as if driving the screw backward. To understand this movement of energy, however, is only the beginning. The only way to achieve high skill is to practice it regularly. Practice makes perfect!

Although Yang Lew-Shan, the greatest known Tai-Chi master, did not look at all like a boxer since he was short and of small build, he could lift and easily throw adversaries twice his own weight. How did Yang Lew-Shan achieve such power? The answer lies in the long and arduous development of his psychic energy. According to Chen Yen-Lin's (陳炎林) Tai-Chi Chuan book, Yang Lew-Shan could use a loud Haah to throw his students without touching them. One suspects that the process involved was in fact similar to a hypnotist's using post-hypnotic suggestions to train subjects to go into a trance with a single pass. Obviously the loud Haah would affect Yang's students, who were conditioned and sensitized, much more than it would affect others who were not. Yang, moreover, could make a candle flame flicker or go out from a distance of one foot. He could pull the flame towards him, hold it, and then send it back and put it out. Yang's skills are in fact proof that the individual may generate and control energies that can affect both people and objects.

Today, no one is capable of such an achievement. The reason is clear. Just as one can easily learn to ride a bicycle at a very fast speed, one can strengthen one's muscles in a relatively short time. However, developing the psychic force, like maintaining balance on a bicycle at a very slow speed, necessitates much patient practice over a long period of time. While such an achievement is definitely possible, very few persons will ever take the time, patience and effort required. To do so is strictly a personal matter.

3-7. THE KEY TO TAI-CHI CHUAN

*C*onsider the following situation: a tumbler toy, such as a small solid sphere connected to a large one, will always right itself regardless of attempts by forces from the side to change the toy's original position of static equilibrium. One wonders why such a response occurs. It seems that the tumbler should fall over so that both spheres would touch the platform on which it originally rested. However, an analysis of the physical principles involved uncovers the mystery. The tumbler has a sufficiently low center of gravity to keep its body upright.

The problem of a body's static equilibrium breaks down into three cases. Consider a solid cone supported by a platform. In case A it rests on its base, in case B on its vertex, and in case C on its side, as shown in Figure 3-7a.

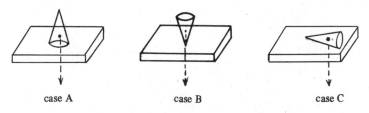

case A   case B   case C

Figure 3-7a

Case A represents the condition of stable equilibrium. Note that two factors contribute to the cone's stability: (1) the center of gravity is relatively low, and (2) the line of the center of gravity, or direction of the gravity field connecting the cone with the center of the earth, remains within the area of the supporting base. It would take considerable force from the side to upset this static equilibrium condition.

In case B, the reverse is true. The center of gravity is relatively high, and the line of the center of gravity is too easily moved off the point of support, thus upsetting the condition of equilibrium. This case is, therefore, called unstable, or precariously balanced.

Case C has an important characteristic. However unevenly the cone may roll on its conical surface, the two critical aspects never change. The distance between the center of gravity and the platform remains constant, and the line of the center of gravity continues to go through the area of contact, although this area itself continues to change if the cone rolls.

To maximize the stability of static equilibrium in case A, therefore, two distances should be considered. The vertical distance between the center of gravity of the body and its platform should be made as short and the base area as large as possible.

Most of the martial arts strongly emphasize the *Ma Pu* (馬步), or "riding horse step", as a model stance; the legs are spread far apart with the knees bent and the body's center of gravity is made as low as possible (see Figure 3-7b). Such a posture is very stable for movements to the left or right in the vertical plane; the center of gravity is relatively low, and the line of the center of gravity is always well within the base between the two feet. However, such a posture is relatively unstable in the fore-and-aft vertical plane. The condition of static equilibrium is rather easily disturbed by a push or pull from the front or back. Since the base area is very narrow (the length of the foot at most), it is relatively easy to move beyond the center of gravity.

Figure 3-7b   Figure 3-7c

An alternate model stance is called the *Kung-Chien Pu* (弓箭步), or "bow-and-arrow stance". The front foot points forward with the knee bent like the shape of a bow, and the rear foot points outward with the knee naturally straight like an arrow (see Figure 3-7c). This stance contrasts sharply with the Ma Pu. The Kung-Chien Pu, which provides more stability in the fore-and-aft vertical plane is somewhat weaker in the lateral direction. However, it also has a relatively greater base area than the Ma Pu.

The art of Tai-Chi Chuan deliberately limits the use of the Ma Pu and emphasizes the more stable Kung-Chien, or "bow-and-arrow" position. In addition to having a larger base and better fore-and-aft stability, one can more easily shift one's front or rear foot to execute the circular Tai-Chi movements when yielding or attacking.

In the original long Yang form of Tai-Chi Chuan, the "Cross Hands" posture, which uses the Ma Pu or double-weighted stance, occurs only at the beginning and end of the form. More recent variations have used an explicit cross hands at the end of the first and second sections of the Yang Tai-Chi, between the forms of "Withdraw and Push" (如封似閉) and "Embrace the Tiger, Return to Mountain" (抱虎歸山). Even if the explicit cross hands is omitted, one must pass through cross hands between sections of the long Tai-Chi. This transitional move provides an example of Wu-Wei-Ehr-Wei, (無爲而爲) or action with the intention of nonaction, a philosophical principle which applies to many aspects of both Tai-Chi Chuan and meditation. In meditation, for instance, one cannot be too Yang, or tense and aware, nor can one be too Yin, or relaxed and forgetful of one's self. One must balance awareness with relaxation to achieve a true meditative state.

In Tai-Chi Chuan as a martial art, the basic principle is to upset the balance of one's adversary while maintaining one's own. This principle is implemented by keeping the weight, or the line of the center of gravity, through one foot at a time. The reader will ask how stability can be maintained with such a small area as a base. This question comes to grips with the central principle of Tai-Chi Chuan and the reason for Tai-Chi Chuan's name. Chapter Two explained that the Tai-Chi diagram represents a dynamic three-dimensional sphere, not a circle in a plane as it is regularly depicted. The purpose of Tai-Chi Chuan is to train the individual to become like a dynamic Tai-Chi or rotating sphere which, for the martial arts, is the most balanced and beautiful of all shapes. Note that the center of gravity and the point of support are always aligned with the line of the center of gravity in every possible orientation of the sphere; that is, the point of contact and center of the sphere are always perpendicular to the supporting platform at the point of contact and, hence, no instability can be induced (see Figure 3-7d).

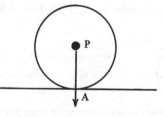

Figure 3-7d

Trained to become like a sphere, the individual, who cannot be caught in a position of unstable equilibrium, can also return immediately to a position of improved stability when attacked. The outside of this sphere is static and relatively soft while its inside is moving and hard. Imagine attempting to strike a blow directly at a solid rotating sphere. The sphere's reaction has two distinct components: the rotational inertia deflects the thrust sideways in the direction of the thrust's motion at the point of contact, and the elastic surface causes the energy of the thrust to be used for its own repulsion. When encountered by a specialist in any other martial art, Yang Lew-Shan, the founder of the Yang Tai-Chi school, reacted like a solid rotating sphere. Any attempts to attack him proved ineffective.

How then can one be trained to become like a rotating Tai-Chi sphere? A candidate should have natural talent, cleverness, good intuitive understanding, diligence and good physical endurance. In general, he or she needs to be highly motivated to submit to the discipline of arduous training. Li Yi-Yu (李亦畬 1833-1892), a Tai-Chi master in the Wu school, has said with great emotion that in 100 years only one or two individuals ever achieved total mastery in Tai-Chi Chuan. Today, however, combining what we can learn from not only Tai-Chi's experts and classical theories but also the application of modern scientific methods, I am trying to design a direct, efficient training program to attain such mastery. This training program contains the following:

1. One must know where the center of the Tai-Chi sphere or the center of gravity in his or her body is located. According to the Taoists, this point is the Tan-Tien (see Chapter 3-1). The beginner is always instructed to sink the Chi to the Tan-Tien, and to concentrate the mind and will in the Tan-Tien. This principle is emphasized so much that one learns to keep this awareness at all times, even in sleep. The purpose of focusing on the Tan-Tien is to become centered within one's being, not only to promote proficiency in the martial arts but especially to maintain a serene, peaceful demeanor. So Tai-Chi Chuan attempts to unify the three aspects of Tai-Chi: the physical movement, the mental attitude, and the philosophical concept.

2. Consider a sphere moving as shown in Figure 3-7e.

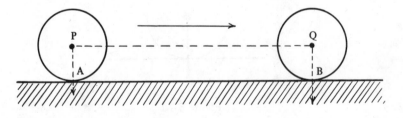

Figure 3-7e

The line PQ, traced by the center of gravity as the sphere moves along the point of contact, or line AB, will always be at a constant radial distance which is directly above and parallel to the point of contact. If the direction of the sphere's motion changes, the curve traced by the center of gravity will still remain in a plane parallel to that traced by the point of contact.

A basic feature of training in Tai-Chi Chuan is that one learns to think of oneself as a sphere with the Tan-Tien as the center. Moving in any direction (without being affected by an external force), advancing or retreating, one must keep the Tan-Tien at a constant vertical distance from the floor or ground. One may not, when not reacting to an externally applied force, raise or lower the body.

3. The head should be positioned as though suspended by a string from above, and the coccyx, the tail bone of the spine, should also remain in the normal standing unbiased position, that is, not rotated or tilted. These two points are always emphasized in the classical theories of Tai-Chi Chuan. Consider the trunk of the body as a cylinder with a vertical axis. The purpose of paying attention to the head-to-coccyx axis is to keep the body's position straight (see Figure 3-7f).

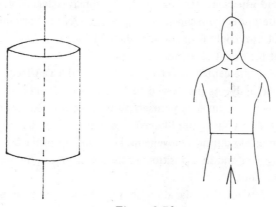

Figure 3-7f

4. There are two types of movement to be analyzed: translation and rotation. Translation of a cylinder from position A to B (see Figure 3-7g) shows that both the cylinder and its axis are moved equally. During the translation, the axis

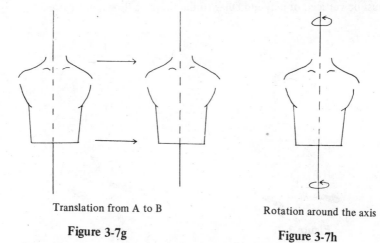

Translation from A to B   Rotation around the axis

Figure 3-7g   **Figure 3-7h**

must remain parallel, not wobbling between extreme positions. Rotation is defined as motion about an axis in which the axis itself remains unmoved (see Figure 3-7h), e.g. the rotational movement of a flywheel whose axis is stationary.

According to Wu Yu-Hsing (武禹襄), "When going back and forth, one should draw into folds. When advancing or retreating, one should turn the body and vary the steps" (see commentary in Chapter 4-3). In terms of translation and rotation, folds refer to bending the knees to ensure the proper translation of the body axis and to maintain a constant height of the Tan-Tien above the floor (when no externally applied force is present). During such motion the whole body, and especially the legs, must be totally relaxed, yet completely aware. Otherwise correct movement is impossible. As for "turning the body", the Yang school's principle is to consider the body as a mill stone, turning on its vertical axis, yet the axis itself remains motionless.

5. The line of the center of gravity starts from the Tan-Tien and is parallel to the axis of the body. As mentioned before, a sphere makes contact with the floor at only one point. Imagine yourself as a sphere with one foot as the point of contact. Now align your center of gravity to pass through that foot. When this posture is not possible during a movement, keep the line of the center of gravity between the two feet and in a position where one can move the weight as easily as possible to one foot.

Ending the theoretical explanation above, we follow with an application of the theory. Four basic postures for the student to practice are provided below:

1. Start with the Kung-Chien Pu, right foot forward. The body is totally relaxed, the mind fully aware, and the head held as if suspended on a string with the coccyx in the natural standing position. The line of the center of gravity is as close to the heel of the right foot as possible. The calf of the right leg must be vertical, or perpendicular to the floor, as shown in Figure 3-7i.

Figure 3-7i

Figure 3-7j

2. Maintaining a constant height, translate the body backward until the entire weight is on the rear (left) leg. The right leg is now totally relaxed or empty, with no weight on it, but the sole is touching the floor and the right knee is slightly bent. Since the line of the center of gravity passes through the left foot, the left leg now becomes solid (see Figure 3-7j).

3. Rotate the vertical¹ body axis to the left, up to say fifty degrees. Turn the body only around this axis without moving or changing the center of gravity from the left foot (see Figure 3-7k).

Figure 3-7k

4. Return to the position shown in Figure 3-7j, keeping the line of the center of gravity through the rear foot.

5. Return to the position shown in Figure 3-7i. This move completes one cycle, which can be repeated a number of times until one feels the strain in the legs. Then the entire sequence is done symmetrically in the bow-and-arrow step with the left leg forward.

The steps for training to be like a Tai-Chi sphere are summarized below:

1. One becomes aware of one's body as being like a homogeneous solid sphere with the Tan-Tien as the center of gravity.

2. All movement is done in such a way that, when no externally applied force is present, the Tan-Tien moves only in a horizontal plane.

3. The body's axis falling from the head through the coccyx remains vertical throughout.

4. The line of the center of gravity always falls through one foot, or as close to it as possible, and always remains within the base of the two feet.

5. All body movement is a translation or a rotation of the vertical body axis.

Following these principles is like doing what is said in "The Classics of Tai-Chi Chuan" (Chapter 4-2): "Stand like a balance and move acting like a cartwheel".

3-8. THE THIRTEEN TORSO METHODS

*T*he Chen and Yang schools of Tai-Chi Chuan base their methods of practice on the principles of Tai-Chi's classical theories. The Wu school, however, also emphasizes the torso method (身法). This method provides a concrete step-by-step approach to understanding the applications of the classical theories, which alone are too refined and abstract for the beginning student. The torso method gives the student a series of techniques which are easy to apply, allowing for gradual and obtainable achievement. Wu Yu-Hsing (武禹襄1807-1871), the founder of the Wu school, developed eight of the torso methods; Li Yi-Yu (李亦畬 1833-1892), Wu's nephew and student, described the other five. The thirteen torso methods are explained below.

Method 1: "Hollowing the chest" or *Han-Hsing* (涵胸)

The chest above the heart should be relaxed downward, not lifted up as soldiers do when standing at attention. The shoulders are kept very slightly forward. Properly cultivating this posture can let the mind's awareness lead the Chi to every part of the body. The tendency to store excess tension in the chest area explains the sense of deep relaxation after a heavy sigh and the importance of hollowing the chest during meditation as well as Tai-Chi Chuan. By applying the torso method for hollowing the chest, one can release tension, lose inner anxiety and meditate longer.

Method 2: "Lifting the back" or *Pa-Pei* (拔背)

While practicing Tai-Chi Chuan, one should pay attention to three aspects of the posture for the back: (a) showing an upward and outward tendency of the spine between the shoulders, (b) letting the shoulders be relaxed, flexible and agile, and (c) not allowing the head to droop forward but rather keeping it erect. Since this concept of lifting the back is hard to understand, here is a method to help one practice it. Stand erect with arms stretched forward and the palms extended outward and overlapping. Next, the arms are dropped with the hands still together. Finally, slowly separate the arms to the sides. One can feel, by moving the shoulders alternately forward and back, that the arms are connected through the back, in effect forming one articulated unit. When practicing Tai-Chi Chuan, one must keep an awareness of this connection between the two arms.

Method 3: "Biding the crotch region" or *Kuo-Tang* (裹襠)

The knees are always at least slightly bent; that is, they are never rigidly locked. Moreover, in order to protect the crotch region, they are kept in relaxed proximity to one another rather than separated. In this method one is aware of the connection between the two legs through the coccyx.

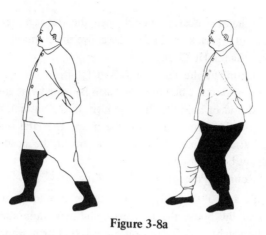

Figure 3-8a

In posture where the line of the body's center of gravity goes through one leg, that leg is referred to as substantial, or solid, while the other, carrying no weight at that moment, is called insubstantial, or empty. However, when one leg is solid and the other is empty, one still imagines that both legs are connected as though they were one leg. Imagine that the legs are hollow inside and that the body weight is like a liquid that can flow through the legs as the weight shifts from one leg to the other (see Figure 3-8a). In this way, one can realize the interchange between solidity and emptiness. Kuo-Tang makes this interchange possible.

Method 4: "Sheltering the stomach" or *Hu-Chun* (護肫)

To keep the rib cage "closed" or protected, one imagines that the lower ribs come together and the higher ones "fold inward" (see Figure 3-8b). This posture gives one a feeling of relaxed comfort.

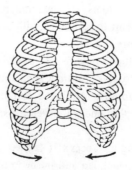

Figure 3-8b

In contrast, an expansive posture would open the rib cage, leaving the torso vulnerable to a frontal attack so that a blow above the stomach would be felt as much more severe than in Hu-Chun.

Method 5: "Lifting up the head" or *Ti-Ting* (提頂)

The head and neck must be kept erect as if hanging by a string from above; don't let the head nod or hold the chin too high. In the natural, relaxed posture the vertebrae carry the entire weight of the head. The vital spirit, or Shen, is felt to be pulled straight upward through the top of the head, as though the body were a fish net being raised from above.

Method 6: "Rounding the groin" or *Tiao-Tang* (吊襠)

The lower the area of the body controlling the movement, the more relaxed the upper parts of the body, thereby preserving maximum stability. Thus for shifting the body weight, one focuses on the calves. Furthermore, one uses the imagination to keep the space between the legs round, the pelvis in (so that the buttocks do not protrude outward), and the lower abdomen a little bit forward and upward.

Method 7: "Skipping" or *Teng-No* (騰挪)

Like a cat waiting for a rat, one assumes a state of relaxed intention, as if preparing for action, yet holding back for the right moment. Then with precise timing one "skips" to accomplish one's goal. This method is characterized by relaxed concentration.

Method 8: "Blitzkrieg" or *Shan-Chan* (閃戰)

Unity in action characterizes the body, limbs and waist. The mind is kept alert and coherent, prepared at any moment to release energy, or Chin, like an arrow ready to leave the bow. The mind and body are both prepared for action, as swift as a sudden clap of thunder. Just as an eagle swoops down to catch its prey, move with direct intention as if no opponent could block the way.

Method 9: "Relaxing the shoulders" or *Sung-Chien* (鬆肩)

When broadening the shoulders but remaining relaxed, one allows the Chi to sink downward. It is important to seek inner stillness and to use one's consciousness rather than a stiff posture.

Method 10: "Sinking elbows downward" or *Chen-Chou* (沉肘)

To allow the elbows to sink naturally one must first will the Chi to the arms. Keep the shoulders loose and relaxed and the wrists flexible and agile. By adhering to these principles, one will develop a sense of the elbows' naturally downward inclination.

Method 11: "Positioning the coccyx" (尾閭中正)

Normally the coccyx is inclined and pushed outwards but in Tai-Chi Chuan it is tucked inward. To correctly position the coccyx, locate one's center of gravity and allow the coccyx to be in a central stable position. This process is almost totally directed by the mind. One must develop a sense that the coccyx cradles the Tan-Tien.

Method 12: "Sinking Chi to the Tan-Tien" (氣沉丹田)

When one has mastered Methods 11, 1, 4, 9, 6 in that order, one can direct the Chi to the Tan-Tien. The practitioner should concentrate on keeping the Chi in the Tan-Tien area rather than allowing it to float upwards towards the chest.

Method 13: "Distinguishing emptiness and solidity" (分清虛實)

Since some Yang exists within Yin, an empty leg must still have some kind of solidity. The empty leg, therefore, must be connected to the ground through the sole of the foot, which adheres to the ground with full awareness. At the same time, one must imagine and concentrate on the connection between the upper end of the leg and the rest of the body so that the whole body is flexible. If one lacks this sense of the connection at both ends of the leg, one possesses a fault called "partial sinking", or *Pien-Chen* (偏沉). The solid leg, accordingly, must be loaded with the entire weight of the body. In addition, one must introduce emptiness into the solid leg by putting one's will there and letting the vital spirit, or Shen, ascend freely to the top of the head. Not distinguishing between empty and solid results in the fault of double-weighting (雙重). At the same time, if in an attempt to avoid double-weighting, one sinks all the weight onto one leg without the mental awareness of Yin within Yang, one still does not distinguish between empty and solid.

CHAPTER FOUR

CLASSICS

Since the following theories describe the fundamental principles of Tai-Chi Chuan, the serious student needs to conscientiously examine their meaning. In the first three texts, quotation marks will offset the translation of the original Tai-Chi classics from the commentary which follows. The last three texts are translated without additional commentary.

4-1. TAI-CHI CHUAN LUN (太極拳論) OR "THE THEORY OF TAI-CHI CHUAN", BY CHANG SAN-FENG

*C*hang San-Feng identified a number of practices and guiding principles for the student of Tai-Chi Chuan while he lived on Wu-Tang Mountain.

The purpose of this work was to relay his knowledge to those interested in enjoying a long, healthy and happy life, not simply to teach Tai-Chi Chuan as a martial art.

"In any action, the whole body should be light and agile, or Ching and Lin. One should feel that all of the body's joints are connected with full linkage". (一舉動，周身俱要輕靈，尤須貫串)

Every movement of Tai-Chi Chuan is expressed from Wu-Chi to Tai-Chi, or from preconsciousness to actual internal consciousness. Movement is never initiated merely by the hands, arms or legs; instead the mind itself directs the body to function as a single unit with every joint linked. The body should be agile and natural; the movement, continuous and constant, like the mountain spring flowing unceasingly into the stream.

"Chi should be stirred. The spirit of vitality, or Shen, should be concentrated inwards." (氣宜鼓盪，神宜內斂).

One can understand how the Chi is stirred by practicing the Tai-Chi Chi-Kung (see Chapter 3-2), which will eventually lead to the circulation of the prebirth Chi throughout the entire body.

The practice of meditation can help one realize how to concentrate and internally cultivate the Shen. The Taoist theory of meditation describes one-to-one correspondences between the energy and the kidneys; the spirit and the heart; the soul (魂) and the liver; the Po (魄), or "unconscious soul", and the lungs; and awareness and the spleen. If all of these vital energies and organs were free to relate as was naturally intended, one would experience a wonderful kind of communion with the natural way of Tao. However, five thieves (五賊) can disrupt the natural interaction of organs and energies, thereby disturbing meditation and/or daily life: the eyes, ears, nose, mouth and mind. If too active, these thieves will steal the inner energy from the body. Therefore, certain precautions have been suggested in order to keep them controlled. It is said that one should hold the ears beyond hearing so that the energy will be concentrated in the kidneys. The eyes should be closed beyond seeing so that the conscious or waking soul will be concentrated in the liver. One should shut one's mouth beyond talking so that the spirit will be concentrated in the heart. The nose should be held beyond smelling so that the Po will be directed to the lungs. One should hold the mind still beyond disturbing so that the awareness will be concentrated in the spleen.

"Do not show any deficiency, neither concavity nor convexity in movement. Do not show disconnected movement." (毋使有缺陷處，毋使有凸凹處，毋使有斷續處。).

One can understand the meaning of these concepts through the practice of the Chan-Ssu Chin, where one's hand must perfectly trace the curve of the Tai-Chi Diagram. A "deficiency" means placing the hand sometimes inside and sometimes outside of the curve (see Figure 4-1a). Having a "deficiency" can be compared to trying to fit a square object into a round hole or trying to fit a screw improperly into its threads; the application of force will be of no use. A deficiency in the Chan-Ssu Chin will weaken the Peng-Chin (explained in Chapter 6) causing one to lose one's chance to entangle one's opponent.

Normal   Deficiency (wavy, not smooth)

Figure 4-1a

Concavity and convexity will also disrupt the proper movement, as illustrated in Figure 4-1b.

Normal   Depiciency (choppy, interrupted)

Figure 4-1b

The path of the Chan-Ssu Chin should be like nature, soft and smooth, but elastic, like a lasso. The body should be like a soft tire being filled with air. If you are not soft, elastic and smooth, you will resist your opponent's force and be unable to rotate like a screw. The Chan-Ssu Chin should be smoothly connected from one movement to the next. When movements are disconnected and gaps show, the opponent has an opportunity to strike.

"The Chin is rooted in the feet, bursts out in the legs, is controlled by the waist and functions through the fingers. From the feet to the legs, legs to the waist, all should be moved as a unit. By moving as a unit, one can advance or retreat with precise timing and the most advantageous position." (其根在腳，發於腿，主宰於腰，形於手指，由腳而腿而腰；總須完整一氣，向前退後，乃能得機得勢 。).

The concept of body unity is delicately intertwined with the very important principle of moving the body continuously. The question which persists is how does one move the body continuously. The answer can be found in the practice of the Chan-Ssu Chin. Let us look at the movement of the Chin through the lower body. Whereas the Chi moves directly from joint to joint, the Chin spirals through the leg like a turning screw. Starting at the heel of the foot, the Chin passes through the ankle, winds around the leg to the knee and then continues winding up through the thigh to the buttocks. The Chin's spiralling movement is possible only if the leg moves as a unit; if the leg does not move as a unit, the Chin lacks continuity, jumping from joint to joint.

"If precise timing and good position are not achieved and the body does not move as a unit, then the waist and legs need more development. They may not be strong or flexible enough. This often shows when moving up or down, backwards or forwards, left or right." (有不得機不得勢處，身便散亂，其病必於腰腿求之，上下左右前後皆然 。).

Beginners or other people unfamiliar with the practice of the Chan-Ssu Chin are sometimes inclined to move the waist without moving the legs, the legs without moving the waist, or even their hands without moving the waist or legs. The ancient Tai-Chi experts were able to remedy this situation by learning to *Chen* (沉), "sink", their bodies as though the full weight of the body could flow through to the feet. In order to strengthen the waist and legs, they trained in the Ma Pu (馬步), or "horse stance", and Kung-Chien Pu (弓箭步), or "bow-and-arrow stance". When studying the Tai-Chi form, they also practiced the Chan-Ssu Chin and ward-off, roll-back, press and push until their minds could totally control their forward and backward steps. Today, because many students take short cuts and do not diligently follow the principle of waist-leg coordination, they could conceivably practice Tai-Chi Chuan for twenty or thirty years without being able to keep the waist and legs moving continuously.

"Use internal consciousness, not external forms." (凡此皆是意，不在外面).

Tai-Chi Chuan stresses mental awareness and concentration. Outer movements only express this "internal consciousness". Being conscious of one's movement leads to control of that movement. For example, it is necessary for one to concentrate on the movement of one's hand when pouring water from a glass into a ¡small hole. If one does not concentrate well, the water will spill.

"Where there is something up, there must be something down. Where there is something forwards, there must be something backwards. Where there is something left, there must be something right. If one intends to move up, one must simultaneously show a contrary tendency (downwards), just as one who wishes to pull a tree up pushes downwards first to loosen the roots, so that it can be easily uprooted." (有上即有下，有左即有右，有前即有後，如意欲向上，即寓下意，若將物掀起而加以挫之之力，斯其根自斷，乃壞之速而無疑 。)

> According to Lao-Tzu in the *Tao Te Ching*,
> What is to be shrunken is first stretched out.
> What is to be weakened is first made strong.
> What is to be thrown over is first raised up.
> What is to be withdrawn is first bestowed.

Yang represents up, forward, right, etc., and Yin represents down, backwards, left, etc. These opposites coexist and are inseparable in character, as illustrated by the Tai-Chi diagram. Because Tai-Chi Chuan is based on this principle, if one wants to show an upward tendency, there must simultaneously be a downward tendency. For example, to drive a nail into the wall, one must first withdraw a hammer and then swing it forward.

"One must distinguish substantiality from insubstantiality. Where there is substantiality, there must be insubstantiality. In all ways, one has to distinguish one from the other." (虛實宜分清楚，一處有一處虛實，處處總此一虛實).

Think of substantiality, or solidity, and insubstantiality, or emptiness, as right or wrong for just a moment. Consider two men discussing the weather. If man A states, "Tomorrow will be sunny," but man B asserts, "There will be a rainstorm," it may seem that only one of these men can be correct; however, tomorrow may be a sunny day with nearby clouds bearing rain. In this discussion both men are correct in their statements; however, they are also both wrong. If one can think of the body in terms of a discussion, then one can clearly see that the body can be both "right" and "wrong", or solid and empty at the same time. Theoretically, one can imagine one's body as the Tai-Chi diagram, in which half is Yang and half is Yin. Yang represents solidity and Yin emptiness. The body must remain equally balanced in terms of Yin and Yang. Where one part of the body is solid, another part must be relatively but oppositely empty. If one puts 70% of one's weight on the right leg, then the right leg is considered 70% solid and 30% empty. The left leg, therefore, becomes 30% solid and 70% empty as demonstrated in Figure 4-1c.

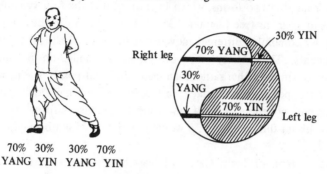

70%   30%   30%   70%
YANG YIN   YANG YIN

Figure 4-1c

Every movement of Tai-Chi Chuan must differentiate between the solidity and emptiness in the two arms, the two hands, the two legs, the two feet, as well as in the left hand and the left leg, the right hand and the right leg, etc. When the left hand is solid, the left leg is empty, and so on. To distinguish between solidity and emptiness, beginners should start with large steps; then one gradually decreases the step and learns to differentiate the substantial and the insubstantial internally, while allowing the external movement to become indifferentiable. One of the Tai-Chi Chuan practitioner's ultimate goals is to make movements which can not be outwardly differentiated as solid or empty.

"The whole body should be linked together through every joint; do not show any interruptions." (週身節節貫串，毋令絲毫間斷耳).

It is important to exercise nine groups of bone joints in the body: the neck, spine, waist, buttocks, knees, ankles, shoulders, elbows, and wrists. To link them all together, one must combine the waist and spine into the center for unifying the body. The waist-spine combination is essential because the waist is the axis for twisting to the right and left and the spine is the basis for bending forward and backward. One must think of the spine as a row of small beads and the Chi as the string which holds them together. Because the Chi has the natural inclination and awareness to stay straight, balance can be maintained throughout the body at all times. The waist-spine combination, which is the most important linkage of the nine joints, thereby frees the Chi to circulate throughout the entire body.

The concept of body unity must also be applied to the practice of the Chan-Ssu Chin. The reverse is also true; by practicing the Chan-Ssu Chin one can find body unity.

"Long Chuan, like a great river, flows unceasingly." (長拳者如長江大海，滔滔不絕也).

Basically, Tai-Chi Chuan has only eight postures. Why then is it called "Long Chuan"? According to the theory of the *I-Ching*, the Tai-Chi produced Yin and Yang, the two forms, which in turn created the four symbols, leading to the eight trigrams (see Chapter 2-3). Tai-Chi Chuan can thus be performed infinitely by combining different movements based on the Eight Gates and the Five Elements. The subtlety of Tai-Chi Chuan is founded on the continuation of one posture into another rather than many different postures. The movement cannot be stopped, nor interrupted, just as in the Tai-Chi diagram which has no beginning and no end. Even if one were to practice a form of a thousand postures without this continuity, it would not and could not be considered Long Chuan.

"The *Pa-Men*, or Eight Gates, of Tai-Chi Chuan are ward-off, roll-back, press, push, pull-down, split, elbow and shoulder-strike. The first four gates represent the Four Directions: south, north, west and east. The last four gates in turn reflect the Four Corners: southwest, northeast, southeast and northeast (as shown in Figure 4-1d).

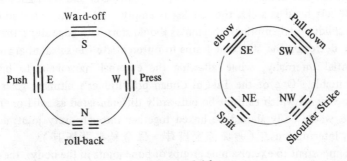

Figure 4-1d

The *Wu Pu*, or Five Steps, of Tai-Chi Chuan are advance, retreat, look to the left, gaze to the right, and central equilibrium. These steps equate to the Five Elements: metal, wood, water, fire and earth. The Eight Gates plus the Five Steps are termed the Tai-Chi Chuan Thirteen Postures." (掤、攦、擠、按；採、挒、肘、靠，此八卦也。進步、退步、左顧、右盼、中定，此五行也，掤攦擠按，即乾坤坎離；四正方也。採挒肘靠，即巽震兌艮，四斜角也。進退顧盼定；即金木水火土也。合之則爲十三勢。).

4-2. TAI-CHI CHUAN CHING (太極拳經) OR "THE CLASSICS OF TAI-CHI CHUAN", BY WANG TSUNG YUEH

"Tai-Chi is born of Wu-Chi. It is the origin of dynamic and static states and the mother of Yin and Yang. If they move, they separate. If they remain static, they combine." (太極者，無極而生，動靜之機，陰陽之母也，動之則分，靜之則合。).

Review Chapter 2-1.

"Neither overextend nor underextend. The crooked should be made straight." (無過不及，隨屈就伸).

*O*verextension of movement, meaning "strong Yang, weak Yin", is as incorrect as underextension, representing "strong Yin, weak Yang".

The only natural and desirable condition is balance between Yin and Yang as indicated in the Tai-Chi diagram. Therefore, when practicing Tai-Chi Chuan or Push-hands, it is better by far to maintain central equilibrium. Whenever over or underextension occurs, one will be off balance. In order to restore equilibrium, one must use either withdrawal or extension. The same principle holds true for many aspects of daily life.

"To overcome the strong and the hard by the gentle and the soft way is termed *Tsou* or "lead by walking away". To remain in the most advantageous position and let one's opponent be at a disadvantage is called *Nien* or "sticking"." (人剛我柔謂之走，我順人背謂之黏。).

One of the main principles of Tai-Chi Chuan is that the small can overcome the large, the weak conquer the strong and the soft win out over the hard. How can these seeming contradictions be reconciled? The answer is to apply the methods of Tsou (走) and Nien (黏).

If two persons are fighting using only techniques of strength and force, the stronger one will undoubtedly win. By applying Tsou, or withdrawing, in such a situation, one responds like the Tai-Chi sphere, diverting and changing the direction of the applied force. By Nien, or staying close, one's opponents will be prevented from moving wherever or whenever they please. In this way, one always keeps one's balance and good position but causes others to lose theirs.

A striking example of this method was provided by the Vietcong during the Vietnam war. Compared to the U.S. Armed Forces, the Vietcong were outnumbered and under-equipped. However, the Vietcong used the principles of Tsou and Nien in accordance with Mao-Tse Tung's strategies of guerilla warfare to separate U.S. soldiers and then attack with only a handful of men. When U.S. soldiers attacked, the guerillas left their camps, led them to the mountains

(Tsou) and then countered with small and numerous attacks. The U.S. soldiers were defeated by overextending themselves in response to the Vietcong strategy in much the same way as one who is overextended is easily toppled in Tai-Chi Chuan. When the U.S. soldiers retreated, the guerillas stayed with them along the way, applying Nien. Apparently the Americans used a similar strategy during the revolutionary war with the British: Keep this combination of Tsou and Nien in mind as an excellent strategy in Tai-Chi Chuan.

"Fast responses to fast actions and slow ones to slow actions. Although the changes are numerous, the principle remains the same." （動急則急應，動緩則緩隨，雖變化萬端，而理爲一貫。）.

Force consists of three elements: magnitude, direction and point of application. If one of these three elements is lacking, one no longer has to deal with force. Tai-Chi Chuan promotes agility in movement so that the opponent cannot find a point of application. Once this agility has been attained, even if your opponent applies one thousand pounds of force, he or she will be thrown off balance, traveling in the direction of that force since no point of contact can be found. How can one achieve this sensitivity to change? The only way is to follow your opponents closely; no matter what their speed, you respond at the same rate. Implementing this unchanging principle takes a long time unless one practices the Chan-Ssu Chin as a short-cut.

"Understanding the Chin, or *Tong-Chin*, is attained through keeping in practice. Only continuous practice will eventually lead to this sudden illumination or a godlike stage." （由着熟而漸悟懂勁，由懂勁而階及神明；然非用力之久，不能豁然貫通焉！）.

How is it possible to learn to move exactly in time with one's opponent? By diligently practicing the solo-exercise of Tai-Chi Chuan. Experience over a long period of time will teach one how to prevent an opponent from finding any point of application on one's body. Once this is mastered, even the strongest opponent will be thrown off balance for lack of an application point. This skill, called "Tong-Chin", is achieved by practicing the Chan-Ssu Chin and the Tai-Chi Chi-Kung, understanding the application of each posture of the solo exercise, and knowing the technique of Push-hands (which is particularly valuable in teaching one to understand one's own Chin as well as the opponent's). Only continuous and diligent practice can allow one to perceive all three aspects of the opponent's force.

"The spirit, or Shen, reaches the top of the head, and the Chi sinks to the Tan-Tien." （虛領頂勁，氣沉丹田。）.

Review Chapter 3-7.

"Keep the central position; do not show anything substantial or insubstantial to your opponent. When the opponent brings pressure on one's left side, that side should be empty; this principle holds for the right side also. When he pushes upward or downward against one, he should feel as if encountering nothingness. When he advances, let him experience the distance as increasing drastically. When he retreats, let the distance seem exasperatingly short. The entire body is so light that a feather can be felt and so pliable that a fly cannot rest without setting it in motion." (不偏不倚，忽隱忽現，左重則左虛，右重則右杳，仰之則彌高，俯之則彌深，進之則愈長，退之則愈促，一羽不能加，蠅蟲不能落。).

This directive shows that one attains the Tai-Chi sphere when one becomes acutely sensitive, neutralizing and rendering harmless the applied action, regardless of its speed. Since a fly cannot find a point of contact when you are so sensitive, how can somebody else attack you?

"Your opponent cannot detect your intentions, but you can anticipate his. If one can master all these principles, one will become a peerless boxer." (人不知我，我獨知人，英雄所向無敵，蓋皆由此而及也。).

Tai-Chi Chuan is a superior way of boxing. Yang Lew-Shan was called "peerless Yang" because he could detect everyone's moves, yet no one could detect his. In order to implement this technique, you must acquire *Chan-Nien Chin* (沾黏勁), or "adherent tenacious energy". This kind of Chin, sometimes called spiritual energy or inner strength (內勁), is manifested in the ability to stay close to the opponent without using force. The expression "to stick like glue" would be relevant here, since Chan-Nien Chin involves neither pushing nor employing any force. This energy can be acquired through diligent practice of Push-hands and Chan-Ssu Chin.

When first practicing Push-hands with a partner, one will have little or no awareness of the Chan-Nien Chin; the hands and arms may feel wooden. Gradually, starting from the hands and proceeding through the elbows, chest, back and the entire body including the skin, one's sensitivity will develop. Once acquired, adhering, or Nien, to the opponent is possible, leading to conquest. With time, the Chan-Nien Chin will accumulate on your skin. The more advanced one's technique, the thicker the Chin and the larger the area it covers. This condition will eventually enable one to detect whether or not one's opponent has the same Chan-Nien Chin. If not, the meaning of "your opponent cannot detect your moves, but you can anticipate his" becomes clear.

"In boxing there are many teachings about combat. Although they differ with respect to postures, they can never go beyond reliance on the stronger defeating those who are weaker, or the swifter conquering those who are slower. These, however, are the result of physical endowments in many cases and not necessarily of practical application and experience." (斯技旁門甚多，雖勢有區別，概不外乎壯欺弱，慢讓快耳，有力打無力，手慢讓手快，是皆先天自然之能，非關學力而有爲也。).

Although other types of boxing each teach different postures, in theory they are similar in that they depend on physical strength and swift motion, aiming at overcoming those who are less powerful. A disadvantage of this approach is that strength and speed are related to a person's physical condition, which tends to decrease in efficiency with old age. The refinement of Tai-Chi Chuan techniques, on the other hand, will lead to development of the Chi, Chin and Shen, which are enhanced with practice and age.

"The strong and the quick, however, cannot explain nor implement the deflection of a thousand pounds' momentum with a force of four ounces, or an old man's defeating a great number of men." (察四兩撥千斤之句，顯非力勝，觀耄耋能禦眾之形，快何能為。).

Other types of boxing stress strength and speed, not technique. The reverse is true in Tai-Chi Chuan. Here the purpose is to train any human body into a Tai-Chi sphere, so that anyone who applies force to this sphere will have that force deviated by a slight turn of the body. Just like a bullfighter who deflects a charging bull through moving his body and cape slightly, the Tai-Chi practitioner does not compare forces with the opponent.

Practitioners of other forms of boxing usually lose their youthful force and speed as they grow older. Because Tai-Chi emphasizes the mind's control over the body and stresses internal, mental training, it allows those who practice this art to maintain a strong body, a clear mind and the ability to withstand attacks by many men, even well into their seventies or eighties.

"Stand like a poised scale and move actively like a cartwheel." (立如平準，活似車輪。).

The person who becomes a Tai-Chi sphere is very active (see Chapter 3-7). To illustrate what is meant here, I would like to take an example from personal experience. In 1966, shortly after I had begun to study Tai-Chi Chuan, I visited the Tai-Chi expert, Cheng Man-Ching. I watched him pushing hands with his advanced disciple Chi Chang-Tao (綦江濤). Cheng told Chi that he would not attack him, but would deviate the *Hwa Chin* (化勁), or "tenacious energy". Cheng was short and nonathletic looking, while Chi was tall and thin, with long arms and legs. The latter attacked Cheng vigorously but was unable to even touch his clothes. This then is an example of perfect balance where one becomes like a Tai-Chi sphere, which is easily set in motion but not necessarily in the expected way, at least as far as the opponent is concerned.

"With your center of gravity displaced to one side, you can be fluid. If you are double weighted, you become stagnant." (偏沉則隨，雙重則滯 。).

If you are substantial on one side, you can rotate your body along the axis. To avoid being toppled easily, keep your axis in line with one foot and lower your center of gravity. On the other hand, if you spread your weight evenly on both feet, you may feel balanced, but actually you are double weighted and will find it hard to move.

Tai-Chi is based on the *I Ching*, so the unchanging must be seen as controlling the changing. Anything contrary to the Tai-Chi sphere is incorrect.

"Many persons who have studied Tai-Chi for a number of years have not developed properly and continue to be subdued by others because they have not realized the error in double weightedness." (每見數年純功，不能運化者，率自爲人制，雙重之病未悟耳。).

Although many people study Tai-Chi Chuan, they do not necessarily understand its theories. Instead of following the basic principles, they try to compete in force and speed. If they would train themselves into a Tai-Chi sphere, they would not continue the practice of double weightedness which invariably leads to defeat.

"To avoid this fault, the relationship between Yin and Yang must be understood. Nien is Tsou and Tsou is Nien. Yin cannot be separated from Yang and vice versa. When Yin and Yang complement each other, one will interpret the tenacious energy, or Tong-Chin, correctly." (欲避此病，須知陰陽，黏即是走，走即是黏，陰不離陽，陽不離陰，陰陽相濟，方爲懂勁。).

The relationship between Tai Chi and the Yin-Yang principle was demonstrated in Chapter Two. Like Yin and Yang, Tsou, or leading away, complements Nien, or adherence, and each contains some of the other. "Tsou" describes an ability to retreat with a soft movement when a stiff force is applied. This response prevents one's opponent from finding any point of contact on one's body. Then, since Tsou without Nien would be losing one's advantage, the person who was originally attacked will Nien to the now off-balance attacker and, if necessary, attack. Conversely, if one only does Nien without Tsou, a mutual attack will occur. The two opposites must combine and occur simultaneously as in the Tai-Chi diagram. With repeated and prolonged practice one will eventually be capable of Tsou and Nien at the same moment, resulting in an ever smaller circle which will eventually disappear. At this point, anyone touching you can be thrown while you will appear to be still. The opposites will be in harmony.

"Comprehend the Tong-Chin; the more you practice, the more wonderful will be your development. You understand in silence and experience in feeling until you may act at will." (懂勁後愈練愈精，默識揣摩，漸至從心所欲。).

By using the techniques of Tsou and Nien and by practicing Push-hands and Chan-Ssu Chin, you will gradually understand the Chan-Nien Chin. Then you will be at the main entrance of Tai-Chi Chuan. Train with your mind. When meditating, imagine someone kicking at you with the right foot. In response, imagine brushing the opponent's knee, twist-stepping, and using your right palm to push the opponent's chest. Meditate this way, and improvement will occur.

"Forget yourself and yield to others. Learn these techniques correctly, for the slightest divergence will take you far off the path." (本是捨己從人，多誤捨近求遠，所謂差之毫釐，謬以千里，學者不可不詳察焉。).

Practice not letting anyone get a contact point on your body. To do so without resistance, you need to lead your opponent away from the direction of his or her movement. The basic principle is to keep a low center of gravity and so confuse your opponent.

"Every sentence is extremely important and every word in it necessary. Understanding comes easily to those who devote themselves to these lessons." (此論句句切要，並無一字敷衍陪襯，非有夙慧，不易悟也，先師不肯妄傳，非獨擇人，亦恐枉費功夫耳).

4-3. AN INTERNAL EXPLANATION OF THE PRACTICE OF THE THIRTEEN POSTURES BY WU YU-HSING
(十三勢行功心解)

"The mind directs the movement of the Chi, which must sink deeply. Then it (the Chi) can be gathered into the bones. When the Chi circulates the body freely, without any obstacle, it can easily follow the mind" (以心行氣，務令沉着，乃能收斂入骨，以氣運身，務令順遂，乃能便利從心。).

*I*f both Tai-Chi Chuan and meditation are combined with the Tai-Chi Chi-Kung on a daily basis, the mind will gradually become capable of directing the Chi.   Controlling the Chi will result in a process of circulation called the "Small Heavenly Circle" (小周天see Chapter 3-3). This circulation of Chi should be gentle and harmonious.   Concentration is required so that the mind and the movement of Chi will match each other.

"If the Chi is cultivated, the spirit of vitality, or Shen, will be raised. One can feel as if one's head is suspended from above; thus one can avoid any slowness and clumsiness." (精神能提得起，則無遲重之虞，所謂頂頭懸也。).

One can explain the suspension of the head in two different ways: 1) by imagining a thread connected to the top of the head whereby one could be lifted like a puppet controlled by a string, or 2) by visualizing oneself as carrying an object on top of the head without dropping it. Both methods serve the same purpose of focusing the attention on keeping the vertical body axis in a perfectly straight position while rotation or translation occurs. Raising the spirit, or Shen, to one's head can then be viewed as consisting of smooth and harmonious movements, resulting from focused awareness on a perfectly straight spine.

"The mind and the Chi must coordinate and blend with the interchange between the substantial and the insubstantial, so as to develop an active tendency." (意氣須換得靈，乃有靈活之妙，所謂變轉虛實也。).

Substantiality implies Yang, representing solidness without stiffness. Insubstantiality, on the other hand, implies Yin, representing softness or emptiness, but not nothingness.   Changing from solidity to emptiness can promote balanced movement and stabilize the lower part of the body. Solidity prepares for emptiness and vice versa. They seemingly are each other's opposites but depend on each other. An example of how substantiality or insubstantiality of movement are controlled by the mind can be seen in the "Single Whip". Since one concentrates on the left hand, it is substantial, while the right hand would be considered insubstantial. In short, substantiality and insubstantiality come into existence through changes in body posture. One must force oneself to concentrate on using one's mind to understand and direct every such change of movement.

"In attacking, the energy should be sunk deeply, completely released and aimed in one direction." (發勁須沉着鬆淨，專注一方。).

Releasing a Chan-Ssu Chin is like throwing an object. One must not hesitate in one's aim; if one does, one's mind and energy flow are interrupted. One must be sure of oneself in order to sense the opponent's Chi; concentrate, sink and watch the opponent, not the ground.

"In standing, the body should be erect and relaxed, able to respond immediately to an attack from any direction." (立身須中正安舒，支撐八面 。).

Anyone who learns to apply the Tai-Chi sphere can stand up and remain balanced. More practice is needed, however, to be able to respond to an attack from any direction. One must put one's foot solidly against the ground, as if one were going to step into it. Day after day, like a sphere's axis, one's foot must be rooted to the ground so that one can rotate in any direction.

"The Chi is to be directed throughout the body as if passing a thread easily, without hindrance, through a pearl having nine zig-zagging paths. The energy is mobilized like steel refined a hundred times over, enabling it to destroy any object."   (行氣如九曲珠，無微不到，運勁如百練鋼，無堅不摧。).

A pearl with nine zig-zagging paths is hard to pass through unless the thread is like blown air.   Therefore, the Chi should be directed by the mind, as if blowing air throughout the body. Physical force needs guidance; whereas the Chan-Ssu Chin of Tai-Chi Chuan needs spirited concentration.

"One's appearance should be like a hawk swooping down upon its prey; the spirit should be like a cat mousing." (形如搏兔之鵠，神似捕鼠之猫。).

When one practices Tai-Chi Chuan, it is helpful to imagine being a hawk or a cat. Both these animals appear completely relaxed on the outside but act with total concentration. In the same way, one should seek stillness when in motion, movement when motionless and thus be totally concentrated at all times while using no physical force.

"It rests as a mountain; it flows like the current of a river." (靜如山岳，動若江河 。).

The movement should be sunken and quiet, the foot rooted as quiet as a mountain, as flowing as a river.

"Reserving the potential energy, or Chin, is like drawing a bow; releasing it is like shooting an arrow. Seek the straightness in a curve; reserve Chin before releasing it." (蓄勁如張弓，發勁如放箭，曲中求直，蓄而後發。).

The Tai-Chi Chuan schools of Chen and Wu mention that one should have five bows. The torso represents one bow; both arms and legs form four additional bows. All five bows should be united as a whole, then the stored energy can move actively throughout the body.

The tips of the torso bow are the coccyx and the four prominent cervical vertebrae. The Tan-Tien is the midpoint of the bow. The *Ming Men Hsueh*, (命門穴), which is on the back directly opposite the navel, represents the "notching" point, or the point of maximum tension, where the back of the arrow and the bow string meet.

It is possible to pull the bow by means of the Tai-Chi Chi-Kung. During inhalation when the bow is pulled, the bow and arrow tip, which approach each other, are each connected to a kidney. The kidneys will then act like pistons. During exhalation the bow is released, allowing the bow and arrow tip to move away from each other. In the next cycle the bow and arrow tip are again connected to the kidneys, but on the opposite sides.

The two bow and arrow tips of the arm are formed by the wrist and shoulder's connection with the collarbone; the elbow is the midpoint of the bow. How does one draw the arm bow? Maintain a curved line between the wrist and shoulder, imagining the arm as a bow complete with string. Keep one's awareness on the elbow, which is sunk and relaxed but always controlled. The motion of the elbow must always follow the motion of the body. Once the arm bows are developed the two arms will move as a unit. As a result, one's sensitivity in perceiving the opponent's energy increases. One will then be able to control, avoid or attack as the situation requires.

The knee is the midpoint of the leg bow; the tips are located in the thigh joint and the achilles tendon. When the leg bows are developed and properly connected to the waist energy which is rooted in the feet, the Chi can expand through the legs and, under control of the waist, function through the fingers.

Of the five bows the torso bow is of primary, the arm and leg bows of secondary, importance. However, they are all interdependent. That is to say, unless the arm and leg bows are developed, the torso bow cannot store up its energy. The torso bow, whose tips are the coccyx and the first cervical vertebra, must be supported in such a way that the torso remains vertical at all times. Maintaining a vertical torso becomes possible when both arm and leg bows are developed and kept slightly bent in the shape of a bow. Then the five bows can operate as one, and the energy is transmitted without interruption.

"Strength comes from the spine. The steps must be changed following along with changes in the position of the body." (力由脊發，步隨身換).

Do not use the hands to release one's strength; instead use the spine and the waist to release the Shen, or the spiritual power which is developed from the prebirth Chi and the Chan Ssu-Chin. As if resting and relaxed but remaining concentrated, one moves the leg and foot as well as the body.

"To withdraw is also to attack and vice versa. The Chin is sometimes broken off but must be immediately rejoined." (收即是放，放即是收，斷 而復連。).

Withdrawal is a kind of neutralization, or Yin. Attack is a way of advancing, or Yang. Withdraw in preparation for attack, and in attacking prepare for withdrawal. Just as Yin and Yang in the Tai-Chi diagram are inseparable and form a unit, so must withdrawal and attack always be close to each other. Withdrawal without attack is too weak, too Yin. Attack without withdrawal becomes awkward in action, or too Yang. Either extreme is not recommended in Tai-Chi Chuan.

A story about Yang Chian (楊鑑) provides an example of the balance between withdrawal and attack. One day a student approached Yang, who was sitting in an arbor smoking a pipe, with a question on how to release the Chin. Master Yang instructed his student to punch him in the abdomen as hard as possible. Being struck, Yang smiled and said "Haah", whereupon the student, attracted and repelled by the matched speed and force of Yang's energy, was thrown far away. Yang, meanwhile, continued smoking his pipe leisurely.

"When going back and forth, one should draw into folds. When advancing or retreating, one should turn the body and vary the steps." (往復須有摺叠 ，進退須有轉換).

Exiting from a highway, one needs to use a gradual bend or curve because a ninety degree turn might cause injuries to the passengers. If there is a large space between the highway and the side road, a slow curve will suffice. If not, one will need several small S-shaped curves as if one were winding up a mountain.

Like the highway and the side road, any two movements in Tai-Chi Chuan must be linked by a transition. The Chinese call the connection of two movements by one large curve or several small S-shaped curves the "drawing-into-folds" or "plait" technique. To move from ward-off right into roll-back, for example, fold up to the right, then to the left and connect smoothly and continuously to the subsequent downward and backward movement. In other words, be sure to apply a folding up of the body between forward and backward action. In addition, one needs a curved transition rather than a straight-forward advance or retreat, between one step and the next.

"Extreme softness leads to extreme hardness." (極柔軟然後極堅剛).

Westerners often question how hardness can come out of softness. But by studying the Tai-Chi diagram, one can see that at the point of maximum Yin, or softness, Yang, or hardness, is born. To apply this principle in the practice of Tai-Chi Chuan, one must first avoid all stiff and rigid movements. This method of practice is especially difficult for those who have trained in hard martial arts, such as Shao-Lin, Karate or Western-style wrestling. People with such a background must remember to free themeselves from habits acquired in their previous training.

At first, generally for one to two years, one performs the postures and movements without exertion and should appear to be completely relaxed below the surface. The softer and gentler one's movements, the easier it is to observe their defects, such as rigidity, force or incorrect postures. With softness goes slowness. In slowly executed movements incorrect postures can be detected much more easily. Movements done quickly always look good, and an erroneous technique is easily hidden in speedily executed forms. Once one has broken oneself of the habit of using rigid force and executed the movements slowly and continously, calmness and lightness are the inevitable results.

When one has learned to perform the movements without effort it is time to go on to the next stage, for which the softness is a foundation. At this point one must begin to mobilize one's internal movement so as to extend and prolong postures. To do so, have the intention to stretch and extend all parts of the body, such as the legs, arms, and trunk, etc. For example, sinking the Chi to the Tan-Tien while the head is suspended as if from above implies that the spine is stretched. This first example concerns internal movement, but one can more readily observe the application of extension in a posture such as "Separate Right Foot". Here the arms and right leg are extended in a stretch which incorporates the arm and leg bow. Of course, the principle of extending postures must be applied to every movement. The extension of the body will eventually result in "elastic hardness", a natural resiliency difficult to speak of, since it cannot be seen, only felt.

A relevant analogy could be drawn with the tip of a whip. It is soft while it is swung, but hard at the instant it is cracked, then soft again. One must

execute the movements of Tai-Chi Chuan in the same manner, keeping Yin and
Yang in mind. When one withdraws, one is soft; when one pushes one is like the
whip, soft until the last moment of the movement, at which time one becomes
completely Yang, or hard; afterwards one becomes immediately Yin, or soft,
again. It follows then that to be perfectly Yin all the time is only the beginning
stage. Once one is capable of being perfectly soft it is time to build a structure
of hardness. However, like the tip of the whip, one's movement is hard for only
an instant. With the application of this principle, one will develop an inner
elastic energy. Continuing to practice soft movement, however, will fail to
produce this elastic energy. The technical term for the soft part of the
movement is "circle", that for the instant of hardness is "square". Thus it is
said that the circle generates the square and the square generates the circle. This
alternation of hard, square, and soft, circle, is diagrammed in Figure 4-3a.

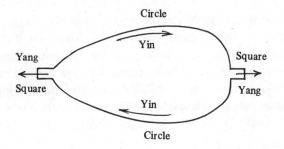

Figure 4-3a

In conclusion, Tai-Chi Chuan is the art of developing the hard out of the
soft. Tai-Chi is like a house, the better the foundation, the larger the structure
which may be built on it; thus the softer one can be, the more power one can
develop. This principle contains the secret of such great masters as Yang
Lew-Shan who was able to defeat all other fighters. This hardness, this energy,
however, must be shown only at the last instant, or else Yin-Yang balance
would be destroyed.

"Alacrity comes about when one's respiration is exact." (能呼吸然後能
靈活).

Practice Tai-Chi Chi-Kung and meditation. The prebirth Chi will become
imperceptible and will match up with action. All movements, although active,
will be undetected by the opponent.

"Chi should be cultivated naturally so no injury will occur." (氣以直養
而無害).

Sinking the Chi into the Tan-Tien is directed by the mind. If the Chi is not
sunk slowly, cultivating the Chi will be very difficult. One must let the breath

become "slender", "long", quiet and slow, keeping one's mind and Chi with the Tan-Tien at all times.

"Chin is stored by moving in curves." (勁以曲蓄而有餘).

The movements in Tai-Chi Chuan should be neither too straight nor too bent. If too straight, the Chin will be broken; if overly bent, postures will be unsupported. A natural curve can store Chin in the bone joints for later use.

"The mind is the commander, the Chi the flag, and the waist the pole." (心爲令，氣爲旗，腰爲纛).

The waist, an important hinge, should be relaxed and loose, so it can turn easily. When the waist turns easily, the spine is flexible so that the Chi can circulate through the entire body. The mind, however, is in charge.

"Movements should be stretched at first and become tight later. In this way one's movements will be perfect." (先求開展，後求緊湊，乃可臻於縝密 矣。).

While practicing, relax the entire body. Initially make big stretching movements and then small compact ones. These changes can be understood in terms of decreasing the size of the circle. Wait until the internal mind can match the external movement and eventually reduce the movement to no circle at all.

"The following is also said: "Concentrate your mind, then your body. Keep the belly completely relaxed; let the Chi adhere to the bones. Always bear these facts in mind." " (又曰：先在心，後在身，腹鬆淨，氣斂入骨， 神舒體靜，刻刻在心。).

To repeat once more, the mind comes first, then the body and next the arm and leg postures. One's mind and Chi should linger around the Tan-Tien. Relax and be at ease.

"Remember that when one part of the body moves, all other parts should move; when one part of the body is still, the rest of the body should be still." (切記一動無有不動 ，一靜無有不靜 。).

The movement in Tai-Chi Chuan can be compared to the gears in an engine. When one gear moves, all connecting gears also move, but not randomly. Standing still is meant as an aware stillness. Still movement does exist but may not be perceivable.

"In all movements to and fro, the Chi adheres to the back of the body and gathers into the spine. Inwardly one concentrates one's spirit, or Shen, and outwardly one appears peaceful." (牽動往來，氣貼背，斂入脊骨。內固 精神，外示安逸。).

According to the traditional Chinese medical theory, daily practice of Tai-Chi Chuan with diligence and real awareness will cause the Chi to accumulate. Concentration and awareness will allow the practitioner to direct this accumulation to the spine. Such activity is comparable to saving money by regular deposits in a bank. The more you practice, the more Chi accumulates in the spine.

Have you ever noticed that a really rich man does not have as ostentatious an appearance as one who is not so rich? He does not want to attract attention and thereby let others take advantage of his wealth. In the same way, when one has gathered the Chi and concentrated the Shen, one becomes a "rich" man, but one should not show this accumulation of power through belligerent attitudes and behavior. One should have an outwardly calm and smiling face, and not always be ready to show off and fight. To show one's Chi and Shen to others indiscriminately is like wearing one's price tags all over one's clothes. The proper use of this level of achievement is merely as a foundation for the development of the next level, or at the very least, to provide for one's health and well-being.

"Walk like a cat; mobilize your energy as if pulling silk threads from a cocoon." (邁步如猫行，運勁如抽絲。).

Walking like a cat means to be simultaneously light, agile, quiet and alive. To pull silk threads from a cocoon, one must not overdo the movement in order not to break the thread. To underdo would mean to produce no thread at all. Having lightness enables one to draw out the energy from the internal to the external without interruption.

"One's attention should be on the spirit, or Shen, not on the breath, or Chi. Special care of the breath makes one clumsy. Once one can forge the Chi, one's energy will be strong as steel." (全身意在精神，不在氣；在氣則滯，有氣者無力；無氣者純剛。).

At first, the Tai-Chi breathing should be practiced more and more deeply until it becomes one-pointed and eventually stops. Consider a top, for instance; when it spins at its highest speed it appears motionless. Concentrating totally on the breath, let it eventually become like the breath of a child. Only then is it time to dwell on Shen. Not till then will the motion be smooth and not stiff as in other hard martial arts breathing exercises. The strongest power comes from nonbreathing and the greatest achievement from nonaction.

"The Chi is like a cartwheel, and the waist an axle." (氣如車輪，腰如車軸).

The waist is the master part of the body. Like the axle rotating a cartwheel, the movement of the waist will turn the whole body.

"It is also said that if your opponent does not move, you should remain still. But at his slightest move, you should be ahead of him" (又曰：彼不動；已不動；彼微動，已先動。).

Think of a cat stalking a bird. The cat is motionless, but totally alert so that when the bird intends to fly, the cat anticipates his action and pounces. In the same manner, when you practice Push-hands, your attention should be focused on the point of contact with your opponent. In this way you can anticipate his or her intentions and react. You are the cat and he is the bird.

"The Chin seems loose, but it is not; it seems stretched, but it is not. If the Chin is broken off, the attention of one's mind still remains." (似鬆未鬆，將 展未展，勁斷意不斷。).

Before its release, the energy is not shown outwardly. After its release, the energy cannot be detected. But at the very instant of attack, the energy, like lightning, is quickly discharged, while the mind still concentrates against the opponent.

4-4. "THE FIVE WORDS' SECRETS" (五字訣) BY LI YI-HU

1. Tranquility or Hsin Ching (心靜)

A tranquil mind is the true secret in the practice of Tai Chi Chuan. Without a still mind, concentration is impossible and so movements are aimless. When beginning to learn Push-hands, be alert, attentive to your opponent's movement. Do not resist or lose contact with him. If he exerts strength, answer with strength without force. In this way you can anticipate force. Focusing on the point of contact with your opponent is of the utmost importance. Bear in mind that the sole aim is to employ the Tsou and Nien techniques.

After practicing Tai-Chi Chuan and Push-hands for six to twelve months you will be able to control the whole body. After training the mind in alertness, you will respond to strength with softness and act without force. It takes additional years of practice to understand yourself.

2. Agility or Shen Lin (身靈)

Agility of the body is essential for smooth, flowing motions in advance and retreat. The body should be pliable. When the opponent's strength lightly touches your skin, your awareness should, as it were, penetrate into his bones. Each arm should support the other, continuously linked by Chi. If the left side of your body feels the weight of your opponent's hand, indicating that an attack will come from the left, make the left side light, or Ching, as if giving in, while advancing the right in a seesaw movement. The same can be applied to the right side. In all ways yield the side attacked while advancing the other. The Chi is like a wheel activating the entire body which then moves in unison. Should this not occur because of deficiencies in coordination and strength, the solution can be sought for in the waist and the legs.

First one must use the mind to control the body and then try to follow the opponent's movements rather than your own. Eventually the body will follow the mind at the same time as one is trying to be aware of going with the opponent's movements. To act alone leads to clumsiness, but to follow the opponent's movement is conducive to agility. If one can really stick closely to the opponent's movements, one's hands can "measure" the magnitude and direction of the opponent's force accurately. One can then advance and retreat as necessary. The more time spent practicing, the closer one's skill can be brought to perfection.

3.   Gathering the Chi or Chi Lien (氣歛)

If the Chi is not stored, one can observe that the movements will be unnatural and abrupt. It is necessary to have the Chi penetrate the bones, and so allow the breathing to pass through the entire body. To this end, coordinate all closing movements with inhalation, all opening movements with exhalation. During inhalation it is easy for a person to raise oneself as well as to lift the opponent, while exhalation enables one to lower oneself and throw the opponent. It becomes even more apparent that all movements are done with the mind rather than through the use of force.

4.   Concentration of Chin or Chin Cheng (勁整)

The Chin of the body should be practiced as a whole. Empty and full should be distinguished clearly. Chin must be exerted from the heels, directed by the waist, propelled by the spine, and allowed to flow through the fingers. Most important, the mind must be one-pointed. The best time to use Chin is just as your opponent is about to employ it, but has not yet started, neither earlier nor later. Advance and retreat in response to your opponent, as a unit. Seek the straightness in the curve. Store the Chin before releasing it. Success will be achieved through using the opponent's strength to hit back. Use four ounces of force to move ten thousand pounds.

5.   Development of Shen or Shen Chu (神聚)

When the previous four requirements have been met, the spirit, or Shen, can begin to be developed. With concentration on Shen the Chi can be transferred to the Shen, or *Lien Chi Hwa Shen* (練氣化神), resulting in light opening or closing movements and the clear distinction of empty and solid. To empty the left is to fill the right and vice versa. Emptiness is not to be equated with weakness, however. Inside, one is firm, stable, controlled and strong. By the same token fullness does not mean force, but robust movement and the exhibition of great spirit. All manipulation is generated from the chest and waist. Chi is exerted from the spine and combined with the opponent's force.

How then is the Chi activated from the spine? It is pushed downward from the shoulders to the spine; this process is called "closing". When the Chi is made to move from the spine to the shoulders and on to the fingers, the process is known as "opening" (See Figure 4-4a).

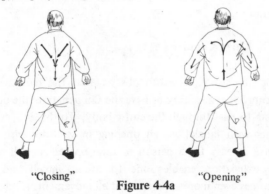

"Closing"   "Opening"

Figure 4-4a

The process called "closing" is involved in the storing of energy, while "opening" indicates the use of energy. The understanding of Yin and Yang is related to comprehending "closing" and "opening"; when this stage is reached one's skill will improve quickly.

4-5. SUMMARY OF THE PRACTICE OF TAI-CHI CHUAN AND PUSH-HANDS (走架打手行功要言), BY LI I-YU

*A*n ancient Tai-Chi expert said, "If one can allow the opponent to lose his balance, then one can use four ounces of force to move ten thousand pounds; otherwise, one cannot handle ten thousand pounds." Let me explain this further:

> If one wishes to allow one's opponent to lose his balance and hopes to use four ounces of strength to move ten thousand pounds, one must first of all know the opponent as well as oneself.
>
> If one wants to know the opponent as well as oneself, one

should forget oneself in trying to follow the opponent.

In order to do this one must use precise timing and be in an alert position.

To achieve this one must move one's body as a unit.

This means that the body cannot show any abruptness.

To this end the Chi should be activated, the spirit must be raised.

This is done by gathering the Chi in the spine.

Gathering the Chi in the spine is achieved through strong calves and perfectly relaxed shoulders, so that the Chi can sink downwards to the Tan-Tien.

The Chin originates in the heels and flows through the legs to the lower part of the body. Above the waist the Chin, which is temporarily stored in the chest, proceeds to the shoulders and arms; the Chin is controlled by the waist. A change in the Chin should be effected. The process of storing energy is called "closing"; whereas releasing energy is referred to as "opening". Keep in mind that in the state of "closing" there is some "opening" while the reverse is also true. At this point one is reminded of the Tai-Chi diagram and the shifting patterns of Yin and Yang. When one part of the body is still all parts of the body should be still; should one part of the body move, all parts should join in. Not moving could be compared to "closing" and moving to "opening". Again, however, there is some "opening" in "closing" and vice versa, much as there is Yin in Yang and Yang in Yin. Consistent practice of this will result in the body's becoming like a Tai-Chi sphere, which will rotate freely when it is touched. It follows then that at that point one can allow the opponent to lose his balance and use four ounces to move a thousand pounds.

Daily practice of Tai-Chi Chuan is necessary for proper understanding of oneself. With each posture one should ask oneself whether it is perfect in every detail and correct it if it is not. Obviously then practice must move at a very slow pace. An additional way of knowing oneself is afforded by the practice of Push-hands. This will assist one eventually in knowing the opponent's intentions. This exercise is done with a partner whose moves one must learn to anticipate. The understanding of the opponent's moves is based on self-understanding. Precise timing and the most advantageous position are helpful. Being touched by your partner you can follow his awareness. Timing is crucial since you must match your opponent precisely. Under these circumstances one can throw one's opponent off balance. A double-weighted position ensues when this is impossible. Additional study of the Yin-Yang, closing -opening concepts will be necessary. The opponent can be understood perfectly if one understands oneself. This is the way to master all adversaries.

4-6. TWO FAMOUS SONGS ABOUT TAI-CHI CHUAN, AUTHORS UNKNOWN

1. **The Song of the Thirteen Postures** (十三勢歌訣).

Never neglect any of the thirteen postures (See Chapter 4-1).
The source of the will is in the waist.
Pay attention to the slightest change from full to empty.
Let the Chi flow through the whole body constantly.
Stillness embodies motion, motion stillness.
Seek stillness in motion.
Surprising things will happen when you meet your opponent.
Give awareness and purpose to every movement.
When done correctly all will appear effortless.
At all times pay attention to the waist.
With abdomen loose and light, the Chi can be activated.
If the coccyx is erect, the Shen rises to the top of the head.
The body should be pliable.
Hold the head as if suspended from a string.
Be alert and seek meaning in the purpose of Tai-Chi Chuan.
Bent and stretched, open and closed,
Let nature take its course.
Beginners are guided by oral teaching.
Gradually one applies oneself more and more.
Skill will take care of itself.
What is the main principle of Tai-Chi Chuan?
The mind is the primary actor and the body the secondary one.
What is the purpose and philosophy behind Tai-Chi Chuan?
Rejuvenation and prolonging of life beyond the normal span.
So an eternal spring.
Every word of this song has enormous value and importance.
Failing to follow this song attentively, you will sigh away your time.

2. **The Song of Push-Hands** (打手歌)

In ward-off, roll-back, press and push,
Use purpose with every action.
Every part of the body in motion is supported by another part.
This way there will be no "opening" to let your opponent attack you.

If your opponent uses force against you,
Use four ounces to deflect a thousand pounds.
Lead your opponent in and allow him to lose his balance.
Yield and assert at the same time.
Do not forget to use the techniques of Tsou and Nien.

CHAPTER FIVE
EXPERIENCES

Just as in other sports where one attains various degrees or belts, Tai-Chi Chuan has specific levels of achievement. Cheng Man-Ching defined the level of a Tai-Chi student's skill in terms of the three powers: humanity, earth and sky. He then subdivided each power into three categories, for a total of nine levels. It is not my intention to use this concept as a method of grading, but rather as a way of defining, for example, what particulars a beginning student should be concerned with and the natural progression of practice for the more experienced student. Thus, the following chapter uses the concept of the three powers to delineate the three main stages of Tai-Chi practice.

5-1. RULES FOR THE HUMAN STAGE

*B*y following the rules of human or first stage, the beginner can establish a firm foundation in Tai-Chi Chuan. However, one will benefit most from diligently practicing one or two basic approaches, rather than trying too many different methods at the same time. In this way one will be well-grounded in one principle before proceeding to the next. Each rule for beginners is described in detail below.

1.   Lightness or Ching

"The Theory of Tai-Chi Chuan" expresses the first principle as follows: "In any action, the whole body should be light, or *Ching* (輕), and agile, or *Lin* (靈)." At first the focus should be on Ching, because lightness is more difficult to cultivate than agility. Even practitioners of other martial arts find Ching problematic; although agile, or Lin, in terms of speed, they generally move using too much outer force and muscular tension. Both athletes and non-athletes learning Tai-Chi Chuan need to develop Ching.

The following examples might be helpful in understanding Ching. Imagine a mother cat swinging playfully at her kittens; she will control her movement in order not to hurt them. In much the same way one can use the principle of Ching to practice sparring. Ching also has special applications to one's step in Tai-Chi Chuan. An old floor may creak when someone steps on it, but stepping with Ching, no sound will be heard.

Understanding lightness, which is Yin, must include the concept of heaviness, which is Yang. Using too much outer force in Tai-Chi Chuan will be experienced by others as heaviness. In nature one would ascribe the characteristics of heaviness to a tornado, whereas lightness would be associated with a gentle spring breeze.

Ching refers not only to outer movements, but also to the control of consciousness or mind. Mental Ching is used to control the Ching revealed in motion. If a cat has a serious intent his bite is designed to hurt, but if playful, with Ching in mind, there will be no pain.

The main purpose of Tai-Chi Chuan is to cultivate inner sensitivity rather than to develop outer strength. Sensitivity is facilitated by reducing force and unnecessary muscular tension. In contrast, using a great deal of outer force numbs sensitivity just as fighting with clenched fists dulls the pain. Therefore, in the beginning stage one should not use awkward force but concentrate on relaxing. Let movements be light and natural, like clouds passing across the sky, or branches blown by a gentle breeze.

As described in "The Classics of Tai-Chi Chuan", practicing Ching opens the door to an extraordinary depth of sensitivity; eventually even "a feather can be felt". By applying Ching to every movement, one paves the way for more advanced techniques. The use of force or heaviness, however, will prevent one from reaching the higher stages of development in Tai-Chi Chuan.

2. Slowness or Man

The movements in Tai-Chi Chuan should be executed extremely slowly, especially in the beginning stage. The slower the movements, the better one can concentrate on their details. In addition, through practicing the forms as slowly as possible, one develops a more acute sense of balance.

The execution of Man (慢), or "slowness", in Tai-Chi Chuan can be compared to riding a bicycle very slowly. This method does not involve making quick transitions and then standing in postures for a long time, just as pedaling a bicycle quickly and then stopping would not be considered slow. Only riding a bicycle continuously as well as slowly can fulfill the requirements of Man.

One can have some experience with Man by walking as slowly as possible at a constant rate while paying attention to every part of the body. It will soon be obvious that the application of Man is very difficult. In Tai-Chi Chuan one's step must be slow, deliberate, and continuous. One must step "in the air" as it were and, if necessary, be able to stop at any time.

Practice the forms with Man uppermost in the mind until there is no possible way to do the solo exercise any more slowly without violating its fundamental principles. For example, if completing the long form, Yang style, at a constant rate takes twenty-five minutes, but going more slowly leads to technical errors, one then needs to speed up the form. But when one feels that one is going so fast as to violate the principles, one must return again to Man. This process should become a regular cycle of learning. Go slowly until one can learn no more from going slowly, then go quickly until one can learn no more from going quickly, finally returning to Man. One will eventually find that for the sake of Man, the optimum time for performing Yang's Tai-Chi Chuan is almost one hour.

The idea of Man is probably familiar to us through its use in various athletic programs, i.e., teaching tennis and golf by videotaping the student's form and providing an instant replay in slow motion. Whereas this system of instruction requires money and special technology, the implementation of Man in Tai-Chi Chuan requires only understanding and perseverance. In addition, calming the outside by practicing slowly and peacefully benefits the inside, one's thoughts and emotions. By relaxing completely, through Man, one becomes more gentle. Eventually, slow, soft practice of the forms will result in the state described as "active outside, empty inside", or "nonaction in action". In other words, by reflecting outer calm, one's inner self will become quiet and still like the water in an old well. When this stage occurs, one may then appreciate the other main advantage of Man. Moving the body slowly and calmly lets one's awareness direct the flow of Chi throughout the body. By focusing attention on the Tan-Tien and then following the Chi as it radiates outward during the movements, one in fact increases that flow. Practicing in this way illustrates the main principle of the Tao-Yie.

Always keep in mind that the movements in the beginning stage must be slow and continuous, like a flying bird's projecting its shadow from moment to moment without interruption (see Chapter 2-5). After the foundations of slowness and lightness have been laid, maintaining a steady speed in fast action will always be possible. In the advanced stages a reduction in speed is no longer necessary since one's movement flows out of the stillness sought from within.

3.   Circular movement or Yuan

All movements in Tai-Chi Chuan are composed of circles as opposed to straight lines. The effects of Yuan (圓), or "circular movement", for defense and attack in a martial art are comparable to those of pitching curves in baseball. A pitcher may be able to strike out an inexperienced batter with a fast ball. However, for an experienced player, the harder, faster, and straighter the ball is pitched, the easier it is to hit. The pitcher, of course, throws curve balls, drops, and sliders most often since they are the hardest to hit and, when hit, usually result in fouls and flies. The Tai-Chi specialist then is constantly "throwing curves" at the opponent, in contrast to the "fast balls" of most other martial arts.

The execution of movements in circles and arcs also generates considerably more force than does linear motion. Yuan's strength is readily illustrated by the wind and the water. A straight, steady wind, no matter how strong, does little damage, but the tornado, cyclone and hurricane destroy without mercy. A straight, steady current of water, no matter how fast, can still be navigated, but a whirlpool or undertow is perilous.

When the beginner starts to practice Tai-Chi Chuan, all action should follow the path of an arc or a circle. With Man and Ching in mind, the movements must be stretched and each arc enlarged to the limit, as long as proper postures are maintained. After one has practiced sufficiently to develop skill in Yuan, the size of the arcs may be reduced. However, no matter how small a movement is, it must still be executed in an arc. Such circular movements may appear easy to do, but practice and constant attention are required to develop natural and unstrained postures. One must have the intention to make all movements circular, starting with the hands and arms. Gradually, these circular movements will "seep" into the rest of the body so that the body eventually leads the hands and arms.

Yuan can be incorporated into one's posture most effectively by daily practice of the Chan-Ssu Chin. Otherwise, when one begins to try to move the hands and arms in circles, one may forget to have the hands follow the body and let the body follow the hands instead. Practicing the Chan-Ssu Chin will not only prevent such errors but will considerably facilitate one's progress.

4.   Constant rate or Yun

Yun (匀), literally meaning "homogenous", describes the smooth pace of Tai-Chi Chuan. In daily life, where movements are usually done automatically, one has no desire to learn to control them. But in Tai-Chi Chuan, especially when first learning the forms, one must learn to execute every movement slowly and deliberately. Although the beginner may have an intellectual understanding of Yun, one's movements will inevitably be performed at an uneven rate. Therefore, one must first learn how to develop the discipline of total consciousness while doing the forms. The proper technique involves concentrating on the movements as if they incorporated a series of still photos each taken a fraction of a second apart. Anyone who has ever observed movements under strobe lighting will know exactly what is meant. Through persistent practice, visualizing a series of stills within each movement will become so internalized and semi-automatic that conscious effort will no longer be needed.

Every day the sun, rising in the east and setting in the west, apparently moves across the sky at a constant rate, but who can actually see the sun in action? Only the keen observer with a quiet and peaceful mind can perceive this constant rate, and only by using a technique, such as observing the movement of shadows.   One should learn from the sun and apply special techniques of perception to oneself when doing Tai-Chi Chuan.

Finally, when one has acquired Ching, or lightness, Man, or slowness, Yuan, or complete circularity of motion, and Yun, or constant rate, one will have completed the human stage.   How can one verify this accomplishment? One will have followed the rules in the human stage when the practice of Tai-Chi Chuan outdoors does not disturb flocks of birds or other animals.   Then one is ready for the second or earth stage.   Remember that although it may take only ten minutes to read this description, the actual completion of the human stage can easily take three or five years.

5-2.   RULES FOR THE EARTH STAGE

*T*he attainment of the human stage is the foundation for all subsequent achievement.   Once this firm foundation is built, however, one's concern will naturally turn to the erection of the rest of the structure; the former attainment so laboriously gained must be forgotten so that effort will be totally mobilized for the earth stage.   In this stage one must understand the principles described in this section so as to guide one's practice to perfection. Again one must at first pay careful attention to incorporating one principle at a time into the Tai-Chi form.   Finally, one will learn to perform the form effortlessly, automatically taking all of the principles below into account.

1.   Agility or Lin

As a result of emphasis on Man and Yun in the human stage, the student usually becomes stiff.   This is allowable for a time since at least the student is now moving the body as a unit.   However, this stiffness must be rebalanced by introducing a type of agility through the application of Lin (靈).   We say "a type of agility" because one generally understands the word "agile" as requiring quick darting movement, or swiftness born of external strength.   On the contrary, Lin must be understood as described in "The Classics of Tai-Chi Chuan": "Stand like a poised scale and move actively like a cartwheel."

Like a well-oiled machine, this agility totally lacks stiffness.   In standing like a poised scale, one is ready to react instantaneously.   One must be able to move like a well-greased wheel, to offer no resistance and spin swiftly.

Fish in a pond with sufficient room to move will swim away swiftly if one disturbs the water.   This example illustrates the usual conception of agility.

Fish confined in a fish tank, however, will wait poised and ready if one sticks a hand in the water and will move only if one attempts to grasp them. Even then the movement will be only what is minimally necessary to elude one's grasp. This is the agility of Lin.

Consider the bullfighter. He stands poised waiting, baiting the bull with his cape and taunting with his shouts. Finally the bull charges, and with graceful, fluid and minimal movement the matador eludes the bull. This is another example of Lin.

One must now include the rest of the meaning of Lin along with the expanded understanding of agility; Lin applies the Tai-Chi principle that Yin is Yang and Yang is Yin. In physical terms the application of this principle means that if you try to grasp my arm, I disappear and simultaneously grasp you, thus converting my Yin to Yang. Or, if you push me I elude your push and simultaneously push you, again reversing the entire interaction. This is the true Lin.

Lin must be a constant and continuous subject of study for the practitioner of Tai-Chi Chuan, for without it such exercises as Push-hands and Ta-Lu become meaningless. Lin can be developed primarily by the practice of the Chan-Ssu Chin, with the following results: 1) weight firmly rooted in the feet, 2) all movements controlled by the rotation of the waist without independent activity of the limbs, and 3) a fluid spatial curve to the arms, hands and shoulders allowing the energy to come to the fingers. When the whole body is mobliized with such controlled movement, one will have entered the gate of Lin and gained the freedom of action that this implies.

2. To relax or Sung

Even though the student of Tai-Chi Chuan hears the word "relax" more often than any other, its meaning is consistently misunderstood because *Sung* (鬆) conveys certain ideas not found in the English word "relax". This problem is compounded by the fact that the average student does need to relax the excess tension in certain muscle groups. Moreover, most Western people have become conditioned, with the popularization of many Eastern systems, to regard "relaxation" as an ultimate goal. The result of these factors is that when the teacher says, "You must relax," the student then tries to exhibit a relaxed body and mind. The teacher then will thoroughly confuse the student by saying, "No! No! You must relax!" The reason for this perplexity is simple; the student conceives of relaxation as that which is experienced by a person who flops down into a comfortable couch and peacefully drifts off into a reverie, totally passive, uncaring, and unguarded. Such a state of mind has no place in the practice of Tai-Chi Chuan. Sung in Tai-Chi Chuan balances Yin and Yang, integrating the hard and the soft. Although easy to say, the integration of these opposites is hard to accomplish. For example, a stiff, tense, "spear hand" exemplifies the maximum of Yang, and a limp, unconscious "dead hand", the maximum of Yin. Neither extreme, nor the combination of half hard and half soft is correct. The proper Tai-Chi hand which is relaxed, or Sung, is balanced so that it can be mobilized immediately to either extreme. The hand may briefly become extremely Yang to attack, or extremely Yin to escape, but only when necessary. The next instant the condition of Sung is reestablished. Think of playing the piano or typing as examples of the need for conscious relaxation or Sung in the hands. The same principle is applicable in Tai-Chi Chuan, for every part of the body as well as the mind.

By practicing Sung, energy (Chi and Chin) will be conserved like money in a bank. One must not strain one's posture and mood as if worrying about money hidden in a mattress, but act composed and serene as if keeping substantial savings in the bank. As energy is conserved and the body and mind become serene, energy will flow through every part of the body. Seeking to send this energy through a stiff body is a common mistake of all beginners. However, one should not be unduly concerned about this event, since with more Sung, more and more muscles will relax. It is known that muscles automatically relax when the mind is cleared and the emotions stilled. This is the Sung the student must attain.

Such relaxed awareness is seen in nature. The snake hibernating all winter does not relax totally, or else it would die. It withdraws consciously, conserving its energy so that it may strike again in the spring. The tree losing leaves in the winter is not withering and dying, but withdrawing into a purposeful state of rest, or Sung, not yielding completely but waiting for what is forthcoming.

The ultimate goals in the study of Tai-Chi Chuan generally involve mastering the martial art and attaining physical rejuvenation, or more properly, an integration and combination of both. An awareness of these goals must be integrated with one's concept of Sung. Achieving Sung leads one into the next step Chen (沉), or "sinking", which is absolutely necessary for the attainment of martial arts skill, since only if one can relax and sink, can one fight effectively. With respect to attaining physical rejuvenation, since one normally loses more and more of the ability to Chen as one ages, Sung can enable one to regain what was lost and then add more to the original store.

Finally, only by understanding and reaching the state of Sung can one pass to the third aspect of the earth stage, the attainment of the three powers.

3. The Three Powers

To achieve proper balance at this stage of practicing Tai-Chi Chuan, one must internalize the concept of the three powers (三 才): sinking the weight down through the feet, which corresponds to the earth; sending the Shen up to the top of head, which corresponds to the sky; and placing the concentration on the Tan-Tien, which represents humanity (see Chapter 2-5). If this concept is correctly expressed, the body will be poised properly in each Tai-Chi posture, neither sunk too low or stretched too high, thereby representing the universe where, according to the traditional Chinese view, the lighter substances ascend to become the atmosphere, and heavier ones descend to become the earth. Versions of the posture "Golden Pheasant Stands on One Leg" (See Figure 5-2a) illustrated correctly by Yang Chen Fu and incorrectly in the other two illustrations.

Only through understanding this concept can one reconcile an apparent paradox which has confused many students of Tai-Chi Chuan: the need to simultaneously implement the principles of Sung, Lin and Chen during the

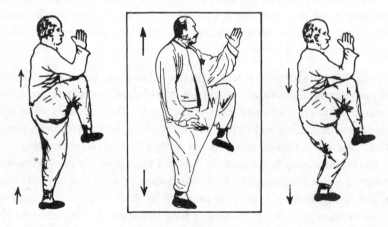

Fig 5-2a

forms. How can one relax, be agile and sink at the same time? These apparently conflicting requirements are resolved by applying the concept of the three powers. First one sinks the weight to the earth. Then one concentrates on the Tan-Tien. Finally, one sends the Shen up to the top of head, becoming balanced, poised and agile.

4. Changes

The concept of change as expressed in the *I Ching* plays a very important role in Tai-Chi Chuan's system. The *I Ching* states that everything changes, or put another way, develops through certain cycles. Nothing is constant but change itself. However, if nothing is constant but change, then the ways that these changes or cycles occur are in fact constant. Thus, the *I Ching* advises one to seek the unchanging in that which changes.

The practical application of this principle in Tai-Chi Chuan has as many aspects as there are possibilities of change; in other words, its application is endless. Three specific points about change will be considered below.

First, Tai-Chi Chuan emphasizes cyclic individual development as opposed to imitation and uniformity. In most physical activities, uniformity of the student's postures is the goal of the teacher, and exact imitation of the teacher is the goal of the student. There are good reasons for teaching this way, but unless the concept of change is introduced, what should be a method becomes confused with an end. Ballet, Kung Fu and many other physical activities require the endless repetition of postures so as to perfect them to a certain uniformity. This approach is excellent, but it neglects the possibility that the student may grow to a greater level of excellence than the teacher. Moreover, this method ignores individual physical differences, intents and desires. In other words, it changes something living and dynamic into something static and dead. In the practice of Tai-Chi Chuan, the concept of change is one with the system of study. Therefore, the student is given the knowledge of what is unchanging and then is allowed to practice in such a way that there is change. For instance, in the posture "Snake Creeps Down" the student is told of the principles which must not be violated: feet flat on the floor, body upright, constant height, etc. (See figure 5-2b, Yaug Chen Fu's Posture) The fact that the execution of this posture, except for these unchanging points, is up to the

Fig. 5-2b

student, allows the posture to change or develop. Instead of attempting to imitate the teacher's posture, the student through time and repetition can develop the posture individually, to his or her best possible actualization of the basic principles. This approach also takes into account differences in individual goals since the person whose orientation is towards improved health may actualize the posture differently from another person whose intent is martial arts skill. Both individuals will be correct no matter how different they look if they do not violate the basic principles of Tai-Chi Chuan.

Secondly, alternating the slow and the fast promotes the correct development of Man. To really be able to go slowly, one must be able to go fast, and one cannot really go as fast as possible unless one can go as slowly as possible. In this instance what changes is the speed at which one performs the form and what is unchanging is the purpose, which is to be able to move as slowly as possible. When the student can go no more slowly, the posture must then be executed quickly. However, even the purpose of this shift is to be able to change back to the slow. By this kind of cyclic alternation, the student returns to the development of Man each time. Being able to go more slowly is possible only by alternation with the fast.

Thirdly, expanding and stretching the postures is designed to develop "no posture" or formlessness. First one stretches and enlarges (開 展) the postures to the individual's limit. When this end is reached, one must reduce the postures until they are "tight" and "close". (緊 湊) Since further contraction would violate basic principles, the cycle must return to expansion. In this example, the size of the posture changes; whereas the unchanging idea is to finally contract the posture into a point, that is to achieve no posture.

One can see how applying these three pinciples of change depends totally upon the individual's goals and ability. So it is with all of Tai-Chi Chuan. Only the individual can really develop his or her own course of study. Only the individual can in fact teach him- or herself Tai-Chi Chuan. No one taught Chang San-Feng but himself; he learned through discovering Tai-Chi's basic principles. This should be the goal of all students of Tai-Chi Chuan. One must seek the unchanging in change and hold firm to the source. In this way, change will become the most important tool and technique in the Tai-Chi Chuan student's repertoire.

These ideas may all seem too abstract, so a final suggestion will bring them into practical application. Once the student has mastered the right side of the form through long study, arduous practice and the help of an excellent teacher, the student must then reach an equal level of achievement on the left side, but without a teacher. Only in this way can one determine what one has learned and developed on one's own as opposed to what was only superficial imitation.

5-3.   RULES FOR THE SKY STAGE

*T*he human and earth stages emphasized the development of Tai-Chi Chuan's postures. In the sky stage, however, the methods focus more on mental training. The following advanced principles are explained in this section: sensing emptiness and solidity, controlling one's breathing, disciplining one's consciousness, and finally seeking void and stillness.

1.   To Sense Emptiness and Solidity

In the human and earth stages, one's movement is restrained by the demands of slowness and a constant rate of motion. At the same time, one must pay attention to other points so that it is difficult to feel quiet and at ease. The first step of the sky stage helps one to calm down through another method, that of learning to simplify one's focus of attention, rather than following a large number of rules. During practice, one concentrates only on distinguishing the insubstantial, or empty, from the substantial, or solid, (分清 虛實) and tries to forget all the other points mentioned before. One must now give up complexity. Most people are aware of this principle only as applied to shifting one's weight. They know that placing the whole weight of the body on one leg makes that leg substantial, or solid, and the other leg insubstantial, or empty. Actually, the principle of distinguishing emptiness and solidity contains more subtleties. For instance, when one is doing the posture Push, the hands are empty at the beginning, but solid at the end of the movement. As the palms gradually stretch out until the ending point, the center of the palm rises a little to display the Chan-Ssu Chin which is "rooted in the feet, bursts out in the legs, is controlled by the waist and functions through the fingers". This stretching results in the maximum point of solidity, or simply the extreme Yang. When the hands are withdrawn, going from solid to empty, the extreme Yang generates Yin. In this process, the tensed palm relaxes, or becomes the extreme Yin. Striking with the fist follows the same principle. At first the fist must be loose or empty, and only at the end does it become tight, or solid. When the fist withdraws, it becomes loose again, and solidity returns to emptiness. So the fist is either tightened or relaxed in accordance with the Yin-Yang changes which exist in every action. In addition, the waist, legs and every part of the body must match the empty and solid condition of the hand. When the palm rises a little to indicate extreme solidity, tense every part of the body.

The postures where the body is expanded and enlarged like an open door are technically called "opening". When the palm is withdrawn and relaxed to indicate the extreme Yang generating Yin, and the body is contracted and condensed like a closed door, the postures are described as "closing". In addition, when one steps forward, the heel touches the ground first and then the sole of the foot is placed down gradually to match the hand's movements. The inside of the body changes from closing to opening. In the same manner, when one withdraws one's step, the inside of the body is to change from opening to closing, matching the hand's change from solid to empty. All these internal and external combinations of opening and closing movements are based on the Chan-Ssu Chin.

If one masters the ability to sense emptiness and solidity, an adversary can offer no opposition or interference when one is opening to attack. When one is closing, no dodging, bobbing or weaving is needed to avoid any attack. One can change the direction of another's force as if it were being applied against a screw thread.

To practice, one should remember the following principle: Starting with strong will power, open or close inside the body first, then expand to display the movement on the outside of the body. As one part of the body moves into action, all the other parts of the body are mobilized to support this action. The physical body and the mind must be totally harmonized.

In short, the manifestations of emptiness and solidity in Tai-Chi Chuan are complicated. Sometimes the right side of the body is empty, while the left side is solid, and vice versa, or the right arm and the left leg are solid, but the left arm and right leg are empty, and vice versa. At other times, the empty appears among the solid, and the solid appears among the empty, just as the Yin-Yang changes metamorphose in an unpredictable way.

It is fortunate that the *I Ching* tells us to cope with shifting events by sticking to a fundamental principle. So there is an unchangeable rule that dominates all these opening and closing changes. Since Tai-Chi Chuan eventually intends to train one to be like a Tai-Chi sphere, these countless changes between opening and closing finally focus on two essential objectives:

1. Always keep the line of the body's center of gravity passing through one foot, which is solid, and let the other foot be empty.

2. When one's body moves forward, backward, left, or right, the body's center of gravity, the Tan-Tien, should trace a path parallel to the ground just as the center of a ball does when it rolls.

If students can grasp these two essential objectives, they can master the changes of empty and solid.

2. Breathing

Tai-Chi Chuan is based on Lao-Tzu's philosophy that softness will conquer hardness. The series of movements in Tai-Chi Chuan are designed to cultivate one's physical and mental capabilities and develop one's Chi rather than strengthen one's muscles. Long and deep respiration benefits the body's general metabolism, the circulation of the blood, and the functioning of the inner organs. The human and earth stages did not specifically discuss breathing, but emphasized soft, slow movement and a gentle tempo. Following these principles prevents short, rushed breathing. In the sky stage, however, Tai-Chi Chuan lets the breathing itself be an exercise led by soft movement. The motion of the breathing is to match one's awareness of Yin-Yang changes in the hand's movement. One exhales when the hand changes from empty to solid. At the end of the exhalation, the lower abdomen expands and the hand simultaneously reaches the end point of solidity with the palm rising slightly. One inhales when the hand changes from solid to empty. When the hand reaches the extreme of emptiness, one stops the inhalation and contraction of the abdomen. To the beginner, coordinating one's breathing with the movement seems very complicated and difficult. However, if one has been practicing the Tai-Chi Chi-Kung presented in Chapter 3-2, one will be able to combine the breathing and the postures relatively easily. Otherwise, grasping this kind of technique merely by practicing Tai-Chi Chuan may take more than ten years.

3. Consciousness

When one begins to learn Tai-Chi Chuan, one is conscious of remembering the movements and thinking about the correct postures just as in other martial arts, sports and dance. But Tai-Chi Chuan requires a higher consciousness, (意) or greater awareness, to develop spiritual rather than bodily strength. When an exercise involves speed and strength, one can have conscious control only at the beginning and end of one's movements. The movement of Tai-Chi Chuan is different. It is so soft and gentle. When one practices moving from non-action to action, or action to nonaction, one can stop, advance or retreat wherever and whenever one wills and always be in total control. Practicing this kind of control has as its main purpose the use of consciousness to strengthen the movement of the body and the achievement of what is called in Taoist technical terms *Lien Chi Hua Shen* (練氣化神),   or "transferring physcial force into spiritual power". Another reason is to form the good habit of performing any action, even in daily life, with awareness. In order to develop consciousness when one practices Tai-Chi Chuan, the movement should be imagined more than merely physically executed; that is, one should use one's awareness instead of one's strength. For example, if one wants an action such as lifting a hand, to be lighter, or more Ching, one can imagine the whole process in slow motion to reach a higher level of Ching. If one wants to improve their Chen, or become more stable by emptying the strength and tension from the upper body into the legs, it is important to sink the will and mind through the line of the body's center of gravity down to the center of the earth and to imagine that every action develops from there. Thus using the imagination intentionally to exaggerate one's thoughts can promote the effects of Tai-Chi Chuan. Once these principles of awareness and imagination are mastered with Ching and Chen, they may then be applied to all activities, such as the changes between empty and solid, opening and closing, etc.

4.   Void and Stillness, or Hsu-Jing

To seek the empty in the solid is to find *Hsu* (虛), or "the void". To seek nonaction in action is to find *Jing* (靜), or "stillness". The pursuit of Hsu-Jing is the highest level and final goal of Tai-Chi Chuan. The movement in Tai-Chi Chuan, as mentioned before, emphasizes using one's awareness rather than one's strength. In the final stage one attempts to progress to the point where the movement itself, (as opposed to one's strength) has an intrinsic and instantaneous effect, such as turning opponents' actions against them.

Tai-Chi Chuan's principle of using stillness in motion in order to master action by nonaction implies that each outward form should project an inward perception of stillness. Thus in pursuing Hsu-Jing, one has to simplify consciousness into only one idea; that is to say, despite different kinds of movements, whether active or nonactive, one should gather them together to embody stillness. Action and nonaction, represented by Yang and Yin respectively, constantly alternate. After much practice, one's concentration will direct the transition from action to nonaction, or from Yang to Yin, and vice versa. One's aim is to become more peaceful inside in order to affect the outside. Gradually, the outer movements will reflect inner direction and total awareness. As a result, one's spirit will blossom and become peaceful. Tai-Chi's ultimate purpose then is, via greater understanding of its martial art aspect and increased health, to reach a higher spiritual level which would lead to the realization of Tao.

According to Lao-Tzu, "to touch ultimate emptiness, hold steady and still". If one knows how to pursue Hsu-Jing, one gradually can foretell the course of everything under the sun, no matter how complicated. Void and stillness, the essence of the Tao, are applicable to everyone and everything. If people proceed according to the Tao, then the origin of existence is easily observed, since everything returns to its roots. This principle applies to Tai-Chi Chuan as well. The movement flows like the Yantze River, fluently and endlessly, with action and nonaction, opening and closing, solidity and emptiness and numerous other pairs of opposites. It seems very complicated, but all will return to the primal state, or Tai-Chi, that is, to the Yang and Yin. So Lao-Tzu said:

> All things work together.
> I have watched them reverting,
> And have seen how they flourish
> And return again, each to its roots.
> This, I say, is the stillness.
> Retreat to one's roots,
> Or better yet, return to the will of Tao.

All things are of the universe, so all things go back to the universe. This is a natural law, so it is fair. For example, although people may be rich or poor, they have nothing when they are born and take nothing when they die. Understanding this law leads one to an easy coexistence with the world, but not understanding it is dangerous. As this law permeates all things, one who abides by it approaches the essence of Tao. The Tao infiltrates time and space, and humanity must follow the Tao in order to live satisfactorily.

The sky stage of Tai-Chi Chuan uses this law of Hsu-Jing. Although external changes may occur, internally one remains calm and empty without ever being affected by them. With such practice, one will understand the way to enter the four-dimensional world. As Chang San-Feng said, "If one emphasizes only the martial arts, he will miss the most important aspect of the philosophy of Tai-Chi Chuan."

One way to develop an enduring state of Hsu-Jing is to select a quiet place, where there is little external interference, such as a park, seashore or mountain. One must give up all thoughts and become tranquil. Forget all the rules mentioned before. One must return to the primal and change the complex to the simple. Pay attention only to the Yin and Yang changes within and without, from action to nonaction and nonaction to action. Finally, find how each movement returns to its roots.

*T*his section, is excerpted from the book *Tai-Chi Chuan*, written by Chen Yen-Lin (陳炎林 b1906- currently teaching Tai-Chi Chuan in Shanghai. See Figure 5-4a) in the 1920's, describes his experiences and provides valuable information and suggestions for the practice of Tai-Chi Chuan.

Fig. 5-4a

Currently, students begin with the Tai-Chi Chuan thirteen postures and proceed to learn them relatively quickly. Often after three or four months of practice students may finish the form and then think that they have learned all there is to know about Tai-Chi Chuan. They do not bother to consider that Tai-Chi Chuan was developed by our ancestors with great difficulty over a long period of time; so how could beginners possibly learn everything in three or four months? The fallacy of this attitude is more evident when we examine the methods originally used to teach Tai-Chi Chuan as a martial art. The course of study would begin with Ma-Pu (馬步) or the horse stance, which teaches solidity and rooting in the legs, for at least one month and often as long as one year. After students had learned to stand firm, they would progress to the posture, Lift-hand (提手上勢), which was practiced for at least one month, to learn how to empty one leg and root the other. After demonstrating they could use both of these postures effectively, each of the thirteen postures would be studied by itself and all its means of application explored. Each posture, again, would be studied for a minimum of one month. Only then would students proceed to learn the complete form. After completing the form, which would take at least several years, students would begin to study the advanced operations such as Push-hands, Ta-Lu and Tai-Chi Sparring, followed by the weapons forms.

Three positions form the frame of Yang's original Tai-Chi Chuan: high, middle and low. Students begin with the high posture, where the knees are bent only slightly. They then follow the middle posture, sometimes called "The Four-Level Posture" (四平架) by flattening the eyes, hands, feet and thighs. Finally, the low posture is practiced. Each of these three positions is a subdivision of the large, medium and small styles. The large form, which was taught by Yang Chen-Fu, (楊澄甫), requires stretching postures and has a tonic effect. It is a good exercise for health. The medium form, taught by Yang-Yu (楊鈺), requires the application of Tai-Chi philosophy and results in moderation. In this form concentration on the Tan-Tien prevents the flow of too much energy to the top of the head. The small form, taught by Yang Chien (楊鑑), requires compact postures and swift movements. Particular emphasis is placed on moving the waist, arms and legs as a unit. Of these three forms, the small one is hardest to learn, because the movement and speed of execution are condensed so that a great intensity of inner force, or Chin, is developed.

Learning all three forms takes a long time. At the beginning, daily lessons on the use of one or two postures are sufficient. Learning too much at a time leads to incorrect forms and superfluous steps. In addition, exercising quickly and the use of too much force are not permissible at this time. Acquiring speed at this time is harmful to the development of the Chi and the requiring effort damages the blood. If one follows the correct procedure, one can benefit from one or two postures as much as someone practicing the entire form of Tai-Chi Chuan several times.

While practicing, one should pay attention to the following details. Set the tongue against the roof of the mouth, close the teeth and place the lips together, breathe through the nose, straighten the body, lift the chest and back, loosen the shoulders and elbows, and keep the neck and head erect. Begin the exercise with the whole body as a unit, experiencing fullness and Ching. Stare in front of the hands, distinguish solid and empty, Yin and Yang, purify the mind, concentrate to increase one's awareness and give up all thoughts. Intend to develop perseverance of the spirit and physical endurance, and relax any tension. With continuous, hard practice, the breathing can be controlled. Relaxing one's tension gets rid of awkward force. For each movement of the posture, let the atmosphere of relaxation and softness penetrate from outside forms to the inside of the body. By practicing in this way, vital capacity is enlarged, and the Chi and blood are harmonized. Both body and mind are beneficially affected. Otherwise, the spirit, or Shen, and mind are disturbed, frivolous, and restless and adverse reactions occur.

Hence, learning the set of Tai-Chi Chuan postures, regardless of one's knowledge and talent, requires at least half a year. Proficiency is related closely to the frequency of practice. The more one practices, the better one executes the postures. If someone really wants to achieve martial arts skill, every time one practices, one needs to repeat the set of forms at least three times. The first time acts merely to stretch one's body; practicing more than two times develops energy and improves skill. If someone needs an exercise for health even half a set of practice is sufficient.

Beginners need fresh air and ample room when they practice. In an area which is too small for Tai-Chi Chuan to be performed continuously, one cannot concentrate well and sometimes goes in the wrong direction. However, no special size for the practice area is needed when one achieves a high degree of skill. Even when one sits or lies down, Tai-Chi Chuan can be practiced. At this time, one focuses on mental practice instead of appearances.

Recommended practice times are twice daily: the first, a half hour after awakening and the second, one hour before going to sleep. Each period is to last 20 to 25 minutes.

While practicing the form, the rhythm should be constant from beginning to end. The transition between postures should be smooth. The postures must be done correctly. Do not show any deficiency, such as concavity or convexity in movement. Do not show disconnected movement but perform with awareness.

It is necessary to know the application of each posture, to know the involvement of Yin and Yang in the movements. The beginner should not worry too much about the breathing. The most important thing is to practice the form smoothly. Let the body become full of Chi; keep the mind and body in harmony. Next, practice the whole set of forms from the left side using the opposite hands and feet for every one of the original postures. For example, the left hand and left leg would be used for the right hand and right leg. Familiarity with the mirror image enables one to reach a higher level of skill. Then one can learn the fixed Push-hands, unfixed Push-hands, Ta-Lu, Tai-Chi Sparring and the weapons forms. In any case, one should proceed slowly so the Tai-Chi Chuan can have its expected effect.

Beginners may experience bodily weakness and sore leg muscles as physiological reactions. Sometimes, this condition may persist for several months or more. One does not need to worry about such reactions because they result from the rebuilding of the body; the original physical structure is destroyed and replaced with fresh construction. Another reason is that everyone has so much tension inside the body. Thus since Tai-Chi Chuan teaches the total relaxation of the body, the legs tire easily. With another two or three hours of rest, such phenomena will disappear quickly and be succeeded by an abundance of, and increase in, spirit and energy. In addition, other phenomena, like a better appetite, will also appear. A tired spirit is related to oversleeping by beginners. Still at the same time, because of the increase in blood circulation, 8 to 9 hours of sleep a night is necessary. A normal condition eventually returns within a short period of time, and senior practitioners need only 4 to 5 hours of sleep.

"Is sexual intercourse permitted to people who practice Tai-Chi Chuan?" The answer to this question is yes. We are not superhuman. However, in order to get a greater reserve of energy, intercourse should be less than usual for people in normal health and stopped altogether for the old or infirm during the transition stage from weakness to strength. Smoking and drinking are permitted, but not for thirty minutes before and after the practice of Tai-Chi Chuan. Otherwise, because of the breathing, the inner organs are harmed.

Beginners may experience numbness in the fingers, arms or legs after practice from using too much force. To recover, just shake them for a couple of minutes. Because of lack of practice, beginners often forget the next posture when too much attention is given to correctness. About respiration, it is better for beginners to breathe naturally through the nose and to ignore, temporarily, the use of long and deep breathing in coordination with body and limb movements. If one concentrates on interior breathing at this stage, the outer posture is easily forgotten. In addition, when one reaches a certain level in using the movement of the body to guide the breathing, and the breathing is smooth and continuous, the outer posture then becomes free and flowing. It is hoped that beginners will not hurry to sink the Chi to Tan-Tien, because to do so at the wrong time may cause an adverse reaction. Ask if a posture does not feel comfortable. Question the teacher, and he will make the necessary corrections. Do not continue to do a posture that does not "fit".

The author lists several of the wrong ideas he had before he started practicing Tai-Chi Chuan: 1) The movement of Tai-Chi Chuan is so soft and slow, how could it benefit one's health? How could strength be developed? 2) The action of Tai-Chi Chuan is so gentle, how could one utilize it as a martial art? 3) He believed the operation of the lungs would be damaged by hollowing the chest or Han-Hsiung (涵胸). 4) What is meant by the Tan-Tien (丹田)? He assumed the Tan-Tien was merely the large intestine.

After practicing Tai-Chi Chuan, he corrected his previous misunderstandings as follows: 1) As the use of one's force becomes more effortless, one can move more swiftly. The comfortable posture and natural breathing, which accompany a reduction in the use of unnecessary force or tension, facilitate the free flow of blood and Chi inside the body. In this way one's health is improved, and one's inner force is developed. 2) How can one fight with slow movements? Slow movement is for the purpose of seeking stillness, but one eventually can speed up when necessary. In addition, through Tai-Chi Chuan, one can develop the skills of "listening to the opponent's energy", or Ting-Chin, and "understanding the opponent's energy", or Tong-Chin. Strength is developed through gentleness. Potential speed is hidden in slow movement, because Tai-Chi Chuan movements originate from the center of the body and are controlled by the waist, not just by the movement of the arms or legs. The main axis of a machine turns slowly, then gears allow the smaller flywheels to spin faster. The same principle applies to the body and the limbs. 3) Does hollowing the chest or Han-Hsiung restrict the operation of the lungs? Straightening the chest and back without relaxing the shoulders and sinking the elbows has bad effects. For natural breathing, one might try to hollow the chest and relax the whole body at the same time. 4) Are the Tan-Tien and the large intestine essentially the same? The author, at the beginning, sensed the abdominal area was empty. He lacked any knowledge of the Tan-Tien until three years later when he realized that the Tan-Tien, which is the headquarters of one's body, could be trained to reserve, supply and nourish the Chi. If the Chi is reserved, the Tan-Tien is filled. Then one can tap the Tan-Tien like beating on a drum. The respiration of a Tai-Chi specialist who uses the Tan-Tien to breathe instead of the lungs, is different from that of other people. It is observed that new-born babies breathe through the abdomen. However, as one grows, one breathes increasingly farther away from the Tan-Tien. People dying of old age breathe only through the nose and throat. Hence, there is an important relationship between life and breathing through the Tan-Tien. At first, the author did not know how to reserve the Chi in Tan-Tien. In the same way, how can one know the quality of food if one hasn't tasted it? How can one describe the beautiful scenery of a place if one has never been there?

The presence of random thoughts results from a restless mood. To eliminate these thoughts, one ought to stare in front as if enemies were present there. Beware of any worries arising. When one becomes familiar with the set of Tai-Chi postures, one will achieve perfect peace of mind. Students also may experience an increased flow of saliva under the tongue after practicing four or five postures. The body benefits greatly and feels comfortable from the swallowing of this saliva, which also will relieve one's thirst. The saliva, which is tonic and nourishing, is called "honey-dew". Anyone who practices Tai-Ch Chuan with the correct postures, taking things easy and using prebirth breathing will find that the phenomena described above will be within reach. These

experiences indicate that one is beginning to develop an inner force by
strengthening the mind and will. This process is called the transformation of
Yin to Yang, or "Lead to Mercury". (己身採戰，或謂汞鉛，亦即借陰補陽
之道．非如邪道以男女後天色身爲採捕也 .)

Students then start to learn the fixed-step (not moving the feet) Push-hands.
It is difficult at first to distinguish between the Four Directions, ward-off,
roll-back, press and push, and to connect them together smoothly. The student
must practice Push-hands with someone more advanced than he, like an
advanced student teacher, so as to be able to learn by imitation. During this
time, the teacher will demonstrate each of Four Directions one by one, making
all necessary distinctions so that there will be no questions in the student's mind
as to their differences. After these distinctions are clearly understood, the
student must practice them in continuous sequence so that they become
smoothly connected. At the same time, the waist and legs must be loose and
active when the Four Directions are practiced. It is through the mobility, loose-
ness and fluidity of legs and waist that the neutralizing and sticking energy are
manifested. Neutralizing, or Hua (化), is the ability to retreat from or accept
the opponent's attack. Sticking, or Nien (黏), is the ability to follow so
closely when the opponent retreats that one is attached like a shadow to him.
When one reaches this stage, the techniques of neutralizing and sticking, or
Hua and Nien, are achieved and it is time to learn Na (拿) and Fa (發).

Na is the technique of locating and sticking to a part of the opponent's
body which is called a point of application. Na is a "holding"; that is, once the
point of application is definitely found it is then adhered to, but no technique
is applied. After Na is learned, Fa can be executed. Fa is the application of a
technique, such as a push or punch, through the point held in Na. Therefore,
one locates and sticks to the point of application with Na and then attacks
through that point with Fa. These principles will never be learned by the
student if he tries to apply them indiscriminately during his Push-hands practice.
Before the student can apply the principles of Na and Fa himself, he must
observe how Na and Fa are used against him by his teacher. The student must
approach Push-hands practice as if it were an experimental laboratory where he
is both the experimenter and the subject. He must watch how his teacher sticks
to him and throws him off balance. He must observe when and where the
teacher applies Na and in what direction he applies Fa. He must distinguish
the timing of Na and Fa. To master the principles of Na and Fa, he must choose
one particular technique and practice it over and over again with a partner
who can help with the study of these principles. When the principles are
properly learned, the student will then be able to apply any technique with any
part of the body. To do all of this takes time, so the student must not be in a

hurry to learn these principles. If he tries to rush the acquiring of this skill, he will not achieve anything.

In this writer's opinion, the basis of all achievement in Tai-Chi Chuan is the fixed-step Push-hands so his advice to the reader is to spend as much time as possible practicing, observing and studying this method. To this end, one must practice Push-hands with as many different people as possible. One must practice with those whose skills are less than, equal to and greater than his skills. One must practice with persons harder or softer, taller or shorter, etc. One must also change partners often. Once one is familiar with a particular person's skills, one will always use the same techniques, which at this point will cause one's development to stagnate.

In moving Push-hands (non-fixed step), the whole body, legs, waist and arms, must move as a unit; the sticking energy, or Nien-Chin (黏勁), must be maintained continuously, as must be done when one is using a weapon. At least one point of the weapon must always stick to the opponent's. If one interrupts the sticking energy, or Nien-Chin, one has broken the connection that allows the opponent to Ting (聽), or sense one's intention, whether it is to attack or retreat.

If one is really fighting with hand or weapon, the technique mentioned in the Chinese proverb, "When one's hand moves, one must see red" (出手見紅), must be used; that is, every single move injures the opponent; one draws blood each time one attacks. One's mind must also follow the point of this proverb. One must be serious and not indulge as if practicing and must not be afraid since either of those moods will prevent one from attacking at the instant there is an opening in the opponent's defense.

Tai-Chi Sparring is first learned as a set of movements or form. To learn the real application of these movements, however, each posture must be practiced separately. While practicing the application of a specific posture, one must place special emphasis on examining the operation of three main areas of the body: the hands and arms, the torso, and the feet or step. One must differentiate between the high and low hand, the advancing and retreating step, and the side and front of the body. The basic principle to observe in each instance is that one takes whatever action is necessary to put oneself in superior position, and keep the opponent in a disadvantageous position. To this end, the hands must keep a circular motion, and the step and body motion must be such that one's torso is always vertical and erect. This position is maintained like a closed door guarding the interior, so as not to give the opponent any chance to attack. Each posture must be correct, but the whole set of movements must be smooth and flowing. The empty and solid, or Yin and Yang, must be clearly distinguished. Internal activity must be energetic and flowing.

Should one concentrate only on practicing the external postures in Push-hands, bad health still remains after ten years of practice. In addition, one will never achieve "understanding skill" or Tong-Chin (懂 勁), because Tong-Chin needs more internal and mental training. Learning outer techniques is easy, but learning the inner ones is difficult.

In addition, one may want to know how one's health and weight change with the practice 'of Tai-Chi Chuan. After one year of practicing, thin people gain weight and their fragility turns to strength; Yin is changed to Yang. Fat people lose weight and become stronger; empty is changed to solid. The effect of Tai-Chi Chuan is to rebuild the body both internally and externally. This change results from the rebalancing of the body by practicing Tai-Chi Chuan. Once the body has been broken down from its former state of imbalanced functioning, the body will then correct both external malfunctions such as excessive thinness or fatness and also any internal malfunctions.

Some principles for health during the practice of Tai-Chi Chuan are described below; 1) Meals may not be taken for at least thirty minutes after and thirty minutes before exercise. 2) Activities prohibited after practice include the following: a) deeply drinking cold beverages and eating cold food or fruit, b) drafts of cold air or cold showers, and c) using too much mental activity. 3) Before the pulse returns to normal, walking replaces sitting or lying down. Otherwise, the rising of blood pressure may have bad effects. 4) A sufficient amount of sleep is needed to compensate for the energy consumed during Tai-Chi Chuan. Late sleepers usually give up easily because of a corrupted spirit. 5) Don't practice Tai-Chi Chuan when exhausted.

The way to success in Tai-Chi Chuan practice includes the following elements: 1) *Perseverance:* perseverance is an essential tool for practicing Tai-Chi Chuan. Without perseverance, involvement in Tai-Chi Chuan is a waste of time and energy. The initial period of practice is indescribably boring and dull. If the student continues with strong determination, attraction will replace boredom after one year, excellence will be attained after five years and great success will be achieved after twenty years for those who really practice daily. According to this writer's experience, the three most difficult types of situations are the following: a) the first one or two months of beginning Tai-Chi Chuan, b) the occurrrence of other urgent events, and c) the honeymoon or other traveling which completely disturbs the daily schedule making it impossible to practice regularly. 2) *Concentration;:* This quality increases the success of one's practice two-fold. 3) *Weather:* Continue to practice during both hot and cold seasons. 4) *Studying:* Study intensively. Exclude all other concerns from your mind; greed or anxiety will result in distractions. The ultimate aims are simplicity and expertness. 5) *One step at a time:* No skipping. To follow the proper sequence and make gradual progress,do not try to obtain goals within too short a time. Hoping to learn the next postures when the previous one is still immature or intending to do the Tai-Chi Sparring when the whole set of postures is still not finished ought to be avoided. It is known that climbing starts from a low position, and walking far starts with the first step. A hasty approach goes nowhere. It is a very important principle not to try to do everything at once. In this way, one can become a good Tai-Chi player.

Not mentioned in the above points is the importance of finding a good teacher. Before one starts learning, it is necessary to examine the teacher's talents. Is he really well-experienced, well-educated and superbly skilled? Can he reveal the secrets transmitted from generation to generation? If one finds an excellent teacher, follow him instead of looking for someone else. Otherwise, one will get nothing, only tire the body, and waste time and money. Also, good teaching is useless without humility on the part of the student.

After the student reaches a certain level, one ought to turn to cultivating and disciplining one's capacity for greatness. The main purpose of Tai-Chi Chuan is mental and psychological training, which does not teach someone to be foolhardy. Literally speaking, one ought to open the mind like a valley, look dumb, and never show off. Never try to impress people since pride goes before a fall. Every practitioner of Tai-Chi Chuan ought to have a profound and complete understanding of this principle.

*   *   *

In addition to the experiences described above by Chen Yen-Lin, this writer has observed the occurrence of the following physical signs. After one or two months of practicing thirty minutes daily, one may hear a crackling noise between the limbs and joints, which gradually spreads all over the body. This sound signals an improvement in the circulation of the prebirth Chi. The rumbling glu-glu sound in the belly provides a clue that the mysterious Tan-Tien is starting to work. Practicing lightness, or Ching, results in feelings of bouyancy while one walks. Do not discontinue simply because of sore and painful feelings in legs or on the back. They will subside after one or two weeks. Signs like these do not necessarily occur in everyone, and their duration also differs according to the individual. Beginners do not have to look intentionally for such phenomena.

CHAPTER SIX

PUSH-HANDS

6-1. THE EIGHT GATES OR PA-MEN.

"The Theory of Tai-Chi Chuan" contains the original explanation of the Eight Gates or Pa-Men (八 門) as follows:

> The Eight Gates of Tai-Chi Chuan are ward-off, roll-back, press, push, pull-down, split, elbow and shoulder-strike. The first four gates represent the Four Directions: south, north, west and east. The last four gates, in turn, reflect the Four Corners: southeast, northwest, southwest and northeast.

First we will examine the concept of the Four Directions. The first four gates with their corresponding trigrams and directions are summarized below:

1. *Peng* (掤), or "ward-off", represented by Chien (☰), or "sky", lies south.

2. *Lu* (攦), "roll-back", represented by Kun (☷), or "earth", lies north.

3. *Chi* (擠), or "press", represented by Kan (☵), or "water", lies west.

4. *An* (按), or "push", represented by Li (☲), or "fire", lies east.

The Four Directions and their relationships are shown in Figure 6-1a.

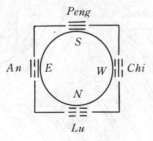

Figure 6-1a

While most people understand that every movement in Tai-Chi Chuan is circular, they do not usually know that the movements are square as well. For example, we see that of the diagram of the Four Directions has a square on the outside, but a circle on the inside. The square and circle are tangent to each other. They represent the outside appearance of the movements Peng, Lu, Chi and An, which form a square at first but later generate an inner circular movement. In the stage of the square every movement should be open and stretched to the extreme; in the stage of the circle, however, the movements are closed and compact.

Clearly understanding the Four Directions is extremely important since they form the basis for all techniques in Tai-Chi Chuan. The only way to know the meaning of the Four Directions is through practicing Push-hands (推手 , See Chapter 6-3). After one has constantly studied and practiced Push-hands, the next step is to learn Ta-Lu, (大擺), which contains the Four Corners (See Chapter 6-4). The Four Corners with their corresponding trigrams and directions are described below:

1. *Chou* (肘), or "elbow", represented by Tui (☱), or "lake", lies southeast.
2. *Lieh* (挒), or "split", represented by Chen (☳), or "thunder", lies northeast.
3. *Tsai* (採), or "pull-down", represented by Sun (☴), or "wind", lies southwest.
4. *Kao* (靠), or "shoulder-strike", represented by Ken (☶), or "mountain", lies northwest.

The outside shape of the Four Corners is a circle, and their inside shape is a square. Their directions and relationships are shown in Figure 6-1b.

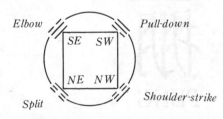

Figure 6-1b

By practicing Push-hands and Ta-Lu, one can gradually understand how a circle generates a square and how a square forms a circle. These transformations exemplify Yin's changing to Yang and Yang's changing to Yin in the Tai-Chi diagram. Practicing Push-hands and Ta-Lu is also the way to understand the more profound concepts of the *I Ching*.

The following section will explain the meanings and postures of the Eight Gates individually.

1. Peng or Ward-off

It is said in "The Secret of Push-hands":

> To ward against an opponent's force, accept it and change its direction
> upward; don't let the force get close to one's body. The posture which
> is used is called Peng, or "ward-off".

Peng's image Chien (乾), or sky, is composed of three Yang-Yao. Therefore, Peng indicates strength, power and untiring energy. These qualities may be
seen in a ball that is inflated with air. Such a ball is elastic and springy. When
you push it in, it reacts and does not let your force go through to its center. If
you push in at one point, the ball springs out at another point and redirects your
force. Anyone who, as a child, tried to sit on a beach ball remembers how
quickly your weight (force) was redirected and you fell off. To use the posture
of Peng, one must react like the beach ball and never let your opponent find
your center.

Using the right arm to ward-off is called Right Peng (右掤). Using the left
arm is called Left Peng (左掤). Figure 6-1c shows the posture of left Peng by
Yang Chen Fu.

掤

PENG

Figure 6-1c

There is a famous song explaining Peng:

Peng is somehow like the water buoying a moving boat.
First one must sink Chi to the Tan-Tien,
Then set the head upright as if suspended from above.
The whole body should be full of elastic energy,
"Opening and closing" in just one moment.
Even if there is a thousand pounds force,
It is easy to float without difficulty.

Once one gains an understanding of Peng's posture, one may take the next step and examine Peng-Chin, or the energy of Peng. The posture of Peng alone is not sufficient for practical application of its Chin. The posture is only the stable balance point from which either defensive or offensive energy is generated. To learn how to use Peng-Chin, one must apply the understanding gained from the practice of the Chan-Ssu Chin exercise.

In Peng-Chin the hand that wards-off must rotate from the inside to the outside. With the palm first facing the body, the forearm twists so that the palm faces out. The torso itself must be stretched by the sinking of the Chi to the Tan-Tien and the upward pull of the Shen in the head. The shoulders must be loose, the elbows lowered and the arms stretched. The crotch between the legs must be rounded so that the Chan-Ssu Chin can develop in the legs. When all these conditions are simultaneously achieved, Peng-Chin may be exerted.

When a person who can simultaneously maintain the above conditions is attacked, he or she will automatically manifest the defensive Peng-Chin. This reaction occurs since the entire body is in a delicate state of balance; once disturbed and set in motion, the body immediately rebalances. In the process of adjusting this balance, the disturbing force is redirected.

The offensive Peng-Chin is generated from the defensive Peng-Chin by lowering the body in coordination with the rotation of the palm so that a vertical circle is developed. This movement turns the attacking force back upon itself and uproots the attacker. In this case, the rebalancing of the body controls the direction of the disturbing force, which is returned to its point of origin.

2.   Lu or Roll-back

Lu's (擺) image, or earth, is composed of three Yin-Yao. Therefore, Lu indicates softness and yielding. It is obedience in the sense that it never opposes.

LU

Figure 6-1d

When mastered, the posture of Lu can control a force of a thousand pounds with only four ounces like the bullfighter who cannot hope to oppose the bull with his own small strength because the bull is too strong and runs too quickly. The matador's solution is to yield, side-step, and confuse the bull with his red cape. In Lu, however, when one yields, one does not step away but maintains contact so as to control the attacker completely while holding a superior position from which to counterattack if necessary.   Figure 6-1d shows the posture of Lu.

The song of Lu explains:

> Let your opponent come in;
> Then rotate with his force.
> Don't resist, but don't lose contact.
> You must be light and agile.
> Let his force go its full range;
> Then it will be exhausted.
> When his force is empty,
> You may let him fall
> Or you may attack if you wish,
> But you must keep your balance
> And not give your opponent a chance to take advantage.

Without understanding Lu, you will always have deficiencies in Push-hands. First, your opponent will always be able to find a point of application to push against. Secondly, you will always resist any attack with force. To correct these problems, you must follow several steps when you use the posture Lu.

Before you can apply Lu, you must use Peng for an instant. This move causes the opponent to exert force. Once he or she is committed to the attack, you must rise a little, then sink and turn the body with the legs and waist. It is important that the beginner turn the body as little as possible and avoid excessive use of the arms so as not to lose balance or expose the sides of the body to attack. You must also follow your opponent with your eyes from the first instant of the attack and continue to watch, even during the follow-through period when, for instance, he or she has fallen down. By watching, one keeps one's attention on the opponent.

The energy of Lu, or Lu-Chin (攦勁), complements Peng-Chin. Whereas the ward-off energy expands, the roll-back energy contracts. Peng-Chin is Yang or hard, and Lu-Chin is Yin, or soft.   In the Chan Ssu-Chin the forward generates Peng-Chin and Ni-Chan generates Lu Chin.   In Lu-Chin the forward palm faces out; then as you roll-back, the forearm rotates so that the palm faces in. Just as Yin develops out of Yang, Lu-Chin develops out of Peng-Ching. First one exerts the ward-off energy; then turning the palm inward develops the roll-back energy.

3.   Chi or Press

To press is to use the hand, arm, shoulder, or back to first stick to your opponent and then press before he or she has a chance to move. Chi's (擠) image Kan, or water, is composed of one Yang-Yao between two Yin-Yao. Lao-Tzu (老子) describes water as follows:

> Nothing is weaker than water. But when it attacks something hard, or resistant, then nothing withstands it and nothing will alter its way.

Water is deceptive because, while is looks soft and yielding, its inner essence is dangerous. In the *I Ching*, Kan is called "the destructive" and is listed as the hexagram indicating the greatest danger. The familiar example of dripping water's wearing away the hardest substances well describes water's deceptive and dangerous nature. The attributes of water characterize Tai-Chi Chuan in general, and the posture of Chi in particular. Tai-Chi Chuan's outer appearance of gentle, yielding movement conceals its inner nature, a most effective and dangerous form of fighting. However, of the Eight Gates of Tai-Chi Chuan, Chi is the one that most completely expresses the nature of water. Therefore, one must execute the posture of Chi like water entering into a crack in a rock in its path. The water first sticks to the rock's outer surface, and then sinks into the rock to destroy it. In the posture of press, stand as in Peng, then place the open palm of the other hand against the wrist inside the forearm. If you stand in a Right Peng position, the left hand is placed against the right arm. The left elbow should sink downward. Figure 6-1e shows the posture of Chi.

CHI

Figure 6-1e

The song of Chi, or press, explains:

> There are two ways to apply Chi.
> The direct way is with an intention,
> "Opening and closing" is just in a moment.
> The indirect way is to use the reaction force
> Like a rubber ball hitting the wall and rebounding
> Or a coin thrown on a drumhead.
> Let the opponent be like the coin
> Bouncing off with a tinkling sound.

Press, or Chi, is the main action in fixed-step Push-hands, which contains the four postures ward-off, roll-back, push and press. Without correctly applying press, practitioners will not be able to develop the proper circular motion for Push-hands. If your opponent does not press you properly, you can't learn how to generate the circle from the square. Conversely, if you don't press your opponent properly, you can't learn how to generate the square from the circle.

Chi-Chin consists of Peng-Chin in both hands and arms. The hands which are close together, rotate slightly as in Peng. However, with Chi-Chin the force is directed to one central point. Peng-Chin forms the basis for Chi-Chin; therefore, one can easily learn Chi-Chin after Peng-Chin has been developed.

4. An or Push

The posture of An (按) looks as if one is simply preparing to push; one or two hands are held in front of the body with the elbows lowered. An's image Li, or fire, contains one Yin-Yao between two Yang-Yao. Fire is very aggressive; its heat extends outwards and its flames reach upward. In the image of An, the two Yang-Yao suggest two forces impacting upon each other, but the inner Yin-Yao represents yielding. Through common sense, it is easy to know that a person with greater force can always "push" a person with less force by using no special techniques. However, when the opponent has a greater force, one has to employ the An technique. In the trigram for An, $\equiv\equiv$, the two Yang-Yao (solid lines) suggest two forces impacting upon each other but the Yin-Yao inside (broken line) represents yielding; i.e. if at first one applies force (Yang-Yao) and finds that the opponent's force is greater than one's own, one must then yield or relax for just a fraction of a moment (Yin-Yao). During this split second, the opponent who is off balance or overextended will try to regain equilibrium. One must take advantage of this time to apply the final force (Yang-Yao) which will enable one to overcome the opponent's force. It is important to note that timing is the key to mastering An. Figure 6-1f illustrates the proper posture for An.

Figure 6-1f

The following song explains An:

> An is like the force of the river water.
> Gently the water flows,
> But how great is the strength concealed within?
> The furious current is difficult to stop.
> It envelops the high rocks with a wave;
> And downwards it drives to fill the hollow caverns.
> Water overcomes all!

An is obviously a very significant aspect of Push-hands. It is important, however, to be conservative in one's push. The arms should move in complete union with the whole body and should not extend beyond one's knees. Awkward or abrupt force should always be avoided.

When practicing the moving-step Push-hands, the practitioner should be aware to develop a vertical circle which consists first of withdrawing the arms counterclockwise to form a neutral semicircle and, secondly, of completing the circle by stepping forward and pushing. An must be applied with direct intention. Therefore, good posture consists of holding the head erect, as if suspended from above, and focusing the eyes in the direction of the push. Other important points to remember include the following: 1. Uproot using the rotation present in the Chan-Ssu Chin with awareness; do not use a straight push. 2. Avoid sudden or abrupt movements because the opponent will see your intention and take advantage of it. 3. Leaning forward beyond one's center of gravity disturbs one's balance. 4. The hands should follow the movement of the legs and waist, and total body movement should follow the opponent, seeking only the moment that he or she is vulnerable.

Finally, An-Chin, which is a form of Peng-Chin where the palm turns from downward to outward contact, is used to push the opponent without outer movement.

5. Tsai or Pull-down

Tsai (採) can be practiced in two ways. The first technique, initially the same as the posture known as "Needle at Sea Bottom" in the Yang school of Tai-Chi Chuan, is used to bring the opponent's force downwards. The second pull-down technique, which is used in response to an attack to the crotch area, involves grasping the opponent's wrist and arm and pulling his or her body force downwards to one's side. The purpose of both techniques is essentially the same. The sudden pull-down movement has the power to shock the opponent, disrupting concentration and balance.

Tsai's image Sun represents the wind. The wind does not blow only in one direction, but changes direction easily. It moves the flexible leaves of the tree but goes around the solid tree trunk. The Yin-Yao which forms the foundation of Sun is topped by two Yang-Yao. This image indicates that the foundation of Sun is free-floating; the posture cannot be fixed into a category of Yin or Yang. Therefore, when one's opponent approaches with force, one responds by pulling down in a Yang fashion.   If the opponent only follows one's movement, however, one simply yields by guiding the opposing force away from one's own body, abandoning the use of Tsai and thereby avoiding the possibility of a counterattack. Figure 6-1g illustrates the proper Tsai posture.

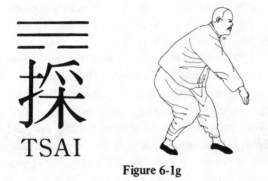

TSAI

Figure 6-1g

A famous song explains Pull-down, or Tsai:

> Pull-down is like Libra's scale.
> Heavy or light-balance can be found.
> Your partner's force may be one thousand pounds;
> Yet your force of four ounces can overcome.
> How can this be?
> The answer is found in the law of the lever;
> Increase the distance from the fulcrum
> And then balance will be found.

Tsai, or pull-down is the main action involved in Ta-Lu. A number of significant factors, although common to all of Tai-Chi Chuan, are stressed in the proper Tsai posture. It is important that one assumes a very balanced, central stance, sitting down on the legs with the elbows sinking downwards. The waist and shoulders should be relaxed to let the Chi travel easily from the Tan-Tien. When executing Tsai, use the body as a total unit, relying on the weight of the body and the power of the legs and waist. The posture will not be effective if one depends only upon the strength in the arms, especially when one encounters a force greater than one's own. Remember that Tsai is used to pull only one of the opponent's arms. Otherwise, one will unintentionally put the opponent in an ideal position to attack. Finally, this posture, in particular, should be attempted only with full intention; i.e., one should not apply Tsai at all unless one is firmly resolved to pull down the opponent.   The posture will be ineffective if employed only halfway. Remember to watch the opponent to the last moment even after one has thrown him or her off balance.

One will know that Tsai has been implemented correctly if the opponent has been stunned, or dumbfounded, so that he or she can then be uprooted, or lifted off balance, by an attack. As always, it is necessary to take advantage of this moment and follow Tsai with a push or press attack, e.g. the "Fan through the Back" posture which follows "Needle at Sea Bottom" in the Yang Tai-Chi Chuan.

6.   Lieh or Split

Three distinguishable steps combine to form the posture known as split, or Lieh (挒). First, one grasps and twists the opponent's wrist. Then one steps behind the opponent, preventing an opportunity for the opponent to withdraw and foiling any attempt to retreat. Now that the opponent has been trapped, one finally uses the arm to strike, or push, the opponent's chest. This move causes him or her to fall backward over the leg which previously had been placed behind. When executed correctly, Lieh is designed to make one's opponent fall backwards.

Chen, image of Lieh, represents thunder and suggests a roaring, tumbling and strapping strength. Two Yin-Yao press down on one Yang-Yao. The Yang-Yao becomes angry as a result of this pressure and reacts with a violent determination to break through and shatter the Yin-Yao. The Yin-Yao takes its own initiative and, like thunder, unexpectedly rumbles with rage. Figure 6-1h illustrates Lieh.

Figure 6-1h

The following song helps to explain Split, or Lieh:

> Lieh is like the flywheel,
> Round and round it spins.
> But far it will send you,
> If you venture too close.
>
> Lieh is like the whirlpool,
> With waves that roll.
> Beware, the spiraling current
> Will sink you without hesitation.

Lieh should be used in Ta-Lu practice in response to an attack of roll-back, or pull-down. Lieh is also very effective in changing the offensive-defensive situation. For example, if one is caught in an unfavorable position by the opponent's use of the posture "Mustang Ruffling its Mane", one can withdraw the step and proceed with Lieh. By employing Lieh one has been able to move from the defensive position of being pushed back to the offensive position of pushing the opponent back. As the saying goes, "whatever you do will come back on you".

Several points of importance should be noted with regards to Lieh. To be effective, Lieh must incorporate the use of one's legs and waist as well as the arms. One must gauge one's distance from the opponent carefully. Clearly, if one is not close enough to the opponent, Lieh will be of no use whatsoever. Finally, one must be aware of the fact one is in a vulnerable position when one attempts Lieh, because one's chest is left unprotected.

Imagine Lieh-Chin rolled up in a tight coil, thus forming a reservoir of Peng-Chin. To apply Lieh-Chin one must allow this reserve of Peng-Chin to suddenly release and spring forward.

7.   Chou or Elbow

Chou (肘) is somewhat self-explanatory because it means using one's elbow to attack or jostle the opponent. When one practices Chou, however, the posture should never be obvious to an observer. Chou should be concealed so as to disguise one's intention from the opponent. One should keep the idea of the elbow attack present in one's consciousness rather than in one's form.

Tui, the image of Chou, represents a lake. One Yin-Yao tops two Yang-Yao. The soft Yin-Yao rests on top and conceals the great force of the two hard Yang-Yao beneath.

The correct Chou posture is illustrated in Figure 6-1i.

肘
CHOU

Figure 6-1i

The following song helps explain the concept of Chou:

> The circle within the square generates the five elements.
> But it is important only to differentiate Yin and Yang, above and below,
> And to distinguish solid and empty.
> When elbow and fist are linked like a chain,
> They cannot be resisted.
> The fist can blossom like a flower,
> And its punch can be especially fearsome.
> When roll-back, press, push, pull-down, split and ward-off are understood,
> The functional use of Chou becomes unlimited.

Because of their diversity, hands are always considered the first method of attack in the martial arts. The fingers can be used to poke a particular point, the palm can grasp, the fist can punch and the back and side of the hands also have specific applications. In many instances, however, the use of one's hands are significantly limited, e.g. when the opponent crowds one into a very tight position. At this time, one can use the elbow as a second line of defense. The elbow has extraordinary power, especially when used for a blow to the solar plexis. This attack is considered particularly atrocious because it can kill. In view of its potential for extreme brutality, the elbow posture remains concealed and is practiced only with inner consciousness.

The basic Tai-Chi concept of utilizing the body as a total unit must be emphasized in this posture. The legs, waist and awareness must be coordinated with the elbow movement. Keep the body straight and the head erect. Remember to watch the opponent, concentrating in the direction of the elbow strike. In particular, for proper posture in *Chou*, check that the elbow and knee coincide; i.e., the elbow should not extend beyond the knee.

When the opponent is close and holds one's hand during the practice of Push-hands, one can respond by using the elbow straight to the opponent's chest. The elbow is also used in the practice of Ta-Lu in response to a roll-back attempt by the opponent.

Chou-Chin is the cultivation of Peng-Chin through the elbow. When the first line of defense (the hands) is blocked, Peng-Chin is sent from the second line of defense (the elbow) and this becomes Chou-Chin.

8. Kao or Shoulder-strike

The use of the shoulder is the most obvious aspect of Kao (靠 ; however, the side of the pelvis and hip should work in unison with the shoulder-strike. This technique is especially effective when the opponent has moved very close. One's step is the key to a successful shoulder-strike. If possible, place one's leg between the opponent's legs so that one's body forms a perpendicular line like the capital letter *T* in relation to the opponent's body. This position will allow one to use the full force of one's shoulder.

靠
KAO

Figure 6-1j

Ken, the image of Kao, represents a mountain. In ancient times, mountains posed a great obstacles to a traveler. The image of a mountain therefore suggests staying, or stopping. Kao prevents the opponent from continuing and poses an obstacle for any attack.

Figure 6-1j illustrates shoulder-strike, or Kao.

As previously discussed, the hands are the first line of defense and the elbows are the second. Now the shoulder and hips are introduced as the third and last line of defense. The elbow was explained earlier as a particularly atrocious assault, but the shoulder-strike to the chest is an even fiercer one.

The following song helps to explain the full meaning of Kao:

> The method of Kao divides shoulder and back technique.
> Within shoulder technique there is some back;
> So, use the shoulder technique in the "Diagonal Flying" posture,
> But remember the back.
> And, only by timing just the right moment,
> Will the technique explode.
> Like rock pounding against rock.
> Beware, all is lost without balance.

When one's hands and elbows are blocked by the opponent's closeness, rely on the power of one's shoulder. Use the legs, waist and total body awareness when attempting the shoulder-strike. A point which cannot be overemphasized is to keep the body erect, being careful not to lean one's shoulder into the opponent. Keep the image of Ken foremost in one's mind, and the attack will be like a mountain, impossible to move.

The cautious student should know that two areas are left vulnerable when applying Kao technique. One's face can be easily attacked if the opponent's hands are free. The opponent might break one's arm. To prevent this break, one can support the elbow with one's opposite hand, as shown in the illustration above. The tremendous power of the Kao technique, when perfected, can be used to overcome an opponent whose force is much greater.

Kao-Chin, as one might suppose by this time, is the cultivation of Peng-Chin through the shoulder. When the first line of defense, the hands, and second line of defense, the elbows, are blocked, Peng-Chin is sent through the shoulder. This Chin is manifest as Kao-Chin.

6-2. THE PRINCIPLES OF PUSH-HANDS

*A*ccording to Chinese Philosophy, the two forces which govern the universe are known as Yin and Yang. Although opposed, they cannot be divided for Yin and Yang cooperate harmoniously. They, moreover, interact as naturally as cause and effect, although Yin and Yang have a circular relationship and cause and effect represent a linear one. Yang is the origin of Yin; Yin is the root of Yang. Yin and Yang represent complementary opposites; e.g. inaction and action, soft and hard, empty and solid, light and heavy, or closed and open. They are intricately connected, relying on, as well as restraining each other's function. They relate in total unity; each helps the other to create perfect balance. For example, day is Yang, night is Yin. Day and night, although opposite to each other, are constantly in transition. This continuous movement finally unites them and, thus, creates a whole.

The concept of Yin and Yang forms the theoretical foundaton for Tai-Chi Chuan. It is absolutely required that Yin and Yang coexist. Where there is Yang, there is Yin; where there is Yin, there is Yang. One must continually seek harmony and balance between these two forces. The process of properly combining Yang and Yin, known as Tong-Chin (懂勁), is considered a significant accomplishment in Tai-Chi Chuan. In the stage of supernatural accomplishment which follows Tong-Chin, Yin and Yang are like the appearance and disappearance of a distant star before one's eyes. The star's apparent changes suggest that Yin and Yang do not coexist like day and night but rather exist simultaneously. The form of the star appears to be there and yet, because it is gaseous in the outer layers, it is not there. This highest stage embodies total oneness; Yin is no longer seen as following Yang because even this sequence would imply a minute separation.

When practicing Tai-Chi Chuan, one must balance Yin and Yang; one's movements cannot be too soft or too hard. If one uses only a single aspect of Tai-Chi, the form is incomplete and really should not be called Tai-Chi Chuan. Tai-Chi Chuan is realized only when the hard and the soft are developed into a Tai-Chi. The method for achieving the proper balance involves first developing the soft, or Yin, to the extreme. Then from the root of the soft, the hard, or Yang, can and should be developed to an extreme. This method is somewhat similar to the way a blacksmith makes shoes. First, he heats the impure pig iron in the fire, thereby making it amorphous. He then pounds the soft iron on an anvil to knock out the impurities. Thus the iron becomes hard, while retaining much of the amorphous, rather than the brittle, structure. The blacksmith repeats this process again and again until he has forged strong steel with the temper and strength to withstand the weight of his horse.

It is important to note that although the steel is hard and strong, it can also bend. Likewise, when practicing Tai-Chi Chuan, one should be totally flexible but maintain an inner awareness. This inner awareness can be seen in a cat sitting very still but totally alert as it prepares to pounce on its prey. To fully realize the meaning of Tai-Chi Chuan, one must put together the lessons learned from the blacksmith and the cat and incorporate the soft and the hard, in the same way as the Tai-Chi diagram encircles the Yin and the Yang. The foundation for Push-hands is laid only when one has understood and incorporated the full meaning of the hard and the soft into the practice of Tai-Chi Chuan.

The practice of Push-hands is vital to the full development of any serious Tai-Chi student. To practice Push-hands one stands opposite a partner in the bow-and-arrow stance. The partners then join hands and alternately use two or more of the Four Directions.

The purposes of Push-hands are described below: 1) Like the Chan-Ssu Chin, it teaches one to fully realize what sensitivity of the entire body means. Externally, the practitioner develops an acute sense of touch transmitted through the skin. Sensitivity and awareness is also developed internally. 2) The practitioner learns how to empty the body of all force. When one rids the body of force, one can experience what it is like to be the twinkling distant star; the body is there and yet it is not there. 3) Through understanding the principles of Push-hands, one can learn to balance Yin and Yang in daily experience. Thus the quality of life as a whole is enhanced.

There are two main views on the proper time to introduce Push-hands to the Tai-Chi student. One suggests that the student should be proficient in the practice of the solo exercise before attempting Push-hands. Adherents of this approach believe that the student should first develop a solid background through a long period of practice in Tai-Chi Chuan and the use of proper body posture. The second maintains that Push-hands should be taught along with Tai-Chi Chuan because they complement each other. This approach holds that Push-hands enables the student to better understand the solo exercise and vice versa.

The practice of Push-hands encompasses all of the Tai-Chi principles previously discussed, e.g. the thirteen torso methods, the Tai-Chi Chi-Kung, the Chan-Ssu Chin, etc. In addition, Push-hands helps the student develop important aspects of Tai-Chi not emphasized in the solo exercise. The following pages will describe these additional principles in order of their development.

1. *Ting* **(聽) or "Listening"**

To succeed in combat, it is important to objectively assess oneself and to know one's own strengths and weaknesses. It is equally important to know both the power of one's opponent and where he or she is vulnerable to attack. In *The Art of War* Sun-Tzu (孫子) wrote the following:

> If you know the enemy and know yourself, you need not fear the result of a hundred battles. If you know yourself, but not the enemy, for every victory gained you will also suffer a defeat. If you know neither the enemy nor yourself, you will succumb in every battle.

To listen, or Ting (聽), one acts like the spy who tries to gain access to valuable information by being constantly alert and investigating every clue. The Push-hands practitioner, however, does not Ting solely through the ears. He or she also listens through the eyes by steadily watching the partner's movement, through the skin by developing a total body sensitivity to touch, and through the mind by awakening the intellect to foresee the partner's moves. Clearly, the art of Ting, or listening, involves mental as well as physical training.

One can understand the significance of Ting through the following example. Consider two people reading the same book. If one really grasps and remembers the ideas and information from the book, whereas the other totally misses the point, the difference between the two is a matter of Ting. One person has developed the ability to listen to the book, but the other has not.

The Push-hands practitioner frees unnecessary tension from the body by relaxing the legs and waist and giving up all awkward movements. In this state of relaxed awareness, one can concentrate and truly Ting, or listen, in order to understand oneself as well as one's enemy. When progress is made, the entire nervous system becomes more alert and sensitive. When high achievement is attained, one can become as swift and agile as a fish or fly.

2. *Tsou* **(走) or "Leading by Walking Away"**

In "The Classics of Tai-Chi Chuan", Tsou (走) is explained as the act of "overcoming the strong and hard by the gentle and soft way". When the opponent offers force, the method of Tsou suggests giving up resistance by becoming soft and thereby evading a direct conflict. Obviously, if one gives no resistance, the oncoming force, no matter how hard, loses its effectiveness and may, in fact, contain its own downfull. Tsou follows the development of Ting simply because one cannot hope to avoid a force if one does not know its direction or magnitude. So, when practicing Push-hands, first Ting, or listen in its full sense, to the opponent's force and then avoid the force by yielding and giving no resistance, or Tsou.

Tsou is used by the bullfighter who cannot hope to overcome the bull by comparing force. The fighter's only chance is to step aside and avoid the bull's attack. When practicing Push-hands, one should always be conscious of the lesson learned from the bullfighter and never compare force with the opponent. This point must be stressed over and over again because one normally reacts by resisting when attacked. One must reverse this tendency, however, and take the path of non-resistance, or Tsou, in order to progress in Push-hands.

Applying Tsou must incorporate the whole body. Relaxing the arms but maintaining force in the body will serve no purpose because the opponent will then simply push the body. If the bullfighter were to move his red blanket but keep his body in the path of the bull, his end would be inevitable. One can learn to turn the waist, bend the knees and coordinate the relaxation of the total body by diligently practicing the Chan-Ssu Chin.

3. *Nien* (黏) or "Sticking"

It is said in "The Classics of Tai-Chi Chuan" that "to remain in the most advantageous position and leave one's opponent at a disadvantage is called Nien (黏), or 'sticking', or 'adhering'," complements Tsou. Tsou is used to retreat from an opponent's advance and to become soft when the attacking force is hard. Nien is used to advance when the opponent retreats and to follow the opponent who tries to escape. Tsou is considered Yin because it involves passivity and following a force, whereas Nien is considered Yang because it suggests initiative and advancing on one's own accord. So, although Tsou and Nien contrast in direction and action, they reciprocate and complete each other's cycle.

Just as Yin is the root of Yang, Tsou is the root of Nien. Therefore, in order to use Nien effectively, one must have a good foundation in Tsou. When the opponent pushes, it is correct to lead by walking away, or Tsou, with the intention of keeping the most advantageous position and putting one's opponent off balance. But, giving up too quickly creates too much distance from the opponent and loses one the opportunity to adhere, or Nien.

Nien, like Tsou, uses the technique of Ting to sense the direction and speed of the opponent's retreat. Timing is the primary factor with Nien because one will meet resistance if one tries to initiate movement too quickly. It is paramount that one attacks only at the exact moment the opponent is at a disadvantage.

Nien can be compared to the process by which a spider catches its prey. The spider waits with alert intention until an insect happens to approach the web. If the insect is trapped and does not resist, the spider will attack immediately; however, if the insect tries to break away, the spider will simply⸲ give more thread to the web and the insect will finally entrap itself with no hope for escape. In this analogy, the web, like Nien, acts to stick and adhere to whatever comes its way. The spider represents the mind, or awareness, which controls Nien. Don't forget! The spider is always in an advantageous position.

4. *Hua* (化) or "Neutralizing"

The following is said in "The Classics of Tai-Chi Chuan":

> The relationship between Yin and Yang must be understood. Nien is Tsou and Tsou is Nien. Yin cannot be separated from Yang and vice versa. When Yin and Yang complemènt each other, one will interpret the tenacious energy, or Tong-Chin, correctly.

To neutralize, or Hua (化), is to combine Nien and Tsou. When an opponent pushes, one should yield, or Tsou, with the intention of maintaining contact or Nien. Thus, we say that Tsou is Nien. As the opponent retreats during your thrust, adhere, or Nien, while maintaining a readiness to yield, or Tsou. Thus, Nien is Tsou. When one wants to develop Tong-Chin, three factors must be kept in mind: (1) yielding, or Tsou, (2) sticking, or Nien and (3) neutralizing, or Hua.

Tsou, the Yin principle, refers to a carefully regulated retreat. One develops an intuitive response to the timing of the opponent's thrust, neither allowing contact to be altogether broken, nor putting needless energy into resisting the attack. And in Nien, the Yang principle, one advances or follows the opponent's yielding, also by maintaining contact while expending the least necessary amount of energy. Hua involves recognizing the equivalence of Tsou and Nien as well as their reciprocal relationship. This concept further implies that one should always maintain an advantageous position so as to be ever ready to catch one's opponent, much as the spider is always ready to trap its prey.

Tong-Chin is well illustrated in the way a mature cat responds to gentle patting or stroking. If one initially touches gently enough, the cat reacts by maintaining the contact ever so lightly. On perceiving the initial contact, the cat knows Tsou, as revealed by its own gentle yielding, and at the same time knows Nien, as indicated by its maintaining the contact.

Both the human being and the cat know Hua instinctively from birth. However, unlike the cat, the human being forgets or loses this instinct through disuse. When practicing Push-hands, one does well to keep in mind the reaction of the cat so as to regain the long lost Tong-Chin. Once Hua is mastered, even overpowering force or quick movement from an opponent can be rendered useless.

The beginner interprets withdrawal linearly, as escape followed by a separate attack. However, Hua consists of a circular movement as represented by the S-shaped curve in the center of the Tai-Chi diagram. Through uniting Tsou, or retreat, and Nien, or advance, one can yield while holding one's ground. As one gains proficiency in Hua, the external movement becomes progressively smaller. The awareness of Hua develops in the mind until there is total inner awareness and practically no external motion.

Hua, the combination of yielding while maintaining contact, is the definitive characteristic of Tai-Chi Chuan. When applying Hua, one must keep in mind the use of the essential Peng-Chin, which was developed from the Chan-Ssu Chin. This motion involves the integrated use of the waist and legs in moving the body as a unit rather than the independent movement of the hands, arms or shoulders. Neutralizing the opponent's force, requires correct movement and timing. If one yields too early, one loses contact; if one responds too slowly, one succumbs to the opponent's thrust. In both cases Hua is not realized. The secret involves being ready to apply full force, yet restraining the total release of that force so that one sensitively applies a minimum of force.

Hua is designed to trap an opponent into an adverse position, one in which he or she is unprepared for the next step. One therefore holds a defensive posture as a precaution against the opponent's attack. This principle is known as the soft aspect of Tai-Chi Chuan. Practicing Push-hands enables one to acquire a good foundation in Hua and thereby maintain a credible defense. Cheng Man-ching advised his students to constantly accept defeat from an opponent. During practice, one must always keep in mind the specter of defeat, so that one can eventually learn to avoid it and thus be free to defeat the opponent. This aspect of Chinese philosophy has much to offer the American people. The competition and the striving to get ahead in much of American daily life results in undue tension for the individual. Cultivating an appreciation of defeat and loss lets one develop a wider perspective on the meaning of life. One can then realize the usefulness and beauty of cooperation which leads to peace and harmony and relationships in which everyone wins.

5.   *Fa* (發) or "Attacking"

In military strategy, it is axiomatic that the best defense is a good offense. After practicing and understanding Hua, or defense, one learns the role of Fa

(發), or offense. Hua without Fa implies Yin without Yang. Finally, when both aspects Hua and Fa, or Yin and Yang, are learned, they must be synthesized to produce a complete, effective whole, as symbolized by the Tai-Chi diagram; half of the circle is Hua, or Yin, and half is Fa, or Yang. With practice of Hua and Fa, the initially large circular movement is gradually reduced and Chin is gradually increased until one reaches a point of such high achievement that almost no movement is required to defeat an opponent. That is, if your Chin is solid enough, you are able to uproot an opponent entirely and throw him or her far away.

Fa, or attacking, consists of three basic factors: (1) circumstance, (2) direction and (3) timing. For successful Fa, or attack, one must take advantage of all three. *Circumstance* connotes taking advantage of the opportunity when an opponent is momentarily off balance or has become stiff in a defensive posture. At this time the opponent's vulnerable posture suggests the direction in which one can apply a minimum of force to push him or her off balance. In other words, one should capitalize on the deficiencies in the opponent's posture and push when he or she is too far back, or pull when he or she is too far forward. By thus following the direction of movement, one can uproot the opponent by pushing sideways at an opportune moment. Proper timing is also essential. An early thrust leads to comparing forces or wasting energy, while a late thrust allows the opponent time and therefore opportunity to correct a disadvantageous position and to take advantage of one's then ineffective push. Finally, all three factors must be integrated to be effective. Taking advantage of an opponent's awkward position without a well-directed attack leads either to a comparison of force or to a disadvantageous position, e.g. finding oneself off balance. So does using an opponent's vulnerability and applying a well-directed thrust without proper timing. Combined, all three insure an effective attack, or Fa, which appears as effortless as the gentle toss of a small object.

The confluence of the three factors to produce a desired attack, or Fa, is well illustrated by what would happen to a swinging door standing between the opponents. As one yields, sticks and neutralizes the Fa in which the door is opened toward one, one may successfully push the door closed. Closing the door too early is both an ineffective defense and attack, while closing it too late results at best in a comparison of force against force. Now, if you control the circumstance, the direction and the timing, just as the opponent draws near to the door, with posture a bit forward and step lifted, but not totally intending to come inside, you can choose the right time to close the door and provide the return thrust, or Fa, that will throw him or her back in surprise.

The distance between the respective opponents has its effect on Fa. When they are too far apart, no attack can be effective; if they are too close together, there is insufficient room to use body, arm and fist effectively. Another factor to consider in Fa is the relative height of the opponents. A short opponent is attacked naturally in the upper body, while a relatively tall opponent is attacked in the middle or lower torso. Also, the opponent may have more, less, or equal strength in the chest, shoulders and arms relative to that in the legs. For an opponent strong in the chest, it is best to attack, or Fa, the upper body in order to uproot the relatively weak legs. For a body strong in the legs, the attack must be low for maximum effect. For the balanced opponent, it is best to attack the middle part.

In addition, and most importantly, one needs to apply the principle of mobilizing and releasing Chin from within as if shooting an arrow from a taut bow. In attacking an opponent, any Fa, or thrust, must carry with it the total energy, of Chin, mobilized from within the body, not just a superficial attack from the arm.

Finally, for Fa, or attack, to be effective, it must be done with total intention to succeed. There is no room here for any considerations regarding the opponent's strength or resistance. You must be convinced that, if it were a mountain before you, you would have the strength and will to accomplish your goal of Fa.

6-3.   HOW TO PRACTICE PUSH-HANDS

*P*ush-hands teaches the application of the movements associated with the Four Directions: ward-off, roll-back, press and push. It also develops the qualities of Ting (聽), Tsou (走), Nien (黏), Hua (化), and Fa (發), explained in Chapter 6-2. Implementing these principles is extremely important and even essential to the mastery of Tai-Chi Chuan.

Try to practice Push-hands with as many different partners as possible because one of the major goals of Push-hands practice is to develop sensitivity and the ability to respond appropriately to any force. Willingness to practice anytime with anyone widens one's range of experience. If one practices with only one person, one may become complacent and adapt the practice of Push-hands to only that person's Chin. If, however, one seeks out a variety of partners, tall and short, men and women, light and heavy, etc., one will eventually be able to sense differing types of Chin more quickly and adapt with facility to new situations. One will also become more peaceful.

Push-hands is more than an exercise that helps to increase the effectiveness of Tai-Chi Chuan as a martial art. Through Push-hands one can begin to see how the principles of Tai-Chi Chuan might transform the world. When we are pushed against, in a train, on the street, or more figuratively, in our jobs or lives, our natural reaction is to push back. When we want something, we get angry or upset with anyone or anything that thwarts us. We expend a great deal of energy throwing ourselves at immovable barriers and at unforeseen or chaotic situations that frustrate us, but over which we have no control. Push-hands confers a peacefulness, a collectedness, a calmness to our efforts. It allows us to sense when it is best to withdraw and when to advance. Best of all, in a martial arts setting, which would. seem to imply opposition and self-interest, Push-hands surprisingly imparts a spirit of cooperation.

There are two major forms of Push-hands: single-handed Push-hands, where each partner uses one hand; and double-handed Push-hands, where each partner uses both hands. These forms have many variations, including fixed-stance and moving-step variations. Some of the great variety of Push-hands exercises are described below.

I.   Single-Handed Peng-An or Ward-Off/Push Practice

1.   A and B stand in the bow-and-arrow stance facing each other with their right feet forward, side by side, and shoulder-width apart. Their right arms are held out in front, with the backs of the wrists touching, and their left hands are held slightly behind their bodies, with palms open, as shown in Figure 6-3a.

Figure 6-3a

2.   Maintaining contact, or Nien, A turns the right hand counter-clockwise so that the palm faces B's chest and touches B's wrist. B assumes the Peng posture. As A shifts weight to the right (forward) leg, the hand moves toward B's chest. The push is from the body, not the arm, and thus the arm is not extended but follows the body forward, as shown in Figure 6-3b.

Figure 6-3b

3. As A pushes, B yields, or Tsou, shifting the weight to the left leg and maintaining the same distance between the arm and the body. Once the weight is completely on the left leg, the body turns to the right from the hips while keeping a straight axis through the center of the body. As the body turns, the palm also turns to face A's chest. B then shifts weight forward to the front leg, pushing against A's wrist. A must now Peng and yield, or Tsou, shifting the weight to the back leg. The cycle is then repeated so that each person alternates between pushing and yielding.

The purpose of this Push-hands exercise is to teach the application of An and Peng by developing Ting, or the ability to listen to an opponent. Also, this exercise provides practice in Tsou, or yielding to a partner; Nien, or maintaining contact; and Hua, neutralizing an opponent's force. The goal for beginners is to develop Tsou, Nien, and Hua, and eventually to learn Fa, or attack. It helps advanced practitioners attain a balance between Hua and Fa.

This single-handed Push-hands exercise has four forms. The version using the right hand and right foot is described above. The other combinations, which should also be practiced, use the following parts of the body: left hand and right foot, right hand and left foot, left hand and left foot. Practicing all of these combinations develops Chin and sensitivity symmetrically.

II. *Variations of Single-Handed Push-hands*

1. In this variation, the backs of the hands adhere at all times. Shifting weight forward, A executes the push palm up, aiming with the fingers to pierce B's throat or chest. At the same time B yields using the ward-off stance, but with the palm down, as described in Peng-An.

2. In this variation, the backs of the hands again adhere, but A attacks B's abdomen, and B attacks A's head. A vertical ellipse is thus described by the hands, from the head of one partner to the abdomen of the other.

As A shifts the weight forward to push B, the palm is vertical, as in shaking hands, with the fingers aiming towards B's abdomen. B wards off by bringing the arm up to the right in a semicircle, piercing with a vertically held palm to A's head. A's posture in avoiding the strike to the head is like "Step back to Drive away Monkey"; B's posture in avoiding the strike to the abdomen is like "Snake Creeps down". This Push-hands variation teaches folding at the hips and relaxation in a sitting-back position.

3.   The following variation is called Chou/Tang-Pien/An, or "Elbow/Single-Whip/Push". Since this exercise is complicated, involving six steps, the individual postures will be described.

   a. Stand in the bow-and-arrow posture with your right arm forward, wrist at chin level and elbow angled down. Your weight should be on your back leg.

   b. Turn your body on its axis from the hips to the right about 45°, your right arm following your body's movement, warding off to the right with the right hand.

   c. With the weight still on your back leg, turn your hips and torso to the left, and follow the movement with your right arm, sweeping across in front of your body with your right palm facing left, pushing to the left.

   d. Sink your weight downward, as if sitting in a chair, and bring your right elbow out in front of your body, stabbing forward with it, keeping your right hand near your chest. Shift your weight to your front leg, elbowing your opponent's chest.

   e. Extend your right arm with the palm up and pierce toward your opponent's neck with your fingers.

   f. With your weight still forward and your arm still extended, change from the piercing-hand position to the crane's-beak or single-whip-hand position, and aim at the chest of your opponent with the second knuckles of your right fingers.

The postures described above are practiced by two persons in sequence: as A performs a, b, and c, B performs d, e, and f. The movements entwine so that as A attacks, B defends, and vice versa.

III. Double-Handed Lu or Roll-back Practice.

1.   Assume the same stance as described for the single-handed practice. Connect left wrists so that the backs of the left hands face one another. With the left hand A grasps B's left wrist and executes Tsai, or pull-down, drawing B's hand down and to the left. A's right forearm

rests just above the back of B's left elbow, controlling it with the implied intention of breaking B's arm. In order to avoid the intended break, B supports the inner left elbow with the right hand, fingers up.

2. To reverse the disadvantageous situation, B must change directions by pushing up to the left against B's own left elbow, turning the waist to the left and simultaneously using the left hand to grasp A's left wrist and turn A's hand counter-clockwise. B then pulls A's left hand downward or Tsai to B's left side. This move puts B in position to break A's left arm with B's right forearm. A prevents this break by supporting A's left elbow with the right hand, *etc.*

This double-handed Lu practice can progress in the same manner as the single-handed practice, with A and B continuously changing the direction of movement. The exercise should also be begun with crossed right wrists, and one should practice the right and left forms to reach equal skill in both. The purpose of the double-handed Lu is to learn how to utilize Lu, or roll-back and how to respond to its application. The practice also develops tsai, or pull-down. You should be aware of and apply the principles of Ting, Tsou, Nien and Hua throughout the double-handed Lu practice.

IV. Variations of Double-Handed Push-Hands

1. One variation is called Lu-An, or roll-back and push. To practice follow the directions described in step one of the double-handed Lu practice: A performs roll-back and the intended break; B supports the elbow. In step two, B begins to turn the waist to the left. When B has turned the waist just enough to squarely face A, B assumes Peng with the left arm. In response, A uses the opportunity to An with both hands. B responds to An by continuing with the double-handed Lu movement, turning the waist to the left while grasping and twisting A's left wrist counterclockwise. This variation can be reversed and interchanged in the same manner as the double-handed Lu practice.

2. Another variation is known as Lu-Chi, or roll-back and press. When A is in the most advantageous position, that is, when A's right forearm is controlling B's left elbow, A opts to release the left hand from B's wrist, places the back of the left hand against B's shoulder, and completes the posture of press by bringing the right hand up and placing the palms together. A then presses against B's left shoulder. B must respond by making a full turn to the left with the waist, down and to the rear, along the line of pressure defined by A's right arm and by the force of the press. B then continues the double-handed Lu movement by executing roll-back and Tsai, or pull-down, bringing A's left arm to B's left side, and so on. One can develop and practice many variations on this

theme; e.g., A uses Lu first, and B uses Chi, then A responds with Chi and B uses Lu, continuing in a repeated cycle.

3.   Four-Directions Practice.

a.   Assume the same stance as described in the single-handed practice. To begin, A must assume left Peng (ward-off left with the right foot forward) with most of the weight resting on the right foot. B assumes An, resting one hand on A's left wrist and one hand near A's left elbow, and pushes forward. See Figure 6-3c.

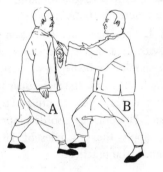

A: Left peng
B: An

Figure 6-3c

b.   A responds to B's An by first relaxing at the waist as if to sit down. Then lifting the right arm, A connects the right elbow with B's left elbow and turns the waist to guide B's movement to the left with Lu. See Figure 6-3d.

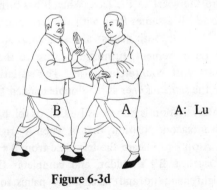

A: Lu

Figure 6-3d

c.   B maneuvers to change the direction of the movement by rotating the left palm counterclockwise until the back of the hand is facing A's chest. B then places the right palm on the left, and executes Chi, or press, as shown in Figure 6-3e.

B: Chi

Figure 6-3e

d.   A reacts to B's Chi by dropping the right hand so that its palm covers both of B's hands and turning the waist right to squarely face B. A then lowers the waist, as if about to sit in a chair, and turns the right hand clockwise, being certain to maintain contact with B's right hand.

e.   B's reaction is to withdraw and assume Peng.   The cycle of movement is completed when A's hands are placed in An on B's wrist and elbow. Then the sequence is repeated from step a with A and B switching moves.

6-4.   THE METHOD OF TA-LU OR FOUR CORNERS

*O*ne should begin the practice of Ta-Lu after a certain level of proficiency has been attained in Push-hands; i.e., knowing and being able to apply each Push-hand posture in a smooth manner. The practice of the Push-hand postures Peng, Lu, Chi and An, which indicate the Four Directions, can form a square illustrating their original nature. To understand the subtler attributes of the Push-hand square, one must realize the circle inscribed within it. The circle is suggested in movement by the way the four postures become a smoothly flowing excercise.

By indicating the Four Corners, the Ta-Lu postures form the outline of a circle. Again, to find the vital subtle meaning of Ta-Lu one must find the square indicated within it. See Figure 6-4a.

This principle of mutual changes or cyclic transitions between the circle and square can be illustrated geometrically. It is possible to visualize this transition by viewing the square as a polygon. One will find that by increasing the sides of any polygon it ultimately becomes a circle. For the reverse process imagine the enlargement of a circle. As the circumference expands, it is possible to

Figure 6-4a

understand that a circle is at each point a straight line, or in fact a many-sided polygon. By decreasing the sides of the polygon, one can find the square inscribed within.

Through the changes from square to circle and from circle to square one can realize the absolute harmony of Yin and Yang and understand how they can become each other. Upon first observation, the method of Ta-Lu appears very complex, and the beginning student may feel that its practice is too difficult to attempt. A competent teacher, however, will be able to instruct clearly and simplify what seems to be an over-abundance of movement. If no teacher is available, do not become discouraged. One can make progress by persistently studying this book and trying to really comprehend the principles presented. It is most important to focus or sharpen one's concentration. When one has made progress with the thirteen torso methods, arm and leg methods, etc., one can grasp the essential concept of whole body unity. Moving the body as a unit will clear the pathway for progress in Ta-Lu and allow one to develop in certain significant ways beyond the practice of Push-hands. One will also find that Ta-Lu can become more fun than Push-hands in that it incorporates the Four Directions of Push-hands as well as the Four Corners specifically associated with Ta-Lu. In addition, the practice of *Shan* (閃), or "lightning attack", and *Chue* (挒), or "breaking", can be studied in Ta-Lu. Shan and Chue are used especially in response to an opponent's shoulder-strike attempt. Shan, designating the use of the palm to hit the opponent's face, is attempted when one's hand is free to move upward. Remember that the arm must follow the body and that the movement must be agile like lightning. The correct application of Chue will break the arm of the opponent. To use Chue, place one hand under the opponent's wrist and lift upward. Place the other forearm on the elbow area of the opponent and move downward. The opponent's arm, which is trapped in this position, will certainly break if sufficient force is applied.

It is important to remember the   principles of Ting, Tsou, Nien and Hua discussed in Chapter 6-2. Thus, one's hands must always maintain contact with the opponent; however, it is paramount that one's touch should be light without force. It is also necessary that one should use the inner consciousness to guard one's own body. Each part of the body has a defensive function; e.g. during shoulder-strike, or Kao, one should place a hand on the inner elbow to prevent the Chue attack by the opponent.

There is no way to discuss all of the combinations or possibilities which exist in the practice of Ta-Lu. A teacher is helpful in pointing out all of the different applications for attack and defense. If you do not have a teacher, however, suffice it to say that one can constantly review the principles and innovate one's own applications.

One basic method of Ta-Lu practice is discussed below. In an attempt to find a simplified system for the study of Ta-Lu, we have indicated the direction of movement and distinguished the postures for each partner, A and B. Through practice, the student should try to eliminate this stiff structure and synthesize the postures into a flowing pattern of movement.

A. Solo Practice

Reminder: In the following Ta-Lu exercises, as with all Tai-Chi movements, the body follows the movement of the feet and the arms follow the movement of the body.

Beginning Stance: Stand facing north with the heels together. Extend right arm up and out in front of the body at head level, keeping the elbow slightly bent and the wrist straight but loose. The palm is facing west. Knees are slightly bent.

Step #1: With the body's weight on the right leg, pivot on the ball of the left foot, turning the heel out to the left at about a 90° angle so that the foot is pointing northeast. Shift weight to left leg.

Step #2:   Step back with right leg so that the bow-and-arrow stance is assumed and the body is facing northeast. As the weight is shifted to the right leg and the body turns clockwise, the extended right arm follows the body's movement describing a counterclockwise downward arc that stops about waist height.

Step #3: Shift weight to left leg. Keeping left foot stationary, step forward with right leg, bringing right arm upward in a counterclockwise arc until the *Beginning Stance* is again assumed. Body is now facing east.

Step #4: Step forward with left leg.

Step #5: Step up with the right leg and close so that feet are again in the

Beginning Stance. Shift weight to right leg as left palm presses against inside of right elbow. This posture is called shoulder-strike. Remember to keep your back straight.

Step #6: Shift weight to left leg. Withdraw right leg, bringing it back to the left leg, as right arm moves upward in a counterclockwise arc (applying ward-off, Peng) until *Beginning Stance* is again assumed.

B. Performance with a Partner

This exercise is performed by two persons so that as A does Step 1, B responds with 4; as A does 2, B does 5; as A does 3, B responds with 6; as A does 4, B does 1, etc. It is important to follow the movement of one's partner so that the performance is smooth and fluid.

Beginning Stance: A and B assume this stance facing each other with the outside of the right wrists touching.

Step #1: (A)/4(B)—A performs Step 1. B performs Step 4, stepping forward with the left leg.

Step #2: (A)/5(B)—A grasps B's right wrist and steps back into the bow-and-arrow stance, pulling B's arm down (Tsai). B brings right foot besides the left and then performs Step 5, or shoulder-strike. A places the back of the left forearm against B's arm above the elbow, hooking the right hand around the inside of B's right wrist, with the intention to break B's arm, or Chue. B's defense against Chue is to push against the inside of the right elbow with the left palm.

Step #3: (A)/6(B)—A releases B's wrist and continues the counterclockwise arc up and aims to strike B's face with an open palm (the lightning attack, Shan). B simultaneously performs Step 6, blocking A's strike with Peng. At this point, B should be facing A. If not facing A, B may need to adjust the left heel before withdrawing from the shoulder-strike.

6-5. *TAI-CHI CHIN*

*T*he Tai-Chi Chi-Kung develops the Chi which includes postbirth Chi and prebirth Chi. Meditation helps to strengthen these two forms of Chi and spread them to every part of the body. When one starts to practice the Chan-Ssu Chin, energy is developed and the whole body works as a unit. Practicing the Tai-Chi solo exercise blends harmoniously one's Chi, or energy, and awareness into Chin. Chin itself is divided into two polar opposites:
1. The hard within the soft, or the soft containing the hard, is called *Tan-Chin*

(彈勁), or "elastic Chin". It is illustrated by a whip in action displaying soft, smooth energy but containing a hard sting at the end. 2. The soft within the hard, or the hard containing the soft, is called *Jin-Chin* (靭勁), or "malleable Chin". It is exemplified by a pliable bar of steel.

Chin is stored in the Tan-Tien much as water is held in a reservoir. The practice of Push-hands and Ta-Lu can be likened to the generation of hydraulic power. Continued practice leads to higher levels of achievement with the goal of total efficiency and the development of a kind of pure quality, wherein the Chin is soft, but weighted and easy to wield. This Chin is similar to an ocean wave in forward motion, looking graceful, but carrying much momentum. The Chinese use the image of an iron bar wrapped in cotton. This achievement, used for health, can lead to rejuvenation and, employed in the martial arts, will not encounter significant opposition. It takes ten years to grow a tree, while this high achievement may require more than twice as long before it takes root.

When Push-hands is done without Tai-Chi Chin, it is done entirely passively, letting the opponent take control without energy input from you. The situation is somewhat like that of the foot soldier in the army who carries only light arms as opposed to the control exercised by the wielder of heavy armaments.

The Yin aspect of Tai-Chi Chuan is fluid and mobile, like clouds moved by a gentle breeze; it is revealed in Tsou and Hua. The Yang aspect is weighted, but not solid: in the sense of being firm and aggressive, it is expressed in Nien and Hua; like a thunderstorm with overpowering strength, it is indicated in Fa. The Tai-Chi diagram shows how Yin and Yang complement each other within a circle showing some Yin in the Yang aspect and vice versa. This same balance must eventually be attained when practicing Push-hands. It is easy to find. If one uses Yang extensively, all one's opponent has to do is neutralize this Yang strength with a small amount of Hua to throw one off balance, just as the bullfighter does. If one emphasizes the Yin aspect in Push-hands, it is possible only to protect oneself, but never to have the chance to attack, or Fa, the opponent. When Yin and Yang are used alternately, it eventually becomes possible to control the opponent, catch him or her off balance, open the line of defense and close in. When Yin-Yang balance is established and the Tai-Chi Chin is developed, a state is reached whereby one cannot be touched by the opponent, yet one can attack anytime. Expertise is the result of long and hard practice. ■

PREFACE
TO THE
FIFTH EDITION

Breakthrough in Tai Chi Chuan

Tai-Chi Chuan is based on the *I Ching*, especially on the idea of "change." No body can perform the forms and postures of Tai-Chi perfectly, for perfection is relative—an ideal dependent on individual perception. In playing Tai-Chi, our aim must be to change again and again; to play with variations in order to make progress each time in our understanding of the principles we are attempting to embody. Even if we try to hold everything constant, even if we strive to reproduce some image of a "perfect form," nature itself insures that conditions within and around us are never the same and no two performances will ever be identical. We can either be frustrated by this or we can learn the way in which change, the only constant, can be employed to attain higher levels of wellness, happiness, and awareness.

Sometimes in our efforts to improve our Tai-Chi, we experience "breakthrough." This does not come from our attempts at humdrum repetition, but is triggered by some modification, some change in nuance or posture, in mood or intent that opens us to a flow of unexpected energy. Sometimes we are able to describe a breakthrough, perhaps with a story or image; other breakthroughs may be nonverbal— a new feeling or heightened perception. Usually, the sensation of breakthrough is exhilarating. It is accompanied by a sense that seemingly difficult things are easier—that seemingly complicated things are simpler. Frequently, breakthrough in one area will have a far broader impact. Breakthrough in a single posture, for example, will often be felt throughout a form.

Goals organize energy

Breakthrough is not unique to Tai-Chi Chuan. Passing an important examination, graduating from school, trying a new method after doing a job the same way for ten years, finding a faster route home, or putting on toeclips after years of only pushing down on bicycle pedals all may result in the feeling of breakthrough. In daily life, we think of solutions to problems as "breakthroughs." I am not talking about the slow, nearly imperceptible progress that comes from daily practice. Breakthrough feels more dramatic, even if it is a relatively small gain. It is like an earthquake—an abrupt release of tension that is measurable and discrete—rather than a series of tremors indistinguishable from one another. I would define breakthrough in Tai-Chi Chuan as "a sudden and exhilarating transition toward enlightenment."

Everyone who persists in Tai-Chi, utilizing the principle of change, will experience many of these transitions. Cheng Man Ching (鄭曼青) told of one such breakthrough which occurred when he was a student of Yang Chen Fu. (楊澄甫) According to Cheng, Yang repeatedly admonished his students to relax. Cheng did his best but still made no progress; his fellow students could still push him around. Then one night Cheng dreamed that his two arms were broken at the shoulder and, like a doll's, were connected to the body only by a string. When he woke, he understood what "sung" (relax) means, and when he pushed with his classmates they wondered how he had made such rapid progress.

I experienced a breakthrough one evening as I watched a cowboy ride a wild horse in a televised rodeo. Suddenly I saw that every motion of the horse had a purpose. The horse's intention to unseat the cowboy was accomplished in a succession of movements that threw the cowboy's center of balance further and further off until it was possible for the horse to toss him to the ground. I realized with excitement that this is also the aim in push-hands—the smallest movements must be related to the goal of defeating one's opponent. Of course, long hours of practice must follow these moments of revelation.

In this article I would like to distinguish between two kinds of breakthrough. The lesser is the personal milestone, of which there can be many. The two examples above belong to this category. The greater marks the boundaries between three major developmental stages which define the road to true mastery in martial art. Each of the three major stages is characterized by a "method." Martial artists in the first stage use hand method, those in the second stage use toso method, and in the third stage mind method. Although many lesser breakthroughs are possible within each stage, the transitions from hand to torso method and from torso to mind method are distinct—requiring a major breakthrough, or what is sometimes termed a "quantum leap." Lesser breakthroughs are individual experiences and will vary widely; the greater breakthrough, however, will be very similar for all who pass from one stage to the next. Most martial artists remain in the first stage. A few reach the second stage. Classical stories tell us of those who have attained the third stage, but I know of no one today who has reached it.

Hand Method: The First Stage. Hand method refers to the execution of techniques by the body's extremities. Techniques include punching, blocking, kicking, striking, locking, and chin na. Stretching is important, and movements are usually large, fast, and forceful. All hard, external schools stay within the bounds of the hand method. For martial artists trained in these schools, the practice of Tai-Chi—defined by its principles, not its forms—represents a breakthrough: the doorway to the second stage of development. Unfortunately, most Tai-Chi players also remain at the first level, for the performance of form and push-hands will simply be the exercise of techniques until players learn to apply the Master Key (the application of the eight trigrams and the five elements) and thereby breakthrough to the next stage.

Torso Method: The Second Stage. The hallmark of the second stage is the use of torso method. Torso method is characterized by use of the body, specifically the waist and spine, to initiate and empower the movements of the arms and legs. That is, the torso learns to lead all movement. In the first stage, muscular dynamics and independent movements generate force. In this stage, suppleness, connectedness, inner movements such as breathing, and the spiral motion pictured in the Tai-Chi diagram unlock the power of innate energy, or ch'i. What do torso method movements look like? No parts of the body move independently; the movement of any part is contingent on the matched motion of all other parts and all parts are continuously alternating between the extremes of yin and yang. Only those who reach this stage can truly be said to be practicing Tai-Chi; yet these are few indeed. Most Tai-Chi players are working on the principles that define the torso method, but the breakthrough that marks mastery of this stage is elusive. It is easy to deceive yourself about progress at this level. Tai-Chi forms can appear very graceful and connected, especially when performed by a player with long experience. Careful study, however, will reveal hands and other parts moving independently, or stagnating and failing to change as weight shifts and the waist moves.

Mind Method: The Third Stage. Finally, there is mind method. It is difficult to talk about this third stage, as I myself have not reached it and I have not yet met anyone who has broken through to this level. The classics attest that it is possible and there are tales of masters whose feats sound as if they had attained this level. In mind method, all movement has been absorbed into the body. Techniques formerly executed with the extremities now begin and are consummated within the energy of the individual. Where previously the torso led, now it is the mind that leads, the energy which follows, and the player's intention is accomplished with little or no external action. In this third stage, physical energy, ch'i, has been transmuted into psychic or spiritual force, called "shen." (神) Tales tell, for instance, of masters who could neutralize the attack of a tiger simply by reflectingthe tiger's fierce energy back at him in a concentrated glance.

It is one thing to say that a breakthrough is necessary to move from stage to stage, but how can we each work toward breakthrough in Tai-Chi Chuan? Imagine the course of your development to be like an endless corridor. If development were merely a function of effort over time, then the corridor would look like a ramp angled upward to the vanishing point. But it is not. The corridor is uneven and interrupted by a series of locked doors. Advancement within each passage comes with patience and perseverance over time; but without a key, the next passage is inaccessible. With effort, you can maintain your skill at the level of the door; but if you become complacent or have no key, you will only remain there without making progress.

Breakthrough is not the automatic result of the passage of time or an accumulation of experience on a particular level. Years of practice will result in smoother technique, but the habit of performance is external. Internal concentration and change are necessary to breakthrough in Tai-Chi Chuan. Think about the history of automobile design. The first cars were essentially a chair or a couch mounted on four wheels. For years, designers allowed these features to dictate what cars looked like on the outside and produced only variations on the theme. The exterior was simply a casing for the interior. For a breakthrough to occur, someone had to adopt an entirely new concept. Aerodynamics provided the key. As designers began to pay attention to the flow of air outside the vehicle rather than to the furniture inside, their designs began to change radically. While it is a simplification, this provides an insight into the nature of a major breakthrough. It is not just a slight improvement on an existing idea; it is a jump to a new arena of creativity made possible by recognition of a different fundamental concept. This is what must occur between each major stage in Tai-Chi development.

I believe the answer for those who wish to go forward is twofold: never be satisfied and always seek diligently for keys to further progress. Let me consider each of these ideas in turn. First, how can Tai-Chi players avoid the pitfall of self-satisfaction, which tempts us to settle for where we are rather than pursue loftier aims? One way is to pay close attention to the reasons we play Tai-Chi and the goals we think we can achieve by practice.

Goals organize energy. They help us use our time and effort more efficiently. Goals are most effective if they are made conscious and meaningful. What is your goal for yourself in Tai-Chi Chuan? One day, if you have achieved skill, what do you think you will do with it? Try to be specific in formulating your goals. For example, "to be healthy" or "to be able to defend myself" or "to feel relaxed and happy" are vague. Vague goals, even if they sound good, will not focus your energy nor inspire you to employ effective means of realizing them. Challenge yourself: sharpen your goals so that they are a reflection of your will to make real progress and to breakthrough. For example, "I want to be healthy" might become "In six months I will be twenty pounds lighter and will be able to walk up to my apartment without breathing hard." I want to be able to defend myself" might become "In one year I will have learned both sides of the sparring form" or "I will demonstrate in X number of sparring or push-hands matches that I can neutralize my partner without hurting him." Specificity helps focus your will and strengthens your belief in your own potential. Focus on something you really want, not just something that sounds nice. The fervor of your desire makes the difference between a fond hope and a goal which empowers your pursuit of it.

Empowering goals are magnetic. They attract energies in your life that contribute to their fulfillment, and repel things that might distract you. Once you have such a goal for Tai-Chi Chuan, you must begin to discriminate between things that contribute to its fulfillment and those that draw your energies away. Do late hours keep you from daily practice? Do you spend too much time in front of TV or in idle reading? Do you often seek companionship instead of valuing time with yourself? You must be willing to push distractions resolutely from you and do what is necessary to accomplish your goal. Your goal, for instance, must compensate you for getting up early each morning for practice!

Let us assume that your Tai-Chi is good. You've worked hard for a number of years and you feel you're on a par with your peers. Other people are better than you only because they have been at it longer. This is a treacherous place. You are losing your "beginner's mind" and you face choices that are critical to your future development. Even after twenty years, if you think "I'm good enough now" or "I'm happy just running this Tai-Chi studio," then you are finished; you will stop there and never breakthrough. If you want to break-through to the next stage you must never be satisfied. When you attain your goal, or see beyond it to something higher, the principle of change suggests that you adjust your sights toward that loftier vision of self-fulfillment. Only your hunger for greater achievement will impel you to breakthrough.

Now let me return to the second concept mentioned above: the importance of seeking diligently for keys to further progress. Where are such keys to be found? I believe that if we sincerely desire breakthrough, keys can be found beneath the mat of the most common experiences of our lives. We must cultivate intuition, however, to discern them. One method of finding keys to break-through in Tai-Chi Chuan is to think deeply about things other people take for granted. Accepting other people's answers at face value, for whatever reason, can block progress. For instance, when I first began studying Tai-Chi, I wondered why there was so much variation among the major styles. Other players told me it was because of differences in the personal styles of the masters, or that the variations were random, or the result of faulty transmission, or that they re-presented alternative martial applications. I sought my own answer by studying three of the major styles and concluded that the Chen, Yang and Wu (武) styles define a continuum, purposefully designed to lead a player from hand method to mind method, from form to formlessness, from the limitations of action in the external world to freedom of action in the internal world. I assure you it would repay your effort to investigate this for yourself as I did.

Another way of finding keys to breakthrough is to relate as much of your daily life and your knowledge of the way things work to the practice of Tai-Chi. Ask continually "how is this like Tai-Chi?" The classics and tales from the lives of earlier masters also will repay your consideration. However, ideas in books or from any source other than yourself must be personalized in the cruci-ble of your own practice. In the earliest classic on Tai-Chi, Chang San-Feng says that Tai-Chi is learned from the movement or orbit of the sun and the moon. Clearly, he watched their movements and related them to his own life. When I first heard this I thought it was superstitious. How can they be related? Then one night, as I practiced Tai-Chi Chuan, I saw the crescent moon rise. Suddenly, I understood the connection Chang San-Feng had made: the back of the hand is yang, the palm is yin. As the hand turns, a crescent of yang appears. We have two hands, so they must match one another like the relationship between the sun and the moon. This breakthrough became possible because I was willing to open my mind and admit that this old story might have something to say to me. From this I was able to recognize that the pa kua, (八卦) representing eight phases of cyclical change, is the key to the torso method in Tai-Chi Chuan.

Suppose you have set yourself a goal to move from stage one to stage two—from hand method to torso method. How might you do this? The hand method rule was to practice a repertoire of techniques over and over until you could execute them smoothly and forcefully. Now you will need to adopt a higher concept: do not move your hands. If the hands cannot move independently, then the body must begin to move in order to cause the hands to approximate the positions you have learned in the form. So to practice torso method, your body must learn to move more and more, as you strive to move the hands less and less. Try this exercise: Stand with your arms at your sides, palms facing to the rear. How can you move the torso so that your palms face outward? If you are not allowed to move your hands, then you must combine the sinking of the body and the use of breath and inner movement to effect a movement in the extremities. As this becomes possible for you, you are on the verge of discovering the difference between Tai-Chi and all other forms of "chuan": every posture in every Tai-Chi form in all styles should be executed with the same inner intent and outer stillness.

Let's carry this exercise a step further. How do you move from torso method to mind method? If you move from hand method to torso method by reducing the movement of the hands and increasing the movement of the torso, then you might expect to move from torso to mind method by reducing the movement of the body and increasing the activity of the mind. This is an advanced concept. To practice torso method, we strive to lead the hands with the body; but what leads the body? The mind—and this will show in the eyes. If we comprehend this, even as we practice at lower stages, we can begin to cultivate the rudiments of mind method. As the mind thinks "I want to move the hand," the eyes lead by looking slightly ahead of the movement. By analogy, when you read aloud your eyes are scanning the text ahead of your voice. This is known as the "eye-voice span." If your eyes focus only on the word you are saying, you comprehend less of what you are reading and your voice loses the appropriate expression. Good readers have larger eye-voice spans than poorer readers. In Tai-Chi, if the eyes focus on the hand, the mind will follow the hand and allow it to lead. If the eyes focus slightly ahead of the hand, the hand will learn to follow the energy of the mind, and the mind might begin to learn from the hand how to act effectively in the world.

Confucius once said every phenomenon has its causes and its effects; every event has its start and its conclusion. If you know what comes first and what follows next, then your actions can be close to the Tao. (物有本末，事有始終，知所先後，則近道矣。) This highlights another important concpet related to breakthrough. A student at the beginning of study has no background. He doesn't know Chen style or Yang style, he doesn't know what to work on first. If at this point he only wants to work on the application of postures and he thinks "I'm right, I'm ready," he'll never get breakthrough, because he is unaware of the requirements of process in his own development. At every stage, there is specific work to be done that cannot be skipped if you wish to make progress. The instructor may suggest routes that have led consistently to greater expertise, but each student must strive to accept responsibility for her own development—to acquire sensitivity to the flow of her own unfolding and her specific weaknesses and needs.

Have confidence in yourself. If the old masters did it, you can do it. Give up negative habits of thought. Excuses will drain your energy and ruin every-

thing. When confronted by a difficult move in a form, such as a jump in the
Chen second routine, if you say "Oh, I'll never be able to do that jump," then in
fact you will never be able to do it. Now, as you read this, sit up straight – lift
your spirit and relax inward toward your center! Remember your goal: to
acquire mastery. There is certainly some truth in the old adage "you are what
you eat;" but how much more true that you are what you think. Our assump-
tions about ourselves and who we are—what we look like, what jobs are possible
for us—create an inertia in our lives. To varying degrees, we are all engaged in
this inertial thinking. Who are you? The more often you think of your goal,
the more it shapes your reality. Once a week is better than once a month, once
a day is better than once a week. Frequency is important and so also is the
intensity of your mindfulness. As often as you remember, ask yourself "If I
were indeed a master, how would I act in this situation? How do I act with this
person from the space of mastery? How does the master sit? How does the
master eat?" Rememberance is the greatest key, linked to the cultivation of
your will and the power of your imagination.

Daily practice of Tai-Chi Chuan is simply an exercise in remembering who
you truly are. If you can remember your goal and yield to the possibility of
change, you will indeed breakthrough and begin to live at higher levels of energy
and consciousness. In his classic on Tai-Chi, Wang Tsung Yueh (王宗岳)
asserts that the energy generated by continuous practice, Tong-Ching, (懂勁)
leads to a sudden illumination or godlike stage. He states that the key to this
stage and to Tong-Chin is understanding the relationship between Yin and Yang
and thereby interpreting energy correctly. He promises all Tai-Chi players:
"Comprehend the Tong-Chin and the more you practice, the more wonderful
will be your development. You understand in silence and experience in feeling
until you may act at will." Of course, the opposite of this is that if you do not
understand, no amount of practice will be of any use!

My purpose in writing this article is to encourage all Tai-Chi players, both
students and teachers, to open their minds and strive to adopt the philosophy
of Tai-Chi, expressed in the principle of change. Unfortunately, some players
are sidetracked by the belief that their teacher is the only teacher. In the
attempt to follow only one way they lose sight of the principle of change and
of the richness of Tai-Chi Chuan. You probably were led to your teacher to
learn certain personal lessons you might not have learned with someone else.
This was a gift to you; but if it fosters an attitude that excludes rather than
includes, one that encourages mockery of other people and ideas, you will very
likely shove away the keys to your own breakthrough. Be open to the lessons
hidden in all that comes your way. Remain flexible and see what works for you.
Do not be afraid to change your practice, to learn another style, or to in-

corporate new ideas into your form. As you change, it changes—as it changes, you change.

I am not advocating change for its own sake, nor am I suggesting that individuals should modify the choreographies of standard forms. The traditional forms within the major styles have been carefully crafted by great masters to accomplish most efficiently the aims of the art. However, individuals must use these forms as personal proving grounds for the classic principles of Tai-Chi philosophy. Forms may change in emphasis as long as the principles are not violated. These principles permit a wide range of physical interpretation, and require you to experiment creatively with movement and energy in your quest for breakthrough to greater levels of mastery.

Jou, Tsung-Hwa

To All of My Students

After 17 years of long, severe self-training, recently I feel I have achieved a break-through in my practice of Tai Chi Chuan. I attribute this largely to the intense practice of Chi Kung or breathing exercise, meditation, silk cocoon chin and the solo form; as well as being well-versed in the Tai Chi classics. I hope for two things in the forseeable future:

First, that my students achieve greater skills, showing advanced progress in Tai Chi and second, that I also continue to achieve higher levels in my training, leading to a second break-through.

These goals fit the larger dream I have, and that is the development of a Tai Chi College to assist in the spreading and sharing of Tai Chi Chuan.

I ask you to do the following:

1) Each day To reflect upon yourself asking:

A) How long have you been practicing Tai Chi?
B) To evaluate your practice:
    How can you improve the quality of your practice?
C) To evaluate your daily life:
    Do you have bad habits?   What are they?   Can you change the bad to the good or the yin to yang to improve the use of your time and your energy?
    Do you make excuses for yourself?
    Do you spend too much time socializing?   Going to parties?
D) Important: Start with yourself. DO NOT CRITICIZE OTHERS, ACCEPT YOUR RESPONSIBILITY AND ENCOURAGE YOURSELF, AND OTHERS.

2) Challenge To Yourself!

A) Compare yourself to me. When I first came to Livingston College I was no more advanced than most of you are now. What can you do to make the kind of progress I have made?
B) For the past 10 years I have had no teacher. There are no secrets withheld from you. Most important is your own practice. I have developed totally on my own. You must also make your development on your own responsibility.
C) Compare your age to mine. Most of you are younger than me. Some of you are not. But I have shown that age is no obstacle in making progress. If you are younger, you should be able to break-through more easily. Also, you have me to ask questions of. How can you use this to your best advantage?   You are more fortunate in that respect, as I have no one to ask questions of.

D) The most significant change you can make towards progress is in your will. How can you develop the strong will I have demonstrated?   It is my will which enabled me to write more books in English despite my poor English.
3) I request that all interested students write out their feelings and responses to the issues I have expressed here and likewise distribute them. Remember!   Where there is a will, there is a way!

Jou, Tsung Hwa
1/20/83

THE TAO OF MEDITATION
Way to Enlightenment

Everyone can be enlightened by this inspiring and informative book. This book now makes available the basic principles of enlightenment in different forms of meditation as well as practical exercises based on traditional Chinese methods.

The book is presented in three parts:

Part One explains the philosophy of all forms of meditation. The uses of the Tai-Chi symbol and the concepts of Yin and Yang are described.

The philosophical ideas of space and time are discussed to open the reader's mind to the fourth dimension. This fourth dimensional view of our three dimensional world has never before been explained so clearly. It is truly the way to enlightenment. The need for students to create their own personal discipline is stressed.

Part Two describes in detail a series of twelve breathing exercises or Chi Kung that can be used to lead and circulate the Chi energy to every part of the body. These exercises are extremely valuable to serious martial arts students and to all who desire to reach higher levels of health and self-awareness.

Part Three deals with the Lien Ching Hwa Chi (練精化炁) or the transfer of sexual energy to psychic energy. Enlightenment through meditation is taken out of the realm of superstition and presented in a realistic, practical way. Detailed guidance to the life-long study of this traditional Chinese method, which is one of the paths leading to the fourth dimensional world, is provided.

Hardcover, 6x9. Price $15.00

THE TAO OF
I CHING
Way to Divination

For the first time in English the I Ching is presented in such a revealing light and told with such elegance through the use of pictures and vivid imagery to finally "Raise the veil of mystery" and encourage personal, practical use of this most valued work of Chinese culture.

The book describes the following:

*How the meaning of Yin and Yang evolved from the Tai-Chi diagram. The basic principles of the I Ching's structure is explained so that the student can determine the meanings of the trigrams directly from the central concept of Yin and Yang.

*Methods of divination including yarrow stalks or coins, but, most importantly, the direct interpretation of time and personal life events. You can use the I Ching to predict coming events and to adjust your behavior to attain harmony in your daily life.

*Three-part divination. The principles of the Five Elements are used for interpretation. Specific examples and exercises to illustrate each divination method are included.

*Pictures based on traditional Chinese wood block prints which are used to summarize the qualities of each hexagram visually instead of in words. This approach enhances the learning of creative, nonverbal, concepts in understanding the I Ching.

*How the traditional meanings of the hexagrams can be translated into relevant, personal terms. Included here are also many details on the lore of divination as applied to the specific hexagrams.

*As a whole, this book takes the reader away from the perception of the I Ching as a series of sayings by some wise person arrived at by a mysterious method and back to its roots as a timeless method of cultivating self-awareness and improving the quality of life.

Hardcover, 6x9. Price $20.00

Name: _____

Address: _____

City _____ State. _____ Zip _____

□ Check or □ Money Order Enclosed.

Yes! Please send me the book listed below:

Qty.	Code	Title	Price	Total
	To1	The Tao of Tai Chi Chuan	17	
	To2	The Tao of meditation	15	
	To3	The Tao of I Ching	20	
Total Order				
Total				

Free postage, autographed by author.

- -

Cut along this line and mail